BUXBAUM

A MURDEROUS AFFAIR

BUXBAUM

A MURDEROUS AFFAIR

BRIAN MARTIN

General PAPERBACKS
Toronto, Canada

General Paperbacks edition published 1986

ISBN 0-7736-7113-7

Printed and bound in Canada

For Nigel

Acknowledgements: Special thanks to Don Murray, Joan Barfoot, Kay and Helen Wigle, Jim O'Neail, Brian and Nancy McAndrew, Dale Wright, Emilie Smith and Len Marucci.

1/The Murder:

"It should have been you..."

It was one of those humid days so typical of summer in south-western Ontario. Scattered thunderstorms had moved through the area in the past couple of hours but the ground was still damp and the air heavy. The temperature had dropped a few degrees from a high of twenty-four Celsius but the humidity of more than 80 per cent made for a sticky day. The only relief would come with the setting of the sun that was now beginning to work its way into the western sky.

The brown Oldsmobile station wagon loafed its way effort-lessly westward along Ontario's Highway 401, its driver wear-ing dark glasses to combat the glaring sun, his thick, drooping, almost Fu-Man-Chu mustache offering sharp contrast to thinning, slicked-back hair. Helmuth Buxbaum checked his watch against the electric clock on the dashboard as the big, air-conditioned vehicle neared London. A little before seven, he noted. In the right passenger seat, his wife, Hanna, stirred from a catnap and saw her husband glance at the time and mutter something.

"What time is it, honey," she asked, preferring his word to anything the dashboard clock might say. "Six-fifty-six," he replied, his precision typical. "We'll be home in fifteen minutes."

Hanna sat up and began to take notice of the light evening

traffic flow on Ontario's major east-west thoroughfare on this July 5, 1984.

It had been a tiring week and she was glad the family's comfortable home in Komoka lay only minutes ahead. She and Helmuth (pronounced hell-mutt) were returning home from Pearson International Airport in Toronto, 200 kilometres to the east. In the back seat of the car snoozed their nephew, Roy, the fourteen-year-old son of Helmuth's older brother, Isbrandt. Roy, whose family lived in Abbotsford, B.C., had flown in from Vancouver, arriving on CP Air Flight 60 about 4 p.m. at the Toronto airport. Soon after "Oncle" Helmuth and "Tante" Hanna collected Roy and his baggage, the weary teenager had slid into the back seat of the big car, slipped off his shoes and exchanged small talk before drifting off to sleep. Behind him in the wagon was a stuffed and mounted fifty-pound halibut he'd brought with him. The frozen meat from the fish accompanied it.

Helmuth and Roy's father had had words during that outing. Isbrandt was worried about losing his cab business and had asked his wealthy younger brother for financial assistance. Helmuth had refused, suspecting that Isbrandt would squander anything he gave him. A deal was struck, however, to have Roy come and work in Ontario during summer vacation. That, Helmuth figured, would help Isbrandt and also demonstrate to his nephew how a successful businessman operated.

Roy was to spend the summer with the Komoka Buxbaums, working in the nursing home his uncle and aunt operated. But before his work of tending the home's extensive grounds was to begin, the Buxbaums were planning to take Roy to the family cottage near Huntsville for a few days.

Helmuth fretted aloud; would the cottage be ready by the weekend? He had sent a nursing home employee to prepare the cottage and wasn't optimistic things would be done to his satisfaction. Hanna assured him everything was bound to be fine, her husband didn't need to worry.

"Remember, honey," she said, "these are holidays. You've got to learn to relax."

Earlier on the westward trip, they'd talked about retirement and the future. Hanna at forty-eight, and Helmuth at forty-five had several years yet to work, but had always enjoyed planning ahead. The Buxbaums had worked hard and made sacrifices in their life. They'd raised a fine family of five children and adopted a sixth. Five of the children were still at home. They were prominent members of the Baptist community in London and they were wealthy; millionaires in fact. They had time to plan what to do with the money they'd earned.

Hanna leaned toward continuing to bring relatives out from behind the Iron Curtain, something she'd done for several years. She had also considered missionary work once the children were old enough to leave home. Helmuth replied that the family could make a more substantial contribution by donating money than tackling overseas projects directly. Other people were paid to specialize in that work.

"Besides, Hanna," he reminded his wife of twenty-three years, "the children will still need our help." He'd found the big woman's soft spot, her big heart. He knew there was nothing more important to Hanna than the children, now aged from twelve to twenty. He, too, was deeply attached to them. And he couldn't see how forsaking the comfortable life the family had built in Canada to work among natives could accomplish much. Let others get their hands dirty, he felt, he'd be glad to contribute money.

Hanna chatted happily about the family's two-week trip to Europe from which they'd returned just two days before after visiting relatives in Austria and Switzerland. Devout Baptists themselves, the Buxbaums had told their Mennonite nephew of the excursion with a Christian group to see the famous Passion Play religious festival at Oberammergau, Germany. It had been a splendid trip in all and Hanna had particularly enjoyed showing off the children to the relatives and talking of the good life back in Canada.

She spoke in English, to please her husband. Born in Poland, Hanna was the product of a German-speaking family and retained a mild accent, while Helmuth, born in East Prussia of Austrian parents, had none. Helmuth preferred to use the language of his adopted land and had worked hard to eliminate his accent, fearing it might hurt his chances of succeeding in business.

It was good to be home for a few days to rest before heading up to the cottage. Hanna's talk of their good times in Europe and the upcoming stay at the cottage didn't seem to have much effect on her husband. But she was used to his appearing preoccupied when she spoke to him; his active mind was always wandering. He'd been a challenging mate. But he seemed to be far off today, rather tense and unable to relax.

London was now butting up against the 401, its industries straddling the four-lane superhighway marking the southern fringe of the city of 275,000, the hub of business and commerce for the rich farming country of southwestern Ontario. The Silverwoods dairy plant, the truck depots and the Northern Telecom factory passed into the rear-view mirror, as did the neon hotel strip of Wellington Road. The skies were clearing from the earlier showers and it promised to be a fine evening.

About eight kilometres west of London lies Komoka, a dormitory village of 1,100 that was home to the Buxbaums and the centre of their financial empire, consisting of a far-flung chain of about ten nursing homes. Several of those homes are in southern Ontario — in London, Chatham, Amherstburg and Watford — while others are in northern Ontario and in Prince Edward Island. Started about seventeen years before with the Komoka home, the chain had grown steadily and would later be estimated to be worth about $20 million on this fateful Thursday.

The fastest route to Komoka from Toronto was to skirt past the southern and western limits of London along Highway 401 and take Highway 402, a new four-lane highway linking London to Sarnia, a hundred kilometres to the west.

Buxbaum eased the Oldsmobile onto the entrance ramp of Highway 402 southwest of London and prepared for the final twenty-two kilometres to the Komoka exit at Middlesex County Road 14.

While this route was longer it saved driving into London and fighting city traffic. Buxbaum preferred it because it was simpler and the scenery more pleasant.

The station wagon continued past the prosperous farms of Middlesex County, through the townships of Westminster, Delaware and Lobo, through the heart of Ontario's bread-basket. The corn was waist high and the well-maintained barns and farm homes were witness to the area's prosperity. Included in the lush green quiltwork of farm fields were occasional groupings of tiny painted barns, called kills, used for drying tobacco leaves.

Just west of the village of Delaware the highway dipped into the gentle valley of the Thames River, at this time of the year a sluggish watercourse that meanders its way southwest to Chatham and spills into Lake St. Clair. Another four kilometres past the Highway 2 exit and it would be time to leave the highway for the last stretch into Komoka.

The Oldsmobile climbed a gentle slope and followed the highway as it took a slight turn to the right. In the back seat Roy stirred. He was anxious to get to their destination. Five hours in a jet and more than two hours in the station wagon had taken their toll; he was tired of travel for this day.

The highway marker indicated the approach of the County Road 14 turnoff leading to Mount Brydges and Komoka. Buxbaum slowed and moved into the deceleration lane.

The overpass ahead carried the county road west into Mount Brydges, another of London's dormitory communities, and east into Komoka. As the big car approached the overpass, another structure appeared beyond it. Several hundred metres farther along and slightly to the left where the highway veered off, was a CN Rail overpass.

On the right-hand shoulder of the road at that next overpass was a dark object, a car, with its trunk open. A figure seemed to be crouched behind its bumper.

Buxbaum noticed the vehicle up ahead and drew his wife's attention to it as he continued to slow the car.

"Hanna, that car, it looks like the Richardsons'," he said. His wife rubbed her eyes and looked ahead and to the left toward the underpass as the Oldsmobile started up the exit ramp to the right.

"You think so, honey?" she asked. She had to take the word of her husband in matters like this. She couldn't tell one make of car from another but she knew Helmuth could. Hanna had seen the big new blue car neighbor Brian Richardson had driven past their home. But was this car the same blue? It was hard to tell. Helmuth would know.

"It looks like car trouble," he said, craning his neck as the wagon continued up the ramp. "I think we should help."

But Hanna was tired. She was anxious to get home. "No, no, don't stop," she murmured. "It may not be them and we're just about home."

At the head of the ramp was a stop sign. It would be a left turn and six kilometres into Komoka and it would be easy to carry on. Helmuth looked to Hanna. Wordlessly he swung the wagon into a tight U-Turn and entered the on-ramp that led back onto 402.

Hanna was more than willing to assist the Richardsons, if the car ahead were indeed theirs. But she wasn't about to argue. Helmuth and Brian Richardson had had a disagreement years ago when Richardson had been the administrator of the nursing home. But time had healed the rift, Richardson had left the home but still lived a few hundred metres from the Buxbaums. He was now pastor at a London pentecostal church.

The Buxbaums had been Good Samaritans before. Helping others was an expression of their Christianity. This wasn't the first time they'd stopped to assist a fellow traveller. In fact, Hanna and Helmuth had stopped along the same highway that very morning on their way to Toronto to help another motorist in a car very similar to this. She'd volunteered her nylons when the driver had asked for them to solve some problem with his car's fan belt. She was still bare-legged from that episode.

The station wagon continued along the ramp until the disabled car came into view. A man was standing beside it, waving his arms. Yes, it was blue, Hanna discovered, and somehow it looked familiar. It appeared someone was in trouble, although the man didn't look like the tall, slender Richardson.

Buxbaum pulled up about a car length behind the blue vehicle. Its trunk was open and something obscured the licence plate. The man who had been waving moved to the passenger side of the Oldsmobile and stood there. The time was about 7:05 p.m.

Suddenly, the right rear passenger door of the station wagon was ripped open. A broad-shouldered man snarled at Roy: "Get your fuckin' head down and keep it down." He meant business. On his head was a gold-and-black ball cap. A nylon stocking covered his face. In his hand was a small revolver, its blue-grey barrel pointed at the terrified youth's face, its barrel, thrust to within an inch of Roy's right eye, was glinting in the sunlight. Roy dived to the floor.

The man, who was wearing a black leather jacket, blue tee-shirt and jeans then turned his attention to Hanna. He grabbed her by the hair and barked: "I want your fuckin' money and jewels."

The gunman moved quickly to the front door, slipped his arm around Hanna's neck and pressed the revolver to her temple. He began dragging her out of the car as Helmuth slipped quietly out the driver-side door and watched from beside the car.

The second man watched from the rear of the blue car. He wasn't masked and wore a blue ball cap, light green pants and cream colored tee-shirt.

The gunman swore at his heavy-set captive and repeated his demand for money and jewels.

The hysterical woman pleaded for her life. She turned to her left, toward her husband. He was no longer behind the wheel; he was watching the struggle from the roadway.

A terrible chill gripped her. Helmuth wasn't moving. He was

just standing there, unflinching. He didn't blink and he made no move to intervene.

In one horrible instant, she realized the truth. Helmuth was behind this.

"No, honey, please, not this way," she screamed as she tried to resist the burly man with the gun.

But he was too powerful. He dragged Hanna out of the car, over a guardrail and back toward a concrete pillar supporting the overpass.

The man at the blue car kept an eye on Helmuth Buxbaum who stood impassively watching the struggle. When he saw Roy stir in the station wagon he ran to the car and ordered the boy to keep his head down. He pushed Roy to the floor.

"Better do as he says," Buxbaum advised his nephew through the window.

The struggle continued in the ditch.

"I've got five children at home," Hanna begged, "don't hurt me. Please."

The gunman eased his grip somewhat, keeping the gun trained on Hanna's head. He suddenly glanced to the side and saw Buxbaum intently watching the scene.

"It should have been you, you son of a bitch," he hissed at Buxbaum.

An instant later, three shots rang out. A .32-calibre bullet crashed into her left temple. It travelled forward, ricocheted off the front of her skull and lodged in her brain. A second bullet grazed her upper left arm. A third shot went astray.

The big woman crumpled, bleeding, into the ditch, her breathing immediately becoming shallow as life began ebbing away.

The gunman and his partner took Hanna's purse and sped off in the blue car. Buxbaum quickly got back into the wagon and turned to his nephew.

"Quick. Put your head up and look," he instructed the

terrified youngster. Roy looked up in time to see the blue car disappear to the west.

It was as though the millionaire knew there were going to be plenty of questions. And he'd want help with the answers.

2/Buxbaum:

"...determined to show he wasn't a wimp."

Helmuth Treugott Buxbaum was born March 19, 1939 in the tiny village of Labiau, East Prussia, to Otto and Luise Buxbaum. He was the last of ten children born to the poor Baptist preacher and his wife and his birth brought them instant recognition. By decree of the Third Reich, Helmuth was — like tenth children everywhere in the land — automatically a god-child of the Fuhrer. Hitler, in his bid to encourage the growth of a greater Germany, had instituted a system of rewarding prolific mothers for their contribution to the Fatherland. They were presented with medals and special identification passes giving them social privileges denied to others. Luise's achievement was duly noted with a document signed by Hitler congratulating her effort and proclaiming god-parenthood.

His middle name had been chosen to reflect his family's profound religious sense, Treugott meaning "true God," literally, or "God is faithful."

Helmuth's arrival meant there were now five boys and five girls in the Buxbaum family, the eldest being Maria at seventeen. The other girls were Elizabeth, eleven; Esther, seven; Lydia, six, and Hildegunde, two. The boys were Friedrich (Fritz), fifteen; Otto, thirteen; Gottlieb, twelve, and Isbrandt, nine.

All but Maria had been born in a variety of towns across

East Prussia and Germany, where father Otto preached to small communities of Protestant adherents.

Otto Buxbaum himself was the product of a large Roman Catholic family. Born in Melk, Austria in 1895, he was one of eleven children of school principal Friedrich Buxbaum. Otto, a non-commissioned officer in the Great War, was captured as prisoner of war by the Russian army and sent to a prison camp in Siberia. During his nearly five years in prison, he became fascinated by the Bible and a fellow prisoner convinced him to convert from Catholicism to the Baptist faith. Otto studied the Bible and decided that when he won his freedom he'd spread the word of God as a Protestant. The academically inclined Otto also studied the Russian language, to challenge his mind and to better deal with his captors.

In the turmoil of the Russian revolution that followed the war, Otto continued to languish in prison camp. In prison he was visited by a pretty Russian girl named Luise, a Mennonite whose German-speaking family had migrated to settle in Siberia in 1908. Luise, the fifth of seven children was born in 1900 in Muntau, South Russia, a Mennonite German community. The two shared a deep belief in God and after a whirlwind romance, were married after Otto's release on July 4, 1920. She was twenty, he was twenty-five. Within thirteen months, Maria, nicknamed Musja (moosey-a), was born in the village of Tolstofka.

Otto and Luise decided the confused state of post-revolution Siberia was not where their future — or that of their baby's — lay. Luise's parents had died the previous year and she felt free to follow her young husband. The family decided they would try to build a future back in Otto's home town of Melk. But getting there wasn't easy. The family made the long trek west to Austria by way of Shanghai, Rangoon and several other Far Eastern ports, through the Red Sea to Venice and from there by train to Austria.

Melk, a town of about 7,000 along the Danube River just

west of Linz is the site of a huge Catholic monastery that dominates the area, being not just a shrine but a tourist attraction in heavily Catholic Austria. Melk would not prove hospitable to the newly converted Otto and his bride. Otto's family was appalled by his abandonment of his faith and upset with his plans to become a preacher. And they were predictably cool to his Mennonite wife, this Russian girl.

With his family shunning him and the small Protestant population in Melk unable to support him financially, Otto was forced to adopt a peripatetic lifestyle, seeking out preaching positions in tiny Protestant communities scattered throughout Austria, Germany and East Prussia.

The outbreak of the Second World War in September of 1939, found the family in Labiau. Despite being forty-five, Otto Buxbaum was conscripted to fight. His three eldest sons, Friedrich, Otto and Gottlieb, were also taken by Hitler's war machine.

As the war dragged on and the tide turned against Germany following Hitler's ill-conceived assault on Russia, Luise was warned to flee if the Russians advanced into town. They were looking for revenge and women and children would not be safe. Luise took the advice seriously and with the Russian armies approaching, she packed the family and left their modest home behind. She moved the family deeper into Germany and safety, joining thousands of others displaced by the war. Shortly after peace was declared, the family reunited in Melk. Miraculously, Otto and his three eldest sons had all survived despite the carnage inflicted on Germany's fighting men.

Melk after the war was a different place, a new order was established and Otto Buxbaum was suddenly thrust into the spotlight. Occupying Russian troops stationed in the town needed a translator and mediator to deal with local officials. Otto, because of his fluency in Russian, became a go-between. The townsfolk finally accepted this Protestant Buxbaum who seemed able to win concessions from the foreign occupiers. The Russians, on the other hand, appreciated someone who could speak their tongue and who had no Nazi connections.

Otto's time had come. He was rewarded after the Russian occupation ended with an appointment as justice of the peace. He took particular pride in this posting, since one of his duties was to conduct the legally required official civil marriage ceremonies for couples before their church wedding. The Protestant Otto looked on his role as that of legitimizing the weddings of Catholics while his teenaged children were put on the payroll to witness the ceremonies.

The Buxbaum family was growing up and in the late 40s the eldest children began taking husbands and wives. At home, however, young Helmuth was developing a passion for religion. He learned and then quoted the bible as much as possible. He was encouraged by his father, who felt the youngster might continue the ministerial tradition. Helmuth would get into scrapes with Catholic playmates, arguing religion and getting his lumps because he would invariably be outnumbered. But he stubbornly stuck to his guns and even though he wasn't a fighter wouldn't shirk from confrontation. ''He was determined to show he wasn't a wimp,'' older brother Isbrandt would say later. Helmuth drew attention to himself with these activities and his parents and older siblings gave him grudging admiration, although some of the older children felt he was a bit of a fanatic. He slept with a bible near his bed and he always sought a role in the evening devotionals conducted by his father. Helmuth was a good little kid, his brothers and sisters would admit, but did he have to be so strident?

But the die was cast. Helmuth had learned to wear his religion like a badge, a trait he was to keep as he grew older.

The economy of Melk, and all of Austria, was depressed and recovery from the war was slow. The Buxbaum children were restless, feeling their horizons were limited. In 1953 Isbrandt, an ambitious young man of twenty-three, decided to travel to Canada where he had acquaintances in an Ontario city called Kitchener. His friends lured him with stories of the job prospects in Canada's bustling economy of the 1950s. Kitchener, formerly called Berlin, had traditionally attracted large numbers of German-speaking Europeans. In the 50s it was to be the magnet to which disillusioned Germans and, in lesser numbers, Austrians would be attracted; a place to start a new life without forsaking language and custom.

Isbrandt tried a variety of jobs including a brief stint at a uranium mine in Elliot Lake in Northern Ontario before returning to Kitchener. His glowing letters back home were examined carefully by his parents, brothers and sisters. He persuaded his parents to come to Kitchener in 1957. They quickly found work on the housekeeping staff at Kitchener-Waterloo Hospital. Then, one by one most of Isbrandt's siblings followed his lead to Kitchener.

In 1958, at age nineteen, the youngest Buxbaum forsook Austria for Kitchener. Shortly after arriving, Helmuth took the advice of Isbrandt and travelled to Elliot Lake where he took core samples and used draughting skills he'd learned in Austria. He didn't care for manual work, however, and returned to Kitchener to plan his future. Among the positions he found was that of junior draughtsman with the city's waterworks department.

Helmuth took part in the Mennonite and Lutheran church and other activities of the substantial German community in Kitchener. Through his mother's efforts he met a quiet, dark-haired woman who caught his fancy.

Hanna Schmidt, three years his senior, had a simple, homespun outlook on things that Helmuth found quite appealing. She dressed simply and lived frugally, carefully saving her money as a factory worker at the giant J.M. Schneider Inc. meat-packing plant. This Mennonite woman proved to be a warm, loving Christian and she completely captivated Helmuth. She was something solid for the young, ambitious Buxbaum, who was dreaming of the future. It didn't take him long to decide he wanted Hanna in that future. She would be stable, supportive and a good mother, he could tell. Her traditional, perhaps even old-fashioned ways were what Helmuth appreciated.

For her part, Hanna, who was being encouraged by her

mother Ottilie to marry another young man in Kitchener, found this bright, young Buxbaum fellow quite appealing. He obviously had good breeding, was handsome, shared her belief in God, and had no shortage of grand ideas about making his mark in Canada. About a year after they met, on June 10, 1961, Helmuth and Hanna were married. He was twenty-two, and two weeks later she would turn twenty-five.

Hanna had been born June 24, 1936 into a German family in Laschingen, southern Poland, the third of three children. She and members of her family had been uprooted by Hitler's war and when the Russians overran Poland, they were placed in refugee camps from 1944 to 1949. Conditions were harsh as the Russians exacted revenge on the Germans who had laid siege to Stalingrad and other cities. Although her father had died in a labor camp, Hanna and the rest of her family survived, holding fast to their faith. In 1949, Hanna, her mother, and older brother Heinrich, came to Canada after escaping from East to West Germany. They joined their older sister, Martha, who had already settled in Kitchener after escaping from Poland in 1944. Hanna became involved in the Mennonite community and immediately started saving money from her work at the meat-packing plant. By the time she met Helmuth she had a nest-egg of more than $13,000. They put the money to use in a solid investment, real estate. Together they started buying houses in the Kitchener area, beginning with a modest home on Southdale Avenue.

Hanna's love for Helmuth was something her mother could not understand. She did not like this Buxbaum, this smooth-talking fellow with the big ideas. Hanna could do better, she thought. Ottilie Schmidt would never fully accept Buxbaum, but she would tolerate him. Her dislike only increased when her daughter announced that she and Helmuth were going to move a hundred kilometres west to the city of London, away from the large German community in Kitchener.

In 1963, Buxbaum reached a decision. With the support of his good woman he was going to go back to school. He announced he wanted to become a doctor and he'd heard the medical school at the University of Western Ontario in London had a good reputation. He and Hanna, who by now was pregnant, moved to a modest home near Hyde Park Road in western London and he took up his studies. Not far from the home was a large Baptist church, West Park, and he and Hanna joined the congregation. Helmuth threw himself into his pre-med courses but he was to have distractions. In early November his sister Lydia, who had finally been persuaded to come to Canada, moved in with Helmuth and Hanna. Two weeks later, the couple's first child, Paul Helmuth, was born. Several weeks after these developments, Helmuth withdrew from the university, disappointed that school was more than he could seem to handle. He, Hanna, the baby and Lydia moved to Kitchener.

The next fall he enrolled at Waterloo Lutheran University, dedicating himself anew to an education. He would return to Western for a summer course and in 1967 he graduated with a degree in biology from Waterloo Lutheran (soon to be renamed Sir Wilfrid Laurier University).

He'd spent many nights and early mornings studying while holding down the waterworks job and supporting his young family. He soon found a job teaching night courses with the board of education and slowly added to his real estate holdings. About this time he became aware of an inexpensive farm that was up for sale back in the London area. Anxious to break away from Kitchener's German community, which he felt would hinder his success in his adopted land, he harbored long-term plans to move back to London. He had a hard look at the farm and felt it would make a fine investment and possibly a future home.

The Buxbaums scraped together $17,000 for the farm. It was a modest property, located just north and east of the village of Komoka. It had two old farmhouses on it and the land was rocky. But Buxbaum saw it had potential.

Meanwhile, his long-time campaign to persuade his parents to return to Canada had borne fruit. They had returned to

Austria in about 1960 because of financial conside.ations relating to Austrian government pension entitlements. Buxbaum had been particularly anxious to show Otto and Luise he could be a success, that he was the one child who could make them proud. "It was very important to Helmuth to get our parents to come over." Lydia recalled later. She felt Helmuth was bothered by the continuing resentment from Hanna's family and he wanted to be accepted. Hanna's love was not enough.

In 1966, Otto and Luise acceded to Helmuth's appeals. Most of their children were in Canada and they felt they owed it to them to make another try. Helmuth was overjoyed. He found them an apartment in Kitchener, but later relocated them to another in London after he purchased the Komoka property. The apartment was just a few kilometres from the farm and Otto would enjoy wandering about the land, removing the smaller rocks and assessing the buildings on it.

Eventually, Helmuth decided to rehabilitate the white two-storey farmhouse for his parents. They could better protect his investment and have more room. Luise and Otto happily moved in and began fixing up the old house. But they soon ran out of things to do and Luise began looking for something to occupy her time. Now approaching her seventies, the woman was still energetic, despite having spent her life raising children under the most trying conditions. She began suggesting to Helmuth that she'd like to provide accommodation in the big house for old people who needed care. Her Christian charity and determination to take on new projects were supported wholeheartedly by Otto.

"Helmuth," she would say to her youngest son, "We have much room here and these old people, they need someone to look after them. I can do something, I want to help." Buxbaum, busy teaching in Kitchener and attempting to get additional certificates so he could earn more money, politely ignored his mother's pleas. He didn't want her having to work, it would only create more headaches.

In Kitchener, he was trying to decide what to do now. Should he try medicine again, or should he tackle some business? Teaching was providing a steady income but the financial future was limited. And he resented being treated like just another employee of a large organization.

One night, relaxing at home, Helmuth announced his goal to his family and his visiting sister Lydia. "I'm not staying poor," he said, determination filling his voice.—"I'm going to be rich and have people work for me."

It wasn't long until something happened that would make those plans attainable. Helmuth's brother Otto, who had been bouncing around in a variety of jobs in Kitchener, met a man about this time who was to change the family's fortunes. Jack Wall had been developing nursing homes and confided to Otto that such homes could be very lucrative. Wall pointed out that the Ontario government was attempting to empty costly chronic care beds in hospitals and psychiatric hospitals. Many of those beds were occupied by the elderly. The budget-conscious provincial authorities had decided it was better to fill those beds with younger patients with more acute ailments. The government embarked on a policy it dubbed "de-institutionalizing" in order to relocate the elderly in smaller, private homes in the community. Money would be made available to assist the move.

Wall argued the trend was bound to escalate; the government was getting tight-fisted at the same time the country's population was aging. The traditional mom-and-pop operators of nursing homes wouldn't be able to cope with the flood of new business. Many of these homes were old, with inadequate safety and fire precautions, Wall said. A sharp operator could step in and fill the void by starting new nursing homes with modern facilities and make a killing. The time to act was now, Wall said, pointing to his own success in operating a few homes.

Otto was all ears. This looked too good to be true. Something he could sink his teeth into. His problem was that he didn't have the capital or the property to undertake such a venture alone. Brother Helmuth was the ideal partner for such an undertaking and the old farm in Komoka would make a perfect nursing home.

At first, Buxbaum was skeptical but he heard his brother out. Then, with his usual thoroughness, he asked hundreds of questions. He peppered Otto with question after question. What kind of daily rate could be charged? Who would pay for these people? What kind of staff would be needed? Was the government likely to change its mind? How many beds would make a viable home? Wouldn't the Komoka farmhouse need to be expanded? Wouldn't it cost a lot of money?

Helmuth slept fitfully that night, his head full of schemes. He was intrigued by the prospects. The next morning, he astounded brother Otto. Using his draughting skills he had come up with detailed drawings of how the old farmhouse in Komoka could be expanded to the north to provide beds for a nursing home. He had seized on the project and with single-minded determination, he knew he'd found the key to wealth and power.

In the coming months, the partner-brothers scraped up financing and contractors and the resulting small operation became the Komoka Nursing Home. Residents were easy to find and the small home was an immediate success.

Helmuth continued teaching in Kitchener and left the day-to-day management to Otto and his parents. His mother, over-joyed at having something to do, cooked for the residents and threw herself into the operation. At last she had an outlet for her Mennonite belief in caring for others. The partners in the home were Helmuth and Hanna and brother Otto and his wife, Elfriede.

Toward the end of the decade, Helmuth saw how healthy the nursing home business was and he left Kitchener and teaching behind. He relocated to London and made plans for a home on the nursing home site for his growing family.

Life was looking bright for the Buxbaums. The next few years were to prove extremely happy and profitable. Helmuth

Buxbaum was about to demonstrate he was a shrewd business-man who could be very successful.

He was also to reveal a personality flaw that would alienate family, friends, church. The boy who had come so far from poverty in war-torn Europe was about to become a millionaire. But he was also going to risk it all.

3/Building Life and Business:

"Money was his God."

Komoka, not far from London's western fringe, is a quiet village noted today for the extensive rectangular ponds along its southern boundary, the legacy of its vast reserves of gravel aggregate.

It was originally named Kamoka by the Delaware and Muncey Indians who inhabited the area. The name means "resting place for slain heroes." Hanna Buxbaum is buried there.

Komoka was to be the base of operations for Helmuth Buxbaum as his nursing home business quickly expanded. He would eventually establish headquarters in an office building on Hyde Park Road in western London, but the Komoka nursing home would remain the flagship enterprise.

This new home was about one-sixth the size of Helmuth's boyhood home of Melk and he came to enjoy his position in it. Once an outcast and poor in his home town, he was to become the richest man in the village. Just as the huge monastery used to look down on Melk, Helmuth Buxbaum's nursing home was situated on a hill overlooking Komoka. He could look down, figuratively as well as literally, on the whole village.

In the early months of the business, Helmuth remained the invisible partner, wrapping up his interests in Kitchener. His brother Otto did the physical work of building and operating the home, which had twenty-three beds and cost $80,000 to create. Otto mingled freely with residents and was generally well liked.

If a patient had fouled his clothes, Otto would pitch in and change the hapless resident. He was willing to work hard and get his hands dirty when necessary. Likewise, the Buxbaum parents toiled to help establish the business. Luise would cook and help with the housekeeping. Often she'd have residents into her living quarters for tea and cookies and choir practice. She and her husband held bible meetings and attempted to meet as many of the needs of the residents as possible. Accustomed to the confusion of a large family, she enjoyed her new role and felt she and her husband were making a contribution to Canada and to their children's success.

Helmuth solicited the help of his other family members, putting to use their talents with a hammer or their willingness to do housekeeping. He ensured the patients themselves were not allowed to vegetate. Their able hands were pressed into service whenever possible, mostly because it was a means of reducing overhead and increasing profit which he would re-invest in other homes. But Helmuth chose not to take on the physical work; others could be convinced to undertake chores through pay or promises. Others could also show their compassion for the residents. To Buxbaum, the old people were merely income-generating units.

Hanna and Helmuth left Kitchener behind and moved into London as a fine new, red-brick home was built behind the nursing home. The sprawling home would eventually have a bomb shelter, indoor swimming pool, aviary, tennis courts, soccer field, and trout ponds. Buxbaum was determined to be a success. He wanted to escape the German ghetto of Kitchener and now he wanted to shed any trace of accent which, he felt, might hinder his progress. His family could recall his taking long solitary walks and repeatedly practising his troublesome ''th''s and ''w''s in order to sound as Canadian as possible. He also became a staunch defender of his adopted country.

Any relative who dared criticize anything about Canada, would feel the sharp lash of his tongue.

In 1967, as work was progressing on the Komoka nursing home, Helmuth approached his brother-in-law back in Kitchener, Heinz Wagner. Wagner was the husband of Hanna's sister Martha, and was operating a painting and decorating business. Buxbaum convinced Wagner to do some work at Komoka and opened the decorator's eyes to the booming nursing home business. He suggested Wagner might want to join him and Otto as a partner in other homes, but Wagner demurred. He had never been fond of Helmuth. His wife and her mother retained an active dislike for him. Wagner was interested enough to contact the Ontario health department to find out where homes were needed. He was advised the London area needed several more facilities. That same year, he established Sun Haven Nursing Home near the village of Lambeth between Komoka and London.

Buxbaum was outraged. This was an invasion of his territory and he would prove to be a ruthless adversary. Helmuth sent Otto to visit Wagner one day with a curt message. "He said he would ruin me," Wagner would later testify in court.

On a subsequent visit to Ottilie Schmidt's in Kitchener, Wagner and Helmuth crossed swords in person. It was an ugly, loud confrontation and Ottilie had to step in to separate her feuding sons-in-law. "She told us to relax, we should get along because we were both going to be in heaven together," Wagner would recall. "But Helmuth said he didn't want to be in heaven with me. He wanted a separate room."

Wagner and Buxbaum refused to speak to each other for the next ten years until Hanna pleaded with the men to be civil so their children could get to know each other. The Wagners sold Sun Haven in 1972, although they would continue to operate other homes elsewhere, away from London. The decade of stoney silence was broken once in about 1969 when a snickering Helmuth telephoned Wagner to inform him he'd told "lies" about Wagner and his operation to health department officials. Buxbaum said he was living up to his threat to ruin his brother-in-law. Another shouting match ensued and before he hung up, Buxbaum exasperated Wagner by informing him that "if you are a Christian you have to forgive me." It was a line Buxbaum was to use whenever he was brought to task for his behavior by business or religious associates.

The Buxbaum nursing home business took another spurt in 1968 when Helmuth bought a vacant Chatham office building for $185,000 and created the first nursing home in the city a hundred kilometres southwest of Komoka. Plans called for 120 beds and a staff of forty. Soon after, an old school was acquired in Amherstburg just outside Windsor and another home established. Others followed in London, the village of Watford, the town of Leamington and the city of Hamilton and plans were prepared for a second home in Komoka. Many of the southwestern Ontario homes Buxbaum established with partners, whom he would then drop when things were running smoothly.

As Helmuth and Otto continued to develop the business, Hanna kept occupied with the children. By the time the Buxbaums had moved from Kitchener to London, Paul (born in 1963) had been joined by Mark (1966), and Phillip (1967). Esther was born early in 1969 and Daniel arrived at the beginning of 1972. Hanna was told she could have no more children, so later in the decade the brown-skinned Ruthie, a nine-year-old orphan from a Costa Rican mission, was added. Despite the pressures of raising the children, Hanna would still find time to drop into the nursing home to chat with patients and staff. But her Christian compassion compelled her to do what she could outside her home. She never became involved in the day-to-day operation. Her prime concern was her children, business was left to Helmuth.

For his part, Helmuth was becoming increasingly preoccupied with maximizing his profits and the realization that he had what it took to be a success in business. The success almost surprised him and he became self-confident. Eventually, he tired of his older brother, whose erratic and sometimes unpredictable behavior Helmuth viewed as unbusinesslike. He convinced his easygoing brother that the 50-50 partnership wasn't organizationally sound and he manoeuvred Otto into reducing his share to 49 per cent. Then one day, while Otto was away, Helmuth convened a hasty meeting of the board of directors and had Otto voted out of the operation. Otto, deeply hurt, took the $500,000 he was offered and returned to Kitchener. He felt he was as much a part of the success of the business as his younger brother and he couldn't understand how Helmuth would treat him so shabbily. After all, hadn't it been he who talked Helmuth into getting into the business in the first place?

Otto Sr., didn't understand what had happened between his sons. He put it down to a business decision and he was the first to admit he didn't understand business. Helmuth, he reasoned, must have solid motives. His youngest son seemed to have real flair for business and he must know what he's doing. The old man was very happy that Helmuth was successful. After a lifetime of having little as a preacher and then justice of the peace, Otto was beginning to enjoy the wealth his family was accumulating. It would be good for the grandchildren; they wouldn't have to struggle as he and his children had. Canada was indeed the land for the future. The septuagenarian automatically assumed Helmuth would share his newfound wealth with his brothers and sisters, some of them having to scrape hard in other endeavors. The Bible urged sharing and Otto hoped his businessman-son would live his faith. Otto proved to be naive. He didn't know how his son operated.

As he grew rich, Helmuth grew greedy — and increasingly manipulative. He would give to the church and he could occasionally donate to worthy causes, but he wouldn't help his brothers and sisters. His parents at one point had convinced him to bail Isbrandt out of debt, but Helmuth vowed afterward he would no longer be the family's financial saviour. He was smart enough to make a lot of money, if the others weren't, too bad: they weren't going to make him their "mark."

On July 4, 1970, Luise and Otto Buxbaum celebrated their fiftieth anniversary. Helmuth organized the event, drawing the family together from Europe and North America and taking everyone to West Park Baptist. The family was growing and new generations were appearing. It was a time for the children to share in the celebration for the senior Buxbaums. It was also important for Helmuth. Not only was he able to show off his large family, but he was able to demonstrate to his relatives how well he, the baby of the family, was doing. He drew the expected accolades on his material success, but he also drew resentment when he declined to support some business ventures proposed by his relatives. He didn't mind resentment, it was a sure sign of jealousy, he reasoned. He was showing the rest of the family he was a power to be reckoned with. He had money and he maintained his parents. It was a glorious time for an insecure boy grown into a man. He started compiling a family history with his older sister Maria, who had moved to Komoka and he orchestrated another family reunion four years later.

Otto Sr. died late the next year. His passing came too soon for Helmuth. He had many more empires to build, to demonstrate even more to his father how much of a success he could become.

On April 1, 1972, the Ontario government decided to formalize its arrangements with the nursing home operators like the Buxbaums through a licensing program to maintain minimum health and safety standards for residents. The health ministry wanted to continue moving chronic patients into the community, but it didn't want them living in firetraps. Staffing requirements would be set out and inspections would be mandatory.

At the same time, the Ontario Health Insurance Plan, the province's version of medicare, was amended to permit payments to cover nursing home beds. The cost of such accommodation was far less than comparable hospital beds, so the government felt it was a good move.

The effect of the government action was to weed out the small operators who could not afford to meet the new standards. It also meant existing homes were being encouraged to join chains in order to better capitalize their overhead and administrative costs. Operators of newer nursing homes would be favored because they had newer facilities and tended to have a more business-like approach to their operations.

Buxbaum was ready for the changes which only encouraged the further growth of his empire. While each of his homes would be established as a separate corporate entity, responsibility for running them would rest with Treugott Management Inc., an independent trust organized for tax purposes in the interests of the Buxbaum children. Helmuth installed the minister of West Park Baptist Church, Paul Fawcett, as one of Treugott's three directors.

Buxbaum impressed the government's inspectors and his growing chain was cited as an example of a good operation to other home owners. The attrition of small operators and rise of chains like the Buxbaums was mirrored in Ontario government figures. At the end of 1972, there were 455 nursing homes in Ontario, providing 22,741 beds. By the end of 1980 there were 351 homes with 28,202 beds and by the end of 1984, 330 homes had 29,476 beds. Fewer operators were providing more beds.

The same year the government formalized its relationship with nursing home operators, 1972, Helmuth detected grumblings from staff on the home front. The Komoka nursing home employed about seventy persons, of whom nearly half were part-time. The nursing assistants, aides, laundry and maintenance workers had complaints about working conditions. Helmuth was aloof and arrogant and paid little heed to their concerns about pay and benefits. He was also a little strange, they felt. He could be particularly pleasant at times and would pay their wages and expenses if they were willing to attend religious conferences with him in Ontario and elsewhere in neighboring states. But he could be moody and volatile, they found. He tended to favor attractive female staff members and asked needlessly personal questions. He was autocratic and stubborn and didn't accept suggestions from staff.

Members of the staff began thinking about a union and when Helmuth heard of an organizing drive he did everything he could to stop it. Midway through the year a certification vote was taken on behalf of the London and District Service Workers Union. By a narrow vote, the workers rejected the union. Buxbaum was overjoyed. He immediately threw a staff party and was unusually sociable. Seeing his reaction, some staffers were angered, offended by his patronizing attitude. Six months later, as soon as legally possible, another vote was taken. The union was in. When Buxbaum heard the result he was furious. He promptly cancelled the staff's Christmas party and stormed through the staff room, ripping out the stereo system.

The first full-time contract started April 1 and Buxbaum was heavily involved in negotiations which eventually broke down and had to be arbitrated. Once again, he proved to be a tough adversary. Charlie Davidson, the union's agent, remembered Buxbaum as disdainful, condescending.

"He was an arrogant person. He acted like he was lowering himself in stature to sit down with us at the same table," Davidson would say later. Buxbaum seemed to exhibit what Davidson described as a "master-serf" relationship with his staff. After the arbitration was handed down, Buxbaum challenged it in court, taking it all the way to the Ontario Court of Appeal, where he lost.

Buxbaum's anti-union sentiment also got him in trouble with the Ontario Labour Relations Board. Nursing aide Madeleine Kish was one of the union organizers and would later become chairman of the home's bargaining unit. While she was on sick leave before the union was voted in, Buxbaum visited her and told her to forget her plans to represent staff: she was fired. The labor board ordered her reinstatement but the bitterness remained.

"He could charm the birds out of the trees as long as you didn't cross him," Kish remembered. "Money was his God."

She found negotiations difficult with him. "You couldn't talk to Helmuth. It was his way or no way. He would cry about going broke during union negotiations."

Because of his activities and attitude, Local 220 of the Service Workers would grow to be a very militant union. In subsequent negotiations, Helmuth used other representatives and hired outside bargainers. The union would be a continuing thorn in his side and he was thankful he didn't have similar problems at his other homes.

He turned back to making money. More homes were added to the portfolio, a chronic care hospital in London, another on Manitoulin Island, another in Midland one in Englehart in Northern Ontario and others in Charlottetown, and Summerside, Prince Edward Island. Even though the home in Leamington, Ont. was sold in 1980 and the Manitoulin Island home disposed of early in 1984, the chain stood at nine homes and one private hospital by the time Hanna died. Business was good and he continued to mix religion with it whenever possible. His minister, Paul Fawcett, sat on his management firm, which he originally named C.I.T.A. Inc. (Christ Is The Answer). The Mennonites continued to spread their word through his homes and the staff continued to take part in religious conferences. Life and business was good in the 1970s.

Helmuth Buxbaum was definitely on a roll.

4/Trouble:

"...much unhappiness in the home."

By the late 1970s, the Buxbaums were well on their way to becoming millionaires. Hanna, however, remained unaffected. Villagers continued to see the simply dressed woman at the grocery store, happily chatting about children as she'd pick up hotdogs and buns for her gang up the hill.

Nearly a decade of child-bearing had taken its toll on Hanna. Always sturdily built, she had lost much of her figure and was inclined toward simple print dresses. She never wore makeup and spent little money on clothes for herself. But she would ensure the children were smartly turned out. She thought of herself last. Typical would be her approach to the rare visits to McDonald's restaurants in London. She would never go for herself; this food wasn't as nourishing as that she could prepare, but she wouldn't deny the children their wishes if they wanted to enjoy a hamburger like other kids. She would order for the children and content herself with eating the scraps they'd invariably leave behind. She was frugal, ensuring she checked the bargains on $1.44 days at Woolco in London. Hanna, as usual, was entirely selfless. She found time to write letters to help get distant relatives out of the Soviet Union, including Georgi Vins, whose family had helped raise Helmuth's mother after the death of her natural parents. Vins, at one time a leader of the underground Evangelical Baptist Church in the U.S.S.R. had been sentenced to five years in hard labor for his activities. In poor health, he was permitted to emigrate thanks to the tireless work of Hanna and was permitted to join relatives in Chicago. Hanna also took her Hungarian-born housekeeper back to her native land to see relatives she hadn't seen in thirty years. Hanna had always found time to consider more the concerns of others than of herself.

Helmuth, meanwhile, was proving the opposite. Money was a narcotic to him. The more he earned, the more he wanted. Anyone who stood in his way would feel his wrath. Money was the benchmark of success and he wanted success very badly. Even when he prospered, he continued to want more money, driven by an inner desire to prove himself a hundred times over.

Money was changing Helmuth. He began to hold in disdain those who didn't have any because they hadn't applied themselves and used their brains as he had. Anyone who wanted to take money from him was an enemy to be destroyed. As he became richer he made more enemies and he didn't seem to care about it. He didn't like being denied and he found he could use money to get others to help him achieve his ends.

The compulsion to succeed was accompanied by another, more ominous drive, the desire for sex. He began smuggling pornographic magazines, movies and paperbacks into the home and hid them away in the bomb shelter he'd created underneath the garage. The glossy photographs and lurid tales fueled his fantasies and made him increasingly dissatisfied with his own sex life. As a Christian, he was bothered by his fantasies. But he gradually set aside his doubts and began to marvel at how readily good-looking young women would disrobe in front of a camera for a few dollars. His tastes grew more exotic; he began bringing back more explicit pornography from trips to the United States and Europe. His fantasies continued. If young women were willing to tout their wares for a few dollars, surely he could find some of these women, if not in Komoka, then in London.

In 1967, following the open house he staged at the new

Komoka Nursing Home — the affair coincided with the Grey Cup game and was practically ignored — Buxbaum and his brother Otto went to a downtown London bar called The Silver Dollar. Otto hired a hooker and treated Helmuth to his first extramarital sexual encounter. Helmuth was delighted. Later, he felt guilty about it all and confessed to a forgiving Hanna. But the urge persisted; images swirled through his brain.

Tentatively at first, he began seeking out women. He started frequenting bars where he'd been told the waitresses were scantily clad. He also dropped into the bars of London's two largest hotels, the Holiday Inn and Park Lane, where he expected to find hookers catering to out-of-town businessmen. Eventually he was able to look prostitutes straight in the eye and say that he, too, was an out-of-town businessman. Once he had broken the ice with these women, initially so foreign to him, he found them interesting. Generally they came from troubled backgrounds and lacked formal education. But he saw in them a kindred spirit — in their appreciation of money and their striving for the better things in life. He also learned which bars were the strip joints and he became a regular. He would approach the strippers and find that most were willing to engage in sex once the fee was negotiated.

In the 1970s he had a string of affairs, beginning in 1970 with a staffer at the Komoka nursing home who became pregnant by him. Buxbaum and his still-forgiving wife agreed to pay child-support to the woman for more than a year, until she was able to find a husband. He had an affair the following year with his secretary and, not long after that, with a woman who lived close to the nearby village of Delaware.

His extramarital escapades only served to make him more discontent at home. He justified his activities by telling himself that Hanna was wrong not to share his sexual desires; he was a man and she shouldn't deny his rights as a husband.

He felt an emptiness in his life. His religion, to which he had always turned, didn't give him enough support. He believed the bible, but it dealt in generalities and it could only give

broad direction to his life. He wanted specifics. Now that he
had achieved much, he wanted to keep it. He had surprised and
delighted himself with his success. But if money was this easy
to make, it might be just as easy to lose, worried the product of
an unstable Europe.

Late in the decade, he became aware of a man named
Howard J. Ruff who addressed many of his deep-rooted
concerns. Ruff, an American in his fifties who raised eight
children, was a Mormon. The operator of a California speed-
reading franchise that in Ruff's words went "spectacularly
bankrupt" in the late 60s, Ruff got into the food-storage and
survival business, becoming wealthy and self-righteous. The
right-wing economic thinker's paranoia was reflected in a
financial advice newsletter, *Ruff Times*, a TV talk show,
Ruffhouse, and several books. Ruff also produced tape recordings of his lectures, which Buxbaum was to acquire and spend
many hours playing.

Ruff predicted a financial Armageddon, an economic disaster from which few would survive. Traditional money would
become worthless in Ruff's scenario, pension plans would
collapse and a "monetary holocaust" result. Exploding
inflation, he predicted, would result in price controls, which in
turn would make paper currency virtually useless, just as in
Germany in the 1930s. Ruff believed that cities would collapse
and racism prevail. Strong stuff, but it had its appeal to
Buxbaum who was concerned his bubble might someday burst.
He'd seen it happen in Europe; he wanted to be prepared if
things suddenly turned sour.

Ruff devised a program to survive after the financial
collapse, which he outlined in his first major book, clumsily
but straightforwardly titled *How to Prosper During the Coming
Bad Years*. Ruff stressed the importance of family and children
in his life as he unveiled his survival scheme. He also noted that
as a Mormon, his basic philosophy was "prudence, avoidance
of unsound debt, and a kind of 19th century rugged self-
sufficiency."

The economic thinker advised that the future of America lies in its small cities and towns. That is where the economic rebuilding would begin and where money should be invested (music, no doubt, to Buxbaum's ears, with nearly all his homes in small cities and towns). Ruff said food should be stored in anticipation of the collapse of the economy and shelters created to give families a place to wait out the expected civil turmoil that would greet the economic collapse. Governments would be forced to return to gold — and silver-based currencies, he said, so hoarding the precious metals would be wise. In addition, in the new world, after collapse, gold and silver bullion and coins could be easily converted into needed goods. Coins were even better than bullion, he said, since they were instantly useable and needn't be assayed. Diamonds and jewellery should also be saved because they, too, could be used to barter for goods and services when the world was rebuilding, Ruff said.

Ruff became Buxbaum's financial evangelist. It was Ruff who inspired him to build and stock the bomb shelter in his home that would be capable of housing fourteen for an extended period of time. He started to hoard food and liquor, the latter for bartering purposes. He also began dealing in gold and silver bullion and coins with local London dealers and always brought foreign coins back from his trips to Europe.

Buxbaum believed Ruff was speaking to him. The men both placed great emphasis on their families and their religion and they were troubled by the future. For Helmuth Buxbaum, Howard J. Ruff's ideology was irresistible.

Ironically, Ruff had some very relevant things to say about sex and the sanctity of the family unit that also had a direct bearing on Buxbaum, but he chose not to heed them.

In *How to Prosper During the Coming Bad Years*, Ruff warned of the dangers of infidelity. "Adultery is also as much of an integrity problem as it is a sexual 'sin', because the adulterer has to lie, sneak and violate his most sacred promises. I don't believe anyone can have a deceitful double life without spiritual and emotional damage which has to reflect itself in tensions in the home.'' The adviser went on to speak again to Helmuth and his growing passion for pornography: ''I am concerned about the consequences of a man moving into middle age, who every day is comparing his wife, as she adds wrinkles and pounds, with the forever young, physically perfect centre-fold and finds that his loyal spouse does not measure up to this fantasyland ideal. No woman can compare with that, and it may well be that this fantasy may be the reason for much male dis-satisfaction and infidelity, and for much unhappiness in the home.''

But Buxbaum was selective in his use of the Ruff philosophy. If he could use the Mormon's advice to find financial comfort, he would. But not even Ruff was going to talk him out of finding comfort with real and fantasy females.

Buxbaum's life, meanwhile, was becoming neatly compart-mentalized. He had hired good accountants and administrators so the nursing homes were being well looked after. He could set priorities in his life and he could afford to live out those priorities. Sundays, of course, were reserved for church. Saturday was a day for the children. The remaining five days were his, provided he made an appearance at the office. Increasingly, he was lured to the bars of London. From Monday to Friday he sought the companionship of women who could appreciate his money. Adultery was very much a part of his life.

It was a spectacularly unsuccessful group of people he began hanging around with. The women had little more than their bodies with which to earn a living. The men with whom they spent time were likewise unimpressive. Fencing stolen property and dealing drugs were among their main pursuits. The women and their male friends lived for the big score: a fat roll of bills and the next high. It wasn't long before the women had Buxbaum trying drugs. He would pay for the drugs and share them with the prostitutes. That way everyone got something they wanted.

Buxbaum, at first viewed as an oddball because of his age

and dress, soon came to be appreciated: he seemed to have no end to his supply of money. But he remained an odd bird to these people, talking about his children and his business and how he enjoyed both. If these people began to appreciate his money, Buxbaum began to appreciate them for his own reasons. Granted, many of them had never seen the inside of a church, but they had a casual, easygoing way with morality and the law that he found both intriguing and appealing. After making sacrifices and working so hard, he liked the lack of experience his new friends had in both. He was seeing a side of life he'd never witnessed before. Life had been a struggle for him. These people seemed to care less. Most of all he liked the fact they respected him for his money. He could be a big wheel in this crowd. He liked causing a stir when he arrived in one of his regular haunts. It was instant acceptance and he loved it.

As he became more involved with women and drugs in the bars of London, he became a bigger supporter of the church, as if to compensate for his life in the bars. Aside from the gift of land for the Mennonite church in Komoka, he was contributing heavily to West Park Baptist. By the 1980s the annual contributions to West Park from the Buxbaums personally and from their companies averaged from $200,000 to $400,000. They were by far the largest contributors to the church. Helmuth made possible a 1981 purchase of a ninety-five-acre parcel of land just northwest of London at Hyde Park and Gainsborough roads where the church had plans to establish a church-school and recreation complex. The price was $370,000, most of while came from the Buxbaums. In recognition of his donations to the church, his photograph was posted alongside that of other benefactors (it wouldn't be long after he was charged with murder in the death of Hanna that the picture would be removed and Helmuth suspended from membership).

He continued sending staff on religious retreats. At the same time, he was keeping close watch on his female employees. Young, single and attractive females were warned early in their employment that the boss might take an unwanted interest.

And he continued to mix business with religion, irritating staffers who felt what they did Sunday morning was their own business.

In March, 1981, he antagonized most of his sixty-five employees at Mason Villa Hospital in London by including a religious-political pamphlet in their pay cheques. Several of the workers went public and told the daily *London Free Press* they were quitting because they were tired of proselytizing in the workplace.

Buxbaum, who had acquired the chronic care facility six years before, had instructed a secretary to enclose a tract called "The Truth About the Trudeau Constitution" published by a Fort Erie, Ont. group called the Freedom of Religion Committee. On the eve of the April 1 enactment of Canada's Charter of Rights and Freedoms and new constitution, the pamphlet condemned the charter for failing to "give a proper place to God, the family or morality." Readers were urged to write letters, opposing the new constitution, to politicians, including British Prime Minister Margaret Thatcher and to sign a petition available from the Freedom of Religion Committee. The proposed charter, according to the pamphlet, "does not protect in perpetuity property rights and the right to life from conception until natural death."

Buxbaum lay low and hoped the controversy would blow over. He was annoyed anyone could be upset with what he thought was merely common sense. He didn't like being challenged, particularly in public.

Around the same time, he was drawing criticism for adding politics to the mix of religion and business. For several years he'd been active in politics, backing the Progressive Conservative party federally and provincially. He would attend political gatherings with a contingent of staff and church members and his appearance was welcomed. In addition, he contributed large amounts to the area's Conservative candidates, his favorite being Gordon Walker, a lawyer and member of the provincial Parliament for London South. Walker, an outspoken right-winger who believed welfare recipients and jail inmates should be made to work to earn their keep, held a variety of cabinet posts in the provincial government. Many of his positions were in the correctional and justice areas and he was a hardliner who believed the system was too soft on criminals.

Before first getting elected to office in 1971, Walker had done corporate legal work for Buxbaum. The two men shared many views and generally got on well. Walker was running for re-election in the March 19, 1981 provincial election and Buxbaum had already contributed handsomely. On the eve of the election, however, Buxbaum acquired a membership list from West Park Baptist and decided to give Walker an extra push.

Under his own letterhead, Buxbaum used scriptural quotations to promote his friend. The two-page letter contained a combination of statements made by Walker on such topics as capital punishment (in favor), abortion (opposed), homosexuality (opposed), care of elderly (in favor) and the scheme of "workfare" under which welfare recipients would have to work for the community to receive benefits (in favor). The letter was sent to about 200 Baptists, some of whom were members of other London churches and Buxbaum had cleverly timed it to arrive between election day and the last Sunday before the election.

One Baptist who didn't receive the letter was Dale Green, the New Democratic Party candidate in the same London South riding. He and Frank Green, no relation, the Liberal Party candidate, expressed concern that they hadn't been approached by Buxbaum who was using religion to promote their opponent.

In the letter, Buxbaum listed ten positions taken by Walker and urged voters to "go out and vote for candidates (such as Mr. Walker) who will take a clear stand for what is right."

In its introduction, the letter said: "Because of my Christian convictions (I have always voted for the person rather than a party) I obtained a complete interview with Mr. Gord Walker ... who is seeking re-election as an MPP and who is a minister in the cabinet, and asked very specific questions and got very exact answers. (I was unable to get an interview with the other candidates.)''

He went on to note Walker's views on children's rights: "children should be under the authority and correction (corporal also) of their parents.''

"Homosexuality should not be accepted as a normal way of life and their rights should not be expanded on in the Human Rights Code.'' Buxbaum continued, supporting Walker's views on workfare: "this way able-bodied recipients must do their community work just to get their normal benefits.''

Each of Walker's ten policies was followed by a scriptural quotation provided by Buxbaum, including one accompanying the workfare position. ''He who does not work shall not eat'' and ''He that is lazy is brother to him that is a great waster.''

The church directory from which Buxbaum got addresses for recipients of his letter contained an introductory warning that it was not to be used for non-church business.

Reverend Paul Fawcett of West Park was contacted by the press about Buxbaum's letter and said he had been aware of it before it was mailed out and that he had known the directory was being used. He said while he didn't favor this type of use of the directory, the statements in the letter were the truth.

The impact of the letter on London South voters was hard to measure. Walker won easy re-election in the riding, as did his party across the province.

Four years later, in May 1985, Walker was not so lucky. Buxbaum was in jail awaiting trial on first-degree murder in the death of Hanna. In that election, Walker, whose outspoken views were becoming an embarrassment to voters in London South, went down to defeat at the hands of a well-organized grandmother who snatched the seat for the Liberals.

Buxbaum was on the sidelines this time, watching the action from his maximum security cell at the Elgin-Middlesex detention centre. He could be forgiven for welcoming Walker's defeat, given the former cabinet minister's no-nonsense views on crime and capital punishment.

5/Rolling Along:

"Is there nothing you people...can do?"

Thrift and hard work had paid off handsomely for the Buxbaums. Helmuth took particular pride in his large family, his rambling home and proving he could make a lot of money in a relatively short period of time. Helmuth, Hanna and most of their brothers and sisters had left Europe for the promise of a new land — a promise fulfilled for Hanna and Helmuth. Helmuth was pleased he'd demonstrated a greater flair for business than any of his brothers and his success was the talk of the family.

Yet he was tormented by feelings of inadequacy. He had money, the benchmark of success in business. He had a large family, proof of his potency as a man. He had respect, sometimes grudging, from the rest of his family. The kid with nine older brothers and sisters had overcome the handicap of arriving on the scene late and certainly made his mark in the world. Hanna had soothed his fears through their sometimes-difficult marriage, but Helmuth remained full of self-doubt. Even when things appeared comfortable, he was plagued by his fears. Was he a success? Had he done something that would come back to haunt him? Were things about to fall apart? The little boy who had been determined to show he wasn't a wimp hadn't changed: he'd merely aged.

Money was no panacea for Buxbaum. It helped him cope

with his doubts but it didn't eliminate them. The Wimp Factor still ruled his life.

Religion helped him compensate for alienating business associates, family members and others who crossed his path. The worse he behaved toward others, the more generous he was in his support of the church.

As a child, he'd sought refuge in the church in order to cope with the Catholic bullies who went after him for being Protestant. He had drawn strength and a sense of power from God. He might get beaten this time, he realized, but the Bible reminded him even the meek are blessed. The little religious prodigy had shown he could out-quote his siblings when it came to the Scriptures.

As an adult, he continued to use the church as a crutch, to be relied upon more heavily when his behavior triggered feelings of inadequacy; when things weren't turning out the way he wanted; when he felt rejected.

By the 1970s, the business was running smoothly and Buxbaum had time to devote to his other energies. The family was in good hands with Hanna, the simple woman, mother for his children, cook and housekeeper. Hanna had given him what he wanted, for the most part. She would even tolerate his escapades with members of the opposite sex, although she couldn't understand his compulsion for them. Didn't he realize he was now middle-aged, she would ask herself. Why did he carry on? In her mind, Hanna associated sex with creating children, and the time for that was over. She had a variety of gynecological complaints that eventually resulted in a hysterectomy in 1978.

Hanna knew her husband enjoyed sex but she didn't understand his underlying need for it. That lack of understanding would prove fatal. Helmuth had grown bored with Hanna. Just as he felt he had to prove himself in business and religion, he felt compelled to prove himself as a man. His large family showed what he could accomplish, but Buxbaum still felt the need to show his manhood. He wanted to demonstrate he was appealing to the opposite sex and that he knew how to please a woman. There was a satisfaction in that, another kind of power. With money available to ensure he was attractive, all he had to do was to remind himself he was potent and desirable; something Hanna would no longer give him the chance to do. Money and power were his aphrodisiacs.

With more time and money on his hands, he chose to indulge himself in the late 1970s. What Buxbaum wanted, he could usually get. His insecurities made him seek out women, who in turn introduced him to drugs, which in turn made him want more women. And both helped him forget for awhile how he'd alienated business associates and members of his family.

He had fantasized about being rich and had realized that dream. Now it was time to live his fantasies about women, and money would be his lure. The millionaire discovered he could always find a woman willing to perform for money. In his mind, Helmuth Buxbaum was Hugh Hefner and Bob Guccione, all rolled into one. Like the publishers of Playboy and Penthouse magazines, he felt he could live the fantasies of other men. He greatly admired the female form and there were always some of those forms looking for appreciation expressed in terms of dollars. Money, power and sex were his.

He got his university degree in 1967 at the age of twenty-eight. But the university experience had an unexpected side-effect, an unsettling impact on him. Universities were reflecting profound social changes in the 1960s. It was the decade of protest, flower power, peace marches, the birth of the women's movement and free love. Even a conservative university like Waterloo Lutheran wasn't immune to what was going on in the rapidly changing North America of the 60s. Helmuth Buxbaum, conservative, religious and serious, had his eyes opened. He couldn't help but notice the young women on campus and wonder if they were part of the change that was occurring. His fantasies were a distraction. Some of these trim young women had to be on the pill, he felt, and if there were a sexual revolution going on around him, Helmuth Buxbaum would gladly enlist as a foot-soldier. The slender, open-minded young co-eds turned his head. He finished his university years with a degree and horizons far beyond his growing family.

He was discreet as he tested the sexual waters in his late twenties. His wife and family would not be aware of his outside interests until a few years later. There was, however, tension in the Buxbaum household. He and Hanna had disagreements as his dissatisfaction with certain aspects of their life grew. The pressures of starting a business weighed heavily on him and sexually he was getting bored with Hanna. The couple realized they needed help and looked for outside counsel. In 1975, Hanna convinced him they should see London sex and marital therapist, Dr. Noam Chernick. He suggested extended counselling. Buxbaum balked at the idea and the therapist's proposal was not taken up. A minister provided some marital counselling instead.

One outlet for his ardor, Buxbaum had discovered, was the nursing home in Komoka. Most of the staff was female. Buxbaum began to look on his employees as able to provide not only respect but also to satisfy the darker side of his personality; his need to continually prove himself. He could dominate them to remind himself he was a boss, a man of substance. And he could look for sex. He didn't like the urges that seemed to drive him. They seemed crude and base and certainly un-Christian; but they were irrepressible. As he exploited his position, his employees took notice. Talk was that the very proper, very polite European man who signed the paycheques was, well, a letch. A nursing aide hired in the early 1970s had heard the talk before she took the job, but felt she could fend for herself. Still, she was shocked when she discovered how Buxbaum behaved. "He treated the nursing home like his own private harem," the woman said years later. At one point it became so bad, she recalled, that Buxbaum was told by his administrator to curtail his nocturnal wandering around the Komoka home, unless he was accompanied by the administrator or the administrator's assistant.

The talk filtered back to Hanna, but she chose to ignore it. She would forgive her husband and find strength in the Bible. Hanna loved Buxbaum so deeply she felt she could surely exert enough subtle control to get him to mend his ways.

Other members of the family were also aware of Buxbaum's activities. One was his father, Otto, who died just before Christmas, 1971, at the age of seventy-six. He and Helmuth's mother Luise had lived in a modest bungalow on the Komoka nursing home property after moving out of the old farmhouse. Old Otto knew what was going on and he tried to get his son to change for the good of his family. Not long before Otto died, Helmuth's sister Lydia remembers the ex-minister's urging his son to "see a doctor" because of his "problem." Around the same time, Buxbaum was advised to go to London Psychiatric Hospital for outpatient treatment. He wouldn't go because he didn't care for anyone rummaging around in his head. And, besides, he was too busy making money.

His forays continued unabated. His staff remained wary of him and there was considerable talk of affairs at other nursing homes he owned, such as the 160-bed Canadianna nursing home a hundred kilometres west in Chatham where he kept an apartment.

Then there was the big blonde. The nursing assistant came to the Komoka nursing home in 1970 and her striking figure and good looks were instantly noticed by the boss. Some of Buxbaum's discretion began to fail and it was common knowledge among staff that Buxbaum and the blonde went horseback riding together. She would disappear inexplicably from work and with a sly wink say she had an "in" with the boss. The affair continued for a number of months and it was glaringly obvious toward the end of her employment that she was pregnant. She was not married and other staffers never heard her talk of a boyfriend. The suspicions were strong although they couldn't comprehend how their boss would carry on this way with a fine wife nearby. The blonde never returned to work after leaving to deliver her child. Buxbaum had proven to himself, once again, that he was a man.

It wasn't long after that he was telling anyone who'd listen that his wife wanted to leave him. The marriage had become very shaky and Hanna was torn between her love for the children and her pain at Helmuth's increasingly open activities. She feared desperately for the future of the young ones. Lacking any skills that would allow her to fend for herself and the children, and fully dependent on her business-minded husband, Hanna realized she was in a fix. Her picture of a hard-working, God-fearing family was under assault, but she was unwilling to ask for a divorce because it would mean failure on the family's part to live the life dictated by God.

Her immediate concerns were tempered by her underlying faith that Helmuth would change his ways and devote himself fully to her and the children. Still, she had to protect her family in case this man, her husband, grew too bizarre and eventually forced her hand. She didn't leave him. Instead, she opted for a form of financial control to protect herself, should the unthinkable ever occur. She and Helmuth spoke to the family's corporate lawyers and Hanna became a minority shareholder in the nursing home business. C.I.T.A. Inc. became Treugott Management Inc., a firm to manage the affairs of the nursing homes and to own the Prince Edward Island home. It was to be a trust administered on behalf of the six children. Helmuth was president. Canadianna Nursing Homes Ltd. was established to own the seven other family nursing homes. Hanna was granted a 42 per cent share of Canadianna, while Helmuth retained 58 per cent. Grace Villa (London) Inc., was Helmuth's own firm and would run the London chronic care hospital.

The corporate reorganization had little effect. Hanna took little interest in her new role and she let the accountants, the administrators and Helmuth run the business. She had achieved some protection for herself and made the depth of her concern known to her husband. For his part, he soon got over his dismay at the distrust his wife had for him. The arrangement was but a truce in the quiet family war.

It wasn't long before Buxbaum's urges caused more pain in

the family. Lydia, who had long ago moved out of Helmuth's home to marry Gerhard Kaufmann, a widower with two girls and a boy, had faithfully kept in touch with her younger brother. "I thought Helmuth was the best brother I had," she later insisted. Helmuth had paid her way to Canada, housed her, helped her learn English and given her work in the Komoka nursing home. Lydia remarked on how good he had been to his parents, providing for them in their last years when the other brothers and sisters had left the responsibility for their care to him. Helmuth liked the situation: he could prove to the rest of the family what a good son he was and how well-off he was to add his parents to his duties. He had continued his contact with Lydia, visiting her at her modest Chatham home when he was in town looking over his nursing home there.

But late in the 70s Lydia's view of her brother changed. She was devastated by what happened. On a visit to the Kaufmann home, Buxbaum made a strong pass at his two young nieces, Maria, just beginning her teens, and Elizabeth, not yet ten. The girls, while unharmed, had previously viewed Helmuth as their favorite uncle. When uncle Helmuth started getting intimate with them, things changed forever. The girls told their mother immediately. Lydia was appalled. Her brother was acting worse than ever. Was he out of control? How could he try this, in her own home and to her own children? He had violated something that was sacred. She complained bitterly to her brother and didn't get the apology or explanation she felt she was owed. She telephoned Buxbaum's minister in London, Paul Fawcett, at West Park Baptist. "Is there nothing you people in your church can do about my brother?," she demanded. "He needs help." Lydia was frantic and her voice underlined her concern. She was looking for assurance from someone who might have the power to convince Buxbaum to change or seek the help she felt he needed. No assurance was forthcoming.

At the end of the decade, Buxbaum's compulsive womanizing led him to find a nice-looking woman who seemed willing to establish a relationship. She was black and Buxbaum found her exotic. He'd always fantasized about making love to a black woman and had long wondered about the sexual prowess he believed blacks to possess. The woman agreed to move into a house Buxbaum owned about five kilometres from the Komoka nursing home. Buxbaum was satisfied with his catch. He'd proven himself as a man who could tame a tigress. The woman stayed as Helmuth's mistress for several months, but in the spring of 1980, Paul discovered what was going on. Only sixteen, he had learned of some of his father's extra-curricular activities through the grapevine that worked so well in tiny Komoka. The teenager was very close to his mother and his discovery hurt him deeply. Raging against his father, Paul said he wouldn't live under the same roof as the man who was doing this to Hanna. The grade ten student moved out and into the home of family friends, the Conleys, who were also members of the church. Paul stayed with them for about seven months before agreeing to move back home.

Hanna, meanwhile, seeing her family unit threatened, would nag Buxbaum, but was afraid of an all-out confrontation; better to persuade him by example. She dug in her heels and prayed for her husband. She took some solace from the fact that he genuinely seemed to maintain his interest in the church. He supported it generously and insisted on reserving his Sundays for religion. She only hoped the faith he professed one day of the week might somehow affect the other six days. Little did she suspect his apparent increasing devotion to the church was compensation for his increasing devotion to an alternate lifestyle she could not imagine. She prayed especially hard for the well-being of her children and was particularly anxious that her husband's activities not affect them. Things remained tense in the Buxbaum household. But the situation didn't deter Helmuth. He just kept rolling along.

6/Stroke and Confrontation:

"...she was bothering him."

Buxbaum continued his Jekyll-and-Hyde lifestyle through 1981 and into 1982. His extra-marital forays increased as he continually sought new women. At the same time, he stepped up his support for his church, making huge donations such as the sum that helped West Park Baptist to purchase $370,000 worth of property for a church-school centre northwest of London. He would often quote scripture and readily embark on theological arguments. The lifestyle he preached was not the one he led. The hypocrisy never seemed to bother him, something those who knew of his sex-and-drugs escapades could never really accept.

On April 17, 1982 Buxbaum's double life was abruptly brought to a halt. A month after his forty-third birthday, he suffered a stroke while putting gasoline into his car. Doctors later attributed the stroke to a freak occurrence. It had come two hours after he had had his neck manipulated by an osteopath as he sought relief from his chronic headaches. It was believed an artery in his neck had been ruptured during this procedure and a blood clot created which produced the stroke. He was taken to University Hospital in London where, four days later, he suffered two epileptic seizures related to the stroke. He was hospitalized for less than two weeks but it was many more weeks before he could return to work. But Buxbaum was lucky. Although it was a serious stroke, he made an almost remarkable recovery. He continued to retain a weakness in his left arm and leg that manifested itself when he became tired. His left eye would twitch and then droop and his left leg dragged when he was worn out. His speech, however was unaffected. His relative youth had helped him to recover.

As he convalesced, his family rallied around him. Hanna smothered him with affection, Paul moved back home, friends from the church and others expressed their genuine concern. In the back of her mind, Hanna wondered if this wasn't some sort of retribution God had visited upon her husband for more than a decade and a half of sin. Buxbaum wondered that, too. For a long time.

The stroke came as a shock to him. His exploits with women and with the drugs they always seemed to have on hand, had convinced him he was virile and young. His fantasy world was shattered and he spent considerable time wondering why this terrible thing had happened to him. As he mended he considered the parts of his life and how he was going to put them together again.

The physical effects of a stroke are not that well understood. The absence of blood from the brain seldom affects two persons the same way, beyond certain common problems with paralysis of limbs or speech impairment. There are sometimes subtle changes that can affect personality. Family members of some stroke victims note that while depression and introversion can result, others have found formerly restrained and polite loved ones suddenly begin using filthy language and abusing others. A hardening of arteries in the brain can cause grandad to get sexually aroused by a tot in his lap. For Buxbaum, it would take some time before his family and others would notice any changes. But when they did, they would be more cause for concern.

He seemed to lose even more discretion, the Old World restraint continued to slip away. His family members noticed he would say inappropriate things in front of his children, making comments about sex and physical anatomy. Not long after the stroke he spoke in front of two young nieces about the absurdity of another relative's love-making with a new spouse. As well, he became more absent-minded and forgetful. Staff at the Komoka nursing home was astounded at one point to see Buxbaum watering a fully mature tree in the pouring rain. Another night he came into the same home with a blanket over his head and proceeded to wander around, apparently thinking he was travelling incognito. He would show up at the home and begin kissing the hands of staff. At home he began sniping at Ruthie, the adopted daughter who was now fourteen. He wanted her out. Tension was so great in the home that Hanna couldn't stand it any longer and arrangements were made to have Ruthie live with the Conleys.

The "governor" in Buxbaum's brain, the mechanism that exercises restraint to control compulsive behavior, was affected by the stroke. He would now say things that immediately came to mind without filtering them through. The governor had served to temper some of his considerable sexual urges, but as soon as he was able he was back in London and seeking out female companions. His appetite for women would prove more voracious than ever.

Some people, facing their own mortality, decide to become better human beings. Others decide it is time to indulge themselves and get the maximum mileage out of what is left to them. Buxbaum chose the latter.

When he returned to the bars of London, he was more determined than ever to indulge himself, to prove his worth. He sought to expand his circle of women and he wanted more and more cocaine. With his business in good hands, his pursuit of the good life became more serious. It was as though he now had to escape from his straight life.

Even the hookers found him to be a bit odd. He spoke to them fondly of his children and of his money; his twin successes. He complained his wife didn't give him sex but he couldn't divorce her. The prostitutes appreciated his money, but soon tired of his demands. Insecure, he would grow jealous if they were seeing other men and he tried to see some of them frequently enough each week they wouldn't need to go elsewhere for money.

Just before Christmas, 1982, he signed up with Taurus Escort Service in London. He couldn't find enough women by patrolling the city's bars. The service, established to provide dates for visiting businessmen and others, had about seventy-five women available for hire. It was a thinly disguised front for prostitution and by early 1984 it was forced out of business when police charged its operators with living off the avails of prostitution. But while it flourished, Taurus did well. Buxbaum, who indicated he was "single/separated" was one of its major customers, company records later revealed. He was a particularly heavy user of the service through early 1983, sometimes hiring more than one woman at a time. The need to demonstrate his vigor and drive had grown considerably.

Two of his more bizarre actions involving women occurred about this time, one with a woman he found through Taurus, another a woman he met through a Taurus escort. The first was a twenty-year-old of East Indian descent, a particularly attractive escort named Nafisha Somani who seemed to catch Buxbaum's fancy. She met him in the spring of 1983 and had nearly twenty dates with him at $150 to $200 a date. On the first engagement, Buxbaum attempted to persuade the raven-haired beauty to perform a lesbian act with the other woman. Somani declined. Most of the time he saw Somani Buxbaum would have another woman along or call for another in the middle of the sex session. Usually he called the women to join him at a South London motel, occasionally one at the northern fringe of the city. By summer, he was asking Somani to find younger girls for him, under age sixteen and "preferably a virgin." She told him she didn't know where to find any such girls. But he kept asking. He was determined to expand the frontiers of his desires.

"Helmuth was very kinky," she later told police. She recalled

a trip she and another hooker had made to Toronto with Buxbaum. He purchased a vibrator and attempted, unsuccessfully,
to get the women to use it on each other.

Several times during their year-long relationship that ended
early in 1984, Somani asked him about his wife. She recalled
his complaining that Hanna was "unappealing, fat." When
Somani pressed about why he wouldn't divorce her, he replied
that Hanna wouldn't divorce him because of her religious
beliefs.

As the relationship developed, Buxbaum made a suggestion
that astounded Somani. He wanted her child. He tried to persuade her to stop taking the birth control pill so she could produce a child for him which he would then adopt. He offered her
$15,000 to get pregnant and another $15,000 upon delivery.
Somani insisted later Buxbaum was serious, and not on drugs,
or drunk, when he made the offer. He repeated it again. She
declined, even though she needed money for a car.

He then made a similar offer to a woman named Debbie
Schaefer, a twenty-three-year-old who was mousey and plain
compared to the striking Nafisha Somani. He offered her
$25,000 to produce a child which he would then raise. She, too,
turned down the strange request. Before this liaison ended,
Buxbaum took her to Zurich where he visited his Swiss bankers
and for a vacation to Club Med in Playa Blanca, Mexico.

In his mind, Buxbaum still needed the proof of his being a
man, the ability to impregnate a woman.

But he seemed to have difficulty keeping his women. Many
of his female companions tired not only of his cocaine habit,
but also his desire to participate in and watch increasingly elaborate sexual acts. (He particularly liked watching lesbian performances.) And they didn't like his possessiveness. Buxbaum
didn't like their seeing other men and didn't like their having
boyfriends. The offer of money for children may have reflected
more his desire to own a piece of these women and keep them
to himself than an innate love of children. Whatever his motives,
the women were not impressed.

The rejection by hookers merely prompted Buxbaum's doubts to grow. Here he was, a man of wealth who could still please women, turned down by women. He had wanted to show he wasn't a wimp; they treated him like one.

Early 1983 was a crucial period in the lives of both Helmuth and Hanna, a watershed. His activities were costing a lot of money. As he slipped further into the nether world of drugs and prostitutes, the costs continued to escalate. By fall, the Buxbaums would learn just how much money was being squandered. At a Florida conference of nursing home operators, the controller for Canadianna Nursing Homes, Nick Potocska, met with them to review the financial health of their holdings. While revenue was satisfactory, Potocska had found there was a serious drain on resources and advised that if Buxbaum continued to spend in this fashion the firm could slip into insolvency. (In months to come, accountants discovered that in 1983 and 1984 Buxbaum had received a total of about $2 million from the operation for his personal expenses. Half of that amount could not be accounted for, they said.) The bank had already complained that the expenditures had caused the Buxbaum companies to exceed their line of credit. Potocska warned there was a liquidity (cash-on-hand) crisis looming on the horizon; the siphoning of funds would have to stop.

Buxbaum, of course, disputed the figures. There must be some mistake, he insisted. "He basically said I was the controller of the corporations but not the controller of himself," Potocska later recalled in court. But the accountant stood firm: stop taking money or the hard-earned empire is in jeopardy.

Hanna was panicky. She knew Buxbaum had been spending a lot of time with friends in London and that he'd made a number of trips to Europe, but she hadn't realized the cost of his behavior. How could he do this to his family?, she fumed. His selfish activities were threatening to undermine everything they had worked so hard for. While she was concerned about her 42 per cent of the business, she was most upset at the threat to the future security of the children. The chain of nursing homes, a legacy she and Helmuth could pass along to their children, was now gravely threatened.

Hanna realized she had to do something. This could not continue. Like a mother bear whose cubs are threatened, she decided it was time to act. Her faith in God wouldn't ensure the children's future. She could no longer afford to sit back, the passive wife, and let Buxbaum carry on. The situation was extremely precarious. She would from now on take a greater interest in the business and find out exactly what Helmuth was up to.

Following the most impassioned confrontation of their shaky marriage, Buxbaum promised to mend his ways for the good of the children. But promises were easy to break and he was soon back to the hookers and cocaine, with greater intensity. Psychologically, he was trapped. Hanna began monitoring his phone calls and asking questions as she never had before. He told his friends in London that he didn't love his wife and complained that she didn't drink or smoke, as he did, and that she was a Bible thumper. The marriage, he claimed, had been arranged, his wife no longer gave him sex and he'd like to get rid of her. His talk was dismissed as just that: talk.

Hanna began to stand up to Buxbaum, to argue with him, to try to make him feel guilty about his activities, telling him he was risking the future of the family. If he wouldn't change for himself or her, couldn't he at least think of the children? How could he be so selfish?

Her tactics were hard for Buxbaum to accept. For most of their marriage, he'd been the undisputed master of the house. Now he was being challenged and made to feel guilty and he didn't like it. The more pressure she exerted, the more he rebelled. He continued to take money from his businesses at the same rate as before. He couldn't face the accusations and the guilt. The need to escape was more desperate than ever.

Back on the prowl, Buxbaum began cruising the bars in London where exotic dancers performed. He enjoyed the scenery and knew if a woman would take her clothes off for money she might do considerably more for more money. One evening in November he dropped into the Fairside Tavern on Dundas Street in an eastern section of London. He thought he saw someone familiar putting money into the jukebox.

"Hi Maria," he called out cheerfully as he came up behind the buxom blonde woman. It was Maria Caully, the married step-daughter of his sister Lydia. They hadn't seen each other for a long time and Maria was stunned to find her Uncle Helmuth in this place. They sat and talked about family and other matters. Maria, an exotic dancer by profession, was wearing a negligee and G-string. She told Helmuth about her dancing and some of the bars where she performed. They agreed to meet again at another east-end bar where she also worked.

Buxbaum again complained that he wasn't getting any sex at home and asked his step-niece to help him meet attractive young women. Maria, who used the stage name Carmen, readily agreed to introduce him as "my uncle and a friend of mine." Most dancers, including herself, augmented their dancing with prostitution. With the helpful Maria setting him up, he engaged many women in the next several months.

One of them was Susan Ambrose, who had just decided to take up exotic dancing to finance some car repairs. She and her boyfriend had been working at an estate near Ilderton, about fifteen miles north of London, she as cook and maid, he as groundskeeper and handyman. After performing her first-ever professional dance at the Abbey Hotel in the east end of London, a fellow-dancer named Carmen asked Ambrose to perform a table dance for her uncle. Ambrose complied and received twice the normal $5 fee from the attentive gentleman. The twenty-six-year-old Ambrose joined him for a drink and then moved to her own table. Carmen approached Ambrose and said the man wanted to have sex with her for $100. Ambrose replied the price wasn't right but she became interested when the offer was raised to $200. Ambrose and Buxbaum repaired to a nearby motel. This was the start of a relationship that lasted into January, 1984, and became increasingly bizarre. Caully promoted the relationship, telling Ambrose she was looking for a "stable" mistress for her uncle. Ambrose promptly quit her dancing career and repeatedly met Buxbaum for sexual relations at another motel on the northern outskirts of the city.

Ambrose pumped Caully for as much information about Buxbaum as possible and learned she had a wealthy man on a string. She kept the relationship going and tried to keep him away from other women. Buxbaum kept talking about how his wife didn't understand him, how she was pushing him around and how he wanted out of his marriage. But, he told Ambrose, Hanna wouldn't divorce him and she was making his life difficult. He said he was afraid of losing his business and his children to his wife. As the relationship with Ambrose continued (at $200 a liaison) Buxbaum grew increasingly determined that something had to be done about Hanna. He began telling Ambrose that Hanna had to be killed; it was the only solution. And when he discovered Ambrose had picked up some knowledge of herbology, he insisted on knowing what herbs could be fatal if mixed with food.

At first, Ambrose felt Buxbaum wasn't serious, that it was only liquor and drugs talking. He talked of a scheme to hire Ambrose as a maid to prepare meals for the family so she could slip some poisonous, undetectable herb into Hanna's food. In another version of the plot, he suggested Ambrose could be hired as a nursing assistant at the nursing home and she went so far as to start filling out an application form he provided. Once Hanna had been killed, Buxbaum promised, he would marry Ambrose.

She tolerated Buxbaum's stories and schemes into late January, even though she realized he was a strange man. The money was good and it was far easier than being a maid. One morning he picked Ambrose up from her apartment north of the city in Lucan and bought her a pre-sex breakfast at a London restaurant. At breakfast, the stone-sober Buxbaum got very serious about the killing plot. "I realized then that he was very serious and he frightened me," Ambrose testified later. If this man could kill his wife, what might he do to someone he'd tried to enlist in the plot?

When he momentarily left her alone to find some cocaine, she fled back to her apartment in Lucan, told her boyfriend to pack, and with someone she believed to be Buxbaum pounding on the front door, ran out the back way and drove off to Toronto in the Volvo that had been recently repaired with Buxbaum's money.

Shortly before the relationship with Ambrose began, Buxbaum's helpful step-niece had also introduced him to a mature-looking seventeen-year-old named Collette Vandenberg. Despite her age, Vandenberg was a regular at Kelly's bar on London's King Street. One day a stripper approached Vandenberg and introduced herself as Carmen. The dancer asked Vandenberg if she knew how to get some cocaine. When Vandenberg told her she did, Caully revealed the coke was for a gentleman who was hovering nearby in the shadows. A touch of panic flashed across Vandenberg's face. She thought the man looked like a "narc". But Caully soothed her fears and told her the man was her rich uncle. Vandenberg located a gram of the drug. Buxbaum paid her and then asked if she'd like to join him at a party at the Park Lane Hotel across the street.

Vandenberg had obtained the cocaine from the resident pusher at Kelly's, a man named Rob Barrett. Barrett asked Vandenberg to introduce him to Buxbaum and all three adjourned to the Park Lane Hotel across the street where they took a room and injected the drug.

A few days later, Vandenberg ran into Buxbaum again at Kelly's. After making a similar transaction Buxbaum led Vandenberg, Barrett and another woman across King Street for another cocaine party at the hotel. After the others left, Vandenberg had sex with Buxbaum and was paid $125. Although there were more escapades with Buxbaum and the Kelly's crowd she refused to have further sex with him. He did ask her at one point if she would find another woman and perform a lesbian act for him, but Vandenberg declined. Vandenberg did see the considerable impact Buxbaum had on the Kelly's crowd, however. He was a bonanza for Barrett and the others. They would do drugs with the millionaire, then pinch money from his pockets, rip him off by shortchanging him on his cocaine purchases and generally take advantage of the wealthy man in their midst. By late January, Vandenberg realized she was becoming a physical wreck from the amount of drugs she was taking and stopped going to Kelly's. Before she dropped out of Buxbaum's world, she introduced him to a much more effective method of ingesting cocaine than by ''snorting'' through the nose. Vandenberg, who had been pushing drugs for Barrett for more than a year, had adopted Barrett's practice of mixing the white powder with water and injecting it into the arm with a syringe. By January 1984 Buxbaum was now getting serious about his drug intake. The pressures at home were too much and he liked feeling wanted by the denizens of the subculture that flourished beneath the surface of reputedly conservative London. He could feel superior to these people, but he also needed them. He was also now firmly in the hands of Barrett. It was a relationship that would culminate in the murder of Hanna.

Barrett, twenty-four when he met Buxbaum, was the product of foster and group homes. By the time he quit school at fifteen, he'd already amassed a considerable juvenile record, mostly for break and enters. Barrett had held a variety of menial jobs but he found a career in dealing drugs. The slightly built man also had a gift for talking himself out of trouble for overdue accounts in which his drug peddling invariably landed him. Pushing drugs helped him pay for his own cocaine habit, which he later estimated cost him $50,000 to fill his veins for a year. Separated and the father of a girl aged four and a boy, two, Barrett spent much of his time at Kelly's, where the regulars knew him as a source for drugs, primarily cocaine, his specialty. The bar was his unofficial headquarters and Barrett had made about a thousand drug deals at the bar by late 1983 when he met Buxbaum. Barrett, also known as Squirrel, had developed considerable street smarts and realized quickly that Helmuth Buxbaum was quite a find. He became possessive of the older man. Barrett didn't want Buxbaum getting his drugs elsewhere; he wanted the exclusive franchise. Squirrel also catered to the older man's need for women and usually took a finder's fee of $100 each time he found one for him. He also introduced Buxbaum to a black prostitute named Dawn Watson who herself would provide other women. As 1984 started, Barrett was supplying Buxbaum with cocaine twice a week, a frequency that would grow to four times a week within a few months. Barrett would supply him with a gram of coke for the going rate of $150 to $200 a gram. But the pusher would hold back as much as half a gram for his own use. Buxbaum knew what was going on but didn't seem to care. Careful of every dollar in the business world, he cared too much about maintaining his drug supply line so he didn't complain. It was a small price to pay to feel accepted and flaunt his power. Occasionally, Barrett would provide a quarter ounce of the drug for $750, holding back a similar proportion. The man known as Squirrel warned other dealers to stay away from the man he would refer happily to as his "mark". Despite Barrett's possessiveness, the presence of Buxbaum in the shadowy world of Barrett and his pals meant everyone would benefit because they seemed willing to do just about anything for money.

Buxbaum began complaining about his wife to Barrett and anyone else who would listen. "She was bothering him," Barrett would say later. "He wanted to have her killed." That was early in January and from that point on, Barrett recalled, every time he saw Buxbaum, the older man kept saying he had to "get rid of her." At first, Barrett, like the others in his crowd, wouldn't take Buxbaum seriously. Accustomed to petty crime, Barrett and his friends couldn't imagine someone telling them this. It must be the drugs that make him talk of murder.

As Buxbaum increased his use of cocaine and kept company with a wide variety of women provided by Barrett and Watson, he pumped thousands of nursing home dollars into the London crowd. He took Watson to Europe at one point and complained he had to get rid of his wife. He spoke ominously of having Hanna drowned, shot or poisoned.

Back home, Hanna was distraught about the amount of time Helmuth was away from home, and quarrelled with him when he did come home. She adopted guerilla tactics. Suspecting he was taking drugs with needles, she would invade his shower, grab him by the arm and look for tell-tale needle marks and bruising. She would find both. Buxbaum couldn't wait to get back to his friends at Kelly's and the Park Lane. He would rest briefly after a binge of cocaine and sex and then head back into London, that much more determined to get rid of Hanna.

As the winter of '84 eased into spring, Buxbaum's cycle continued, but storm clouds were thickening. Hanna had shared with Paul her concerns about his father and the two of them were determined to wean him off drugs. One day in March, Hanna found a plastic package of white powder and confronted Helmuth with it. She demanded to know its contents and when he wouldn't tell her, she decided to get to the bottom of the matter. Their son Phillip had taken karate lessons several years before from a black man in London, Hanna remembered. She didn't know who might be able to identify a drug, but thought if anyone might, it would be Christopher Browne, the karate teacher.

Browne was startled one April evening to answer his door and find Helmuth, Hanna and Phillip. Helmuth, whom he'd met through a friend and spent some time with, seemed upset. "Chris, you gotta help me out," Buxbaum hissed out of earshot of his wife and son. "My wife thinks I am unfaithful." Inside the apartment and in front of Hanna, Buxbaum handed Browne the package and asked him to taste it. Browne, not knowing what else to do in this strange situation, complied. He identified the substance as baking soda. Hanna wasn't satisfied: "She really freaked," he would recall later. She accused Browne of providing drugs to her husband and added: "I don't know what you've done with your relationship but I don't want you to destroy mine,'' she told the recently separated Browne. She demanded Browne look at Helmuth's arm. But Buxbaum was wearing long sleeves and pulled his arm away, refusing to let Browne roll up the sleeve. The three Buxbaums left soon after and Browne was left to wonder about his occasional friend, Helmuth. This Helmuth is a strange cat, thought Browne. Last time he visited me a couple months ago, he tried to buy sex from my girlfriend. What's next?

Buxbaum was furious at the humiliating scene his wife had put him through. He could overlook being ripped off by his pusher; it wasn't the first time. But being humiliated by his wife, never. A man who is a real man does not put up with this nonsense, he muttered darkly.

Meanwhile, Hanna stepped up her campaign to get him off drugs. She and Paul began making some discreet inquiries and discovered there was a program not far away in Michigan where people with drug addiction problems could be treated. Pine Rest Hospital in Grand Rapids seemed like the ideal spot. They spoke to Helmuth about it, but he was angry and upset. He insisted he didn't know what they were talking about. Underneath, he resented this intrusion that threatened to take away his good times, the hours when he could feel comfortable. The tension between Helmuth and Hanna was becoming unbearable. She was desperate to change his ways; he was desperate to get her off his back. He went for assessment at the hospital but delayed signing up for treatment. Later, his still-unsigned application form was retrieved from Hanna's purse which police divers had retrieved from the Thames.

As Hanna got more serious, so did Helmuth. Divorce was out of the question for her on religious grounds. Even if he could leave her, she would take with her 42 per cent of his nursing home empire. Where would that leave him? He would have to retrench, something he was loathe to do. His days of hard work and sacrifice he hoped to keep as just a memory. She wasn't going to take his pride.

Cocaine had fogged his mind, but he knew one truth about

life: Money could buy just about anything he wanted. He felt he was virtually omnipotent. And now he wanted to rid himself of a wife. The euphoria and sense of being above the concerns of mere mortal men made him think he just might be able to shed a major irritant in his life. Helmuth's decisions had been correct before, he reasoned, he was right this time, too. It only made sense. This woman had become a monster in his eyes, she was out to destroy him. She had to be stopped.

Within days, Buxbaum was asking his friend Barrett if he could arrange the death of Hanna. Barrett couldn't believe it. He knew how unhappy Buxbaum was with his wife, but Barrett wasn't inclined toward violent crime. Buxbaum persisted. All Barrett had to do was arrange it, not shoot anyone. With his contacts he must know someone who could use some money. Initially, Buxbaum offered Barrett $50,000 to arrange the death, then, when he was certain he'd interested Squirrel and might actually have to pay the money, modified it to $25,000. Barrett, once he got over the shock, thought about it and decided he could work this situation to his advantage. He could certainly use the money for cocaine, rather than just live off the scraps he hustled from Buxbaum. He decided to humor the out-of-love husband.

"I led him to believe it was going to get done," he confessed later. "I was just going to take advantage of him."

Things would soon change when Barrett realized the threat posed by Hanna to himself and to Helmuth was real.

7/A Plot is Hatched:

"You've got to get going on this."

Early in January, 1984, Buxbaum first mentioned to his drug dealing cohort Barrett that he wanted Hanna killed.

Murder was something Squirrel didn't want to hear about, much less undertake. But as he became aware that Helmuth was sincere, he also realized the millionaire was prepared to pay good money for anyone who would take on the assignment. While murder wasn't something Barrett understood, he did understand money. He humored Buxbaum from the beginning and let him talk freely about what he had in mind. Barrett was glad Buxbaum had taken him into his confidence and he wanted to ensure Buxbaum didn't discuss it with some of his other acquaintances in London's bars. If Barrett could lead him to believe he was talking to the right man, the millionaire would look no further for help. The ever-scheming Barrett was determined not to share his client with anyone else.

Barrett was supplying Buxbaum with cocaine twice a week, sometimes three and four times, usually meeting him at Kelly's then joining him to inject the drug at the Park Lane or another hotel. It wasn't long before Buxbaum was complaining about Hanna every time he saw Barrett and insisting she had to be killed. In April he asked his sympathetic friend if he could arrange Hanna's death.

Taken aback at first, Barrett mulled over the request. He was using an increasing amount of cocaine and his nightly drug deals at Kelly's weren't bringing in enough revenue. He had an outstanding bank loan of $2,300 from the previous year, money he'd needed to move his wife, Kelly, and their two young children back to London from Calgary where he'd been laid off from a foundry job earlier. He and a partner had started breaking into London homes to help finance his drug habits. Barrett estimated his take from the break-ins amounted to $70,000 in the previous year, but his habit had more than gobbled that up. He'd been able to curtail his break-ins once he met Buxbaum and a steady income was assured. But Barrett's use of cocaine and speed was growing with his income. He saw a chance of earning enough money to guarantee his own supply of drugs. So he strung Buxbaum along, keeping others away.

Helmuth kept up the pressure and became insistent that Barrett could arrange the job. The pair talked about it at length, usually high on cocaine, their minds working overtime. Barrett didn't want to dirty his hands with murder while Buxbaum wanted to be sure no one would suspect him of being behind the deed.

The pair concocted a scheme to kidnap and kill Hanna as a perfect solution to the problem. This way Buxbaum could play the distraught husband and an entirely credible ransom target. And Barrett could pay someone to take Hanna away and kill her without his having to know the details.

Over the next several weeks the plot was refined. The killers would come to the Buxbaum home some morning when only Hanna and her recently hired maid were home. They would spirit her away and kill her, keeping her wedding ring. The ring and a ransom note demanding a large amount of money were to be mailed to Helmuth from somewhere in the United States. The contract price for the job was $25,000 plus expenses of which Barrett would pay $10,000 to the actual killers. A bonus of $10,000 would be paid to Barrett if the body wasn't found for a year. In addition, Buxbaum agreed to help Barrett relocate to either New Brunswick or Prince Edward Island. Buxbaum would help Barrett and his estranged wife and two children find a home, furniture and a job so Barrett could start a new life. Kelly Barrett's home was in New Brunswick, but Buxbaum's nearest nursing home where he could hire Barrett was in Prince Edward Island. This detail was to be worked out, they agreed.

When the arrangement was to Barrett's liking, he accepted Buxbaum's money, hoping, however, he could put off actually having to follow through with the scheme. Perhaps Helmuth and Hanna might start getting along; maybe Buxbaum would change his mind or find some real killers in Detroit or Toronto. In the meantime, Barrett encouraged the older man to keep talking to him so he wouldn't start looking elsewhere for hired help.

Barrett had long wanted to escape the streets of London where he was well known as a pusher. The successful murder might be his ticket out. He believed a fresh start with his wife might work. "I wanted to start over where nobody knew me," he would later say.

As the plan was being honed, Barrett indicated he could use some cash, trying to flush some murder money from Buxbaum. Barrett had been fined $500 in early February for cocaine possession and the three-month time limit to pay the fine was approaching. But Buxbaum wasn't willing to part with cash until he had a firm commitment from the younger man who seemed to be wavering.

Buxbaum decided to hire Barrett to do some landscaping work at the Komoka Nursing Home. It would give Squirrel a chance to meet Hanna, survey the geography of the home and earn money at eight dollars an hour toward his fine. Buxbaum, always the shrewd businessman, thought it might reveal how reliable Barrett was before he gave him any large amount for a really important job.

Barrett, aside from his need for money and the chance to try his first straight job in nearly two years, was curious about this woman Buxbaum wanted killed. Could she possibly be as bad as Buxbaum said?

The drug pusher took up his duties at the Komoka home late in April and it wasn't long before he met Hanna. Buxbaum had told his wife that Barrett was an unfortunate chap he'd met in London, had taken pity on and was trying to get back on his feet. With her natural compassion, Hanna began to talk to Barrett, to find out more about this rather scruffy young man.

Each day she invited him into her home and fed him lunch, gently trying to learn about his background. For his part, Barrett was astounded at the spectacular Buxbaum house. For a moment, he couldn't resist thinking what a field day he would have if he ever decided to break in. Buxbaum and his family had it made, he thought. Barrett discovered Hanna was a fine woman and she seemed genuinely interested in his family and situation. It surprised him. Every day for more than a week he joined Hanna for lunch in her kitchen. The food was good, but he would later recall being irritated by only one thing: "She was trying to get me to go to church."

It wasn't long before an opening developed for a grounds-keeper at Buxbaum's Grace Villa Hospital back in London and Barrett was transferred. Barrett had no car and he'd had to rely on Helmuth for his transportation to Komoka. The new place was within walking distance of Barrett's Ridout Street apartment. Things appeared to be working out nicely, but the situation would soon change.

On May 20, Barrett was in the groundskeeper's shed at Grace Villa when Buxbaum's twenty-year-old son Paul informed him he was fired. Paul accused Barrett of supplying drugs to his father and pimping for him. The dismissal was immediate and Barrett was angry. He'd been making some honest money for the first time in a long time and he didn't like this treatment. He knew Hanna was behind the move. Barrett was warned never to come around the nursing homes and never to telephone Helmuth. Paul said his father wasn't well and didn't need to associate with the likes of Barrett. Upset with this sudden turn of events, Barrett took his $192 severance cheque and complained to Helmuth that night when he saw him at Kelly's. He was beginning to see what Helmuth was up against and was now more receptive to Buxbaum's plight. He realized the threat to his best customer was real. Squirrel's new-found affluence and improved lifestyle were under assault.

Buxbaum was apologetic, but said there was nothing he could do. Paul was in charge at Grace Villa and had the authority to hire and fire. Buxbaum said he'd had a fight at home when Hanna and Paul said they'd discovered Barrett was his connection for drugs and women. He promised to make it good.

On May 24, Buxbaum met Barrett at Kelly's in the middle of the day. He gave Barrett two Polaroid snapshots to give to the men he hired for the killing. One showed Hanna reclining in bed, the other showing the front end of the family's brown Oldsmobile station wagon. Buxbaum then drove Barrett to two city banks where the businessman withdrew $2,000 and $3,000 respectively. He placed the cash in envelopes and gave them to Barrett.

It was agreed that when Barrett had to contact Buxbaum it would be through the office. Because Hanna was bound to try to enlist the office staff on her side, Barrett would identify himself as "Andy" whenever he called or left a message. Thanks to Hanna, even communication with his "mark" was becoming more difficult.

Barrett deposited $1,500 of the money in the Kelly's office safe and immediately decided it was time for a holiday. He told Helmuth he was going to Florida where he had contacts who he thought might take on the killing. Americans had ready access to handguns and experienced help was needed for this job, he convinced Buxbaum.

Barrett was hoping the killing would be done while he was miles away but, in fact, the drug pusher had no plans. He carefully left Helmuth believing the trip would be fruitful.

"He was under the impression his wife was going to be murdered while I was in Florida," Barrett was later to tell a judge.

Barrett contacted his brother, John, with whom he had been

staying occasionally since January. John, two years older than his brother, was no stranger to crime, having been convicted several years before of the armed robbery of a submarine shop and sentenced to five years in prison. John had met Buxbaum, and did cocaine with the older man and the younger Barrett. Squirrel explained the trip was an attempt to set up a cocaine connection for Buxbaum; he said nothing about murder.

The Barrett brothers travelled to Detroit where they stayed for a day looking for cocaine, then took a thirty-hour bus trip to Orlando where they booked a room at the Gateway Inn. John stayed several days before flying home. After his departure, Barrett contacted his wife, Kelly, then waitressing in Sarnia, and asked if she would join him, bringing with her the $1,500 he'd left in the London bar's safe. He was hoping for a reconciliation and his wife was willing to join him. She collected the money which was picked up from the bar by Barrett's mother, Sadie and flew to Orlando June 1.

After several days, Barrett telephoned Buxbaum and told him there were snags.

"I got some problems, Helmuth," Barrett reported. "I had some guys lined up for the job but they ripped me off. I've found another guy in London, but I've got to fly him down to give him instructions. I need more money, though. This place is expensive and I need more advance money for the work."

Buxbaum was interested in what was happening. Barrett said he needed still more money because of further problems. Buxbaum advised Barrett he was visiting Florida and would be in Tampa the next day. They should meet to discuss this in person.

The following day, Buxbaum telephoned Barrett from Tampa, then went to the Orlando hotel. He met Barrett in the hotel room and said he couldn't stay long: his son, Paul, was waiting outside in the car. Barrett assured him the killing would happen, he was just encountering difficulties he hadn't expected. Helmuth turned over an additional $2,000 U.S.

"But you've got to get going on this," Buxbaum said, since he and Hanna and the children would be leaving for a week in

Europe late in the month. He was getting increasingly desperate. He had attempted to move out of the home about June 14 but Hanna had reminded him of his responsibilities to the family and had persuaded him to stay. He was feeling trapped and couldn't stand the prospect of spending time with his wife in Europe.

"No problem, Helmuth," Barrett assured him. He agreed to set the plan in motion as soon as possible.

The couple visited Disney World, Epcot Center and Sea World, enjoying the area's tourist attractions and lounging about the hotel pool.

It was beside the pool they met a couple from Montreal, Jean and Brigitte. Jean could barely speak English, but his girlfriend was fluently bilingual. The two couples found they had much in common and became friends.

Barrett took an immediate liking to Jean, who, with a missing tooth and tattoos on his arms and chest, seemed to be the sort of fellow who might not care for the niceties of the law. He also claimed to be a member of Hell's Angels. The pusher from London realized he might be able to pull off the murder with the help of this agreeable couple. As June unfolded under the hot Florida sun, Barrett began to tell Jean and Brigitte of his contract to kill a millionaire's wife back in Canada. They said they were interested in getting in on the action.

Our June 16 Barrett received another $1,500 from Buxbaum via Western Union.

The photographs were turned over to the couple, together with $500 and a road map giving precise directions to the Buxbaum house. Barrett instructed his sub-contractors to arrive in the morning when only Hanna and the maid were home.

Jean and Brigitte seemed to like the plan and said they would fly to New York to rent a car, drive back to Montreal where they would pick up a weapon and go to Komoka. After the killing, they were to return to Florida for their $10,000. In a few days the Quebec couple flew off, leaving behind their clothing and cameras as security on the advance money. Not long afterward they telephoned Barrett, saying they were in New York and the plan was proceeding smoothly. It was the last Barrett heard from Jean and Brigitte.

When Barrett finally ran out of money he and Kelly took the long bus ride back to London, arriving home on about the 23rd. He tried to get in touch with Buxbaum with an involved tale of how he had been ripped off again. But the Buxbaums had left for Europe and weren't expected back until July 3.

Flat broke, Barrett stewed about what to do for more than a week. He'd taken $5,000 initially from Buxbaum, plus another $3,500 in Florida. He'd lost the pictures and $500 to Jean and Brigitte and he had nothing to show for it. And Hanna was very much alive. Helmuth was going to want a good explanation upon his return, Barrett knew. Squirrel also realized if his explanation weren't suitable, he stood to lose his "mark" and would have to go back to hustling for his drug money.

Barrett had moved back into a friend's Ridout Street apartment near the core area of London and Kelly came with him. The reconciliation was still holding. On the Canada Day long weekend the Barretts joined some friends at the Lake Huron resort town of Grand Bend, returning late Sunday to spend the holiday Monday, July 2, in London.

The Barretts and one of their young daughters were strolling through Thames Park near the apartment when two men suddenly confronted them. The smaller man Barrett recognized as Pat Allen, a twenty-four-year-old speed freak who specialized in dealing that drug. Allen and Barrett were long-time friends in the drug underworld and once Allen had helped Barrett through a cocaine overdose. The bushy-haired, bearded Allen was accompanied by a well-developed giant he introduced only as "Big Jim."

A few days earlier, Barrett had confided in Allen that he knew a man who wanted his wife killed and Allen had expressed some interest in getting a piece of the contract. Allen, a former weapons tester in the Canadian Armed Forces who was washed out for flat feet, didn't take long to figure out who Barrett was talking about. "I took it for granted because of the company he was keeping that it was Buxbaum," he would later testify.

At the Thames Park meeting, Allen and Big Jim informed Barrett they were collecting a drug debt, money for a friend who was in jail. They wanted $1,000, Big Jim said, "or I'll break both your legs if you don't come up with the bread in a week."

Thoroughly intimidated by these two, especially by Big Jim, who towered over him, Barrett tried to explain there was no debt. When Big Jim seemed unimpressed, he promised to come up with the money by the deadline. Then, in the next breath, the ever-resourceful Squirrel had a proposal for Big Jim.

"How'd you like to earn a lot of money, say, $10,000 to knock off somebody, a guy's wife," Barrett asked the big man. Big Jim was non-committal. He was an enforcer. Knees, hands and legs were one thing. Murder was another. But he didn't reject the offer outright, mostly to keep the cocaine dealer squirming.

Barrett continued to stew. Now he had to come up with another $1,000 that he didn't think he owed. And he was still broke. It was only a couple of days until Buxbaum would return and he still hadn't found a killer. On Wednesday, the 3rd, Barrett contacted Allen and promised payment on the drug debt was coming. Then, he got around to the real reason for his call. Was Big Jim willing to take the contract for murder?

"Forget about Big Jim," Allen said. "I'm interested." Barrett didn't expect this from Allen, a man whose specialty was break-ins and the fencing of stolen goods. Allen, who later was to estimate he'd injected tens of thousands of dollars worth of speed into his arm in the previous year, also had a conviction for robbery with a pellet gun. But he was at the start of a week-long "run", or burst of hyperactivity stemming from his use of speed, and he knew Barrett would pay $10,000 for the killer. He looked on the money as an investment in his habit. It would keep him in speed for weeks.

Allen had a sideline related to his brief stint as a weapons specialist. He understood guns and had developed a profitable business modifying them for his drug-enforcer friends. Currently, he was converting an American-made 30-round semi-automatic machine gun to fully automatic operation. The 9mm experimental submachine gun, called a KK9, was destined for a Detroit man he knew only as "Duke."

Allen knew he could use the KK9 or an old .22-calibre revolver he'd acquired in a break-in a few months before. He'd never killed anyone before, but he didn't hesitate to take on Barrett's job.

Barrett sounded relieved to finally have found someone to help him out of his jam and said he'd get back to Allen.

Meanwhile, late that same night, the Buxbaum family returned from Europe, tired but happy.

But there was little joy in Helmuth; he was apprehensive. Hanna had talked him into attending the drug rehabilitation program in Michigan. It would begin in a few days and he didn't want to go to it.

Hanna had less than two days to live.

Early next morning Barrett reached Helmuth to report he'd found a new killer but he needed replacement photographs. The man was ready, he said, "but I need more money. This has been hard work."

Later that same morning, in the parking lot behind Kelly's, Buxbaum handed Barrett an envelope containing $5,000 and two more Polaroids to replace the ones lost to Jean and Brigitte. The picture of Hanna showed her standing by her kitchen sink and there was another picture of the station wagon. Buxbaum said he and Hanna would be driving to Toronto the next day to pick up a nephew and he wanted the killing done during the trip. He said he'd call Barrett later at Kelly's to arrange details. The plot to kidnap Hanna from her home had been abandoned.

Barrett met Allen at a nearby restaurant and told him the plan. The contract was for $10,000, but Allen asked for half that amount up front. The wary Barrett, not interested in being ripped off again, said only they'd talk about it more. Allen said he needed money to rent a car and for other expenses. Barrett, grumbling he'd already lost up-front money to the Quebeckers, turned over $400 so Allen could rent a car and cover his other expenses.

Shortly after this meeting, Barrett met Anita Pitcher on Dundas Street in downtown London. The twenty-year-old slender, plain-looking Pitcher, a sometime-hairdresser with a record of fraud, had known Barrett for about a year when he walked up to her and asked if she would be interested in travelling to Toronto for a party. Pitcher readily agreed to the idea and joined Barrett for a couple of drinks at Kelly's. About 4 p.m. they were joined by Allen who said he'd like to go to Toronto, to Canada's Wonderland, while they were in Toronto. While Barrett was up making a series of telephone calls, Allen told Pitcher he wanted to rent a car but he couldn't because no car agency would accept his Alberta driver's licence. Would Pitcher help him?

The pair took a cab to the Rent-a-Wreck franchise on York Street. They asked for the least expensive car on the lot that could travel out of town and were shown R19, a shiny blue 1977 Chevrolet Nova. Pitcher put down $150, given her by Allen, as deposit for two days' rental and the pair drove off, Pitcher at the wheel. A couple of blocks away Allen took over.

Barrett, who had been telephoned as promised by Buxbaum, was back at Kelly's where he was picked up by Allen and Pitcher in the compact Nova. He directed his companions to a McDonald's restaurant along Oxford Street in northwest London. Behind McDonald's the trio found Buxbaum sitting alone in his big brown Oldsmobile station wagon. Barrett got out and spoke to him and returned to Allen and said they were to follow the older man. Buxbaum wanted to go to Komoka to get some money and return to Barrett a stolen fur coat Squirrel had sold him several months before. Helmuth and Barrett had agreed they didn't want the coat at the Buxbaum house in case police investigating the kidnapping conducted a search. Buxbaum was still determined the killing would look like a kidnapping and he told the pair he wanted to show them the route he was planning to take to Toronto the following day.

Barrett rejoined Allen in the Nova and after dropping off Pitcher at a K-Mart next door, the two vehicles headed west to Komoka, the Oldsmobile leading the way. Just outside the village the big car stopped along a country road. Barrett jumped out of the Nova, spoke to Buxbaum and returned to Allen saying they were to wait there while Helmuth drove on to his home to collect the money and coat. Fifteen minutes later Buxbaum returned, gave the coat to Barrett and motioned for the pair in the blue car to follow him. The Oldsmobile continued west to a spot on a paved country road just past Komoka and pulled over near a woodlot. Buxbaum told Barrett he wanted the killing done there. But Allen disagreed.

"This is crazy, man," Allen said. "It's too busy here," he said, pointing to an intersection nearby and a gas station on the corner.

"I can find a better spot than this. Follow me."

Barrett joined Buxbaum in the Oldsmobile and Allen led them off to the west on County Road 14 and onto Highway 402.

The two-car procession drove south and east on the super-highway for about two kilometres where Allen pulled onto the shoulder. To the right was a deep gully filled with bullrushes. The Oldsmobile stopped, staying about six car-lengths back. Barrett got out of the wagon and spoke to Allen who said this would be the place for the murder. Acting as messenger, Barrett relayed this information back to Buxbaum who said "fine," he'd be there the next morning at eight.

The Oldsmobile left the scene and Allen began studying the spot more closely. He and Barrett discovered a culvert in the ditch covered by a metal grate measuring slightly more than one metre by one metre. They removed the lid and found the culvert was fairly deep. They left the lid off, because, Allen explained later: "I planned on stashing the body down there." Barrett said the plan looked okay, but he was leaving all the details up to his companion.

The pair then drove to the South London apartment of Allen's friend, Janet Hicks. Hicks, thirty-one, a cookie factory worker Allen had known for about two months, let Allen store things at her apartment. The tall, slender, frizzy-haired Hicks was home when Allen and Barrett arrived and Allen asked her to go to the living room while he and Barrett went into Hicks' bedroom. Allen retrieved a blue knapsack he'd left in a closet several weeks before. He told Hicks to return to the bedroom as he took the knapsack into the living room and opened it. Barrett let out a low whistle. Inside was the KK9 Allen said he planned to use in the murder. He then asked for another fifty dollars for ammunition from an impressed Barrett. Squirrel coughed up the money and Allen returned the gun to the closet. Allen then asked Hicks if she would accompany Barrett to Toronto to monitor a speed deal Squirrel was going to make for him. Hicks agreed and Allen and Barrett left. Squirrel would return to pick her up later.

Allen and Barrett collected Pitcher at the K-Mart and then Allen dropped off Barrett and Pitcher at Kelly's. Allen drove the Nova to another apartment in the southeastern part of the city and collected a .32-calibre revolver he'd lifted during a break-in six months before in addition to needles and utensils for speed. This done, he went drinking at his favorite bar, the Wellington Tavern, around the corner from Kelly's. The revolver was in the Nova's trunk.

Meanwhile, Barrett bought a supply of cocaine and chartered a black Cadillac limousine. He visited several bars and told everyone he was off to a Toronto party. He planned to be still partying when the murder occurred. With him he took Hicks, Pitcher and a friend and bouncer named Rick D'Iorio. D'Iorio was to act as Barrett's bodyguard with the promise of $300 and a drug-filled couple of days in Toronto. The bodyguard notion was an afterthought, but Barrett planned on raising hell to ensure his presence in Toronto was noticed. D'Iorio was along in case things got out of hand. Shortly before 8 p.m. the foursome got into the limousine and promptly began injecting cocaine, with the exception of abstainer Hicks, who preferred prescription uppers and downers to cocaine and speed. After the two-hour rolling cocaine party they arrived at the downtown Westbury Hotel shortly after 10 p.m. They took neighboring rooms on the fourteenth floor for a night of drinking and injecting coke. Barrett and D'Iorio wouldn't sleep, their drug high keeping them up all night.

Meanwhile, back in London, Allen was joined at the Wellington by a couple of friends. One of them was Terry Armes, thirty-four, thin, pasty-faced and twitchy. His companion, Spider, was a different story. Robust and handsome, he lifted weights. But there was one chink in the bodybuilder's armour: a weakness for speed.

The big man had spent the day drinking beer and playing pool and he needed some speed, *now*, to stay awake. Speed-dealer Allen and his clients left the Wellington for an east-end townhouse where Allen had a cache. Spider bought an eighth of an ounce of the drug for $150 and the trio shot up.

On the way back to the Wellington, Allen told Spider he had some "business" to discuss with him, *later*. Spider let him know that Armes was not to be excluded: "Terry's my partner," he said. "Anything you say to me you can say to him."

Reluctantly at first, Allen began telling the men of his contract to kill someone. He didn't offer names but said he was concerned he might not be able to pull it off by himself. He wanted help. He offered Spider $3,000 to be a part of the job. The men surprised Allen by agreeing to take part without even asking the identity of the intended victim. They drove back to the Wellington and closed the place, leaving at about 1:30 a.m.

They talked more about the plan and the weapons to be used. Spider, expressed interest in the KK9 machine gun. Allen took his companions to the Jalna apartment of Hicks and displayed the weapon. Spider was impressed. Then Allen revealed the identity of the intended victim: Hanna Buxbaum, the wife of Squirrel's mark.

Spider handled the KK9 appreciatively and asked questions about its operation. He decided he had to use it.

After injecting some more speed they put the KK9 into the trunk of the Rent-a-Wreck Nova and, at about 3 a.m., left for the crime site where Allen would explain how the killing was to go down.

He showed them the gulley at the edge of Highway 402 and groped in the darkness for the culvert. Buxbaum, he said, would pull up with his wife at about 8 a.m. and he, armed with the revolver, or Spider, with the KK9, would drag Hanna from the car, shoot her, stuff her body down the culvert, then replace the lid.

A half-hour later, they drove back to London. Sleepless from speed, they picked up some beer from a bootlegger then parked the Nova in Springbank Park at London's west end. In a haze of speed and beer they talked of money and murder.

8/July 5, 1984. On the 402:

"I'll get back to you."

It was foggy in Komoka as Helmuth and Hanna arose on this Thursday morning. They'd slept in, still trying to overcome jet lag from their European vacation. It was just after seven and it seemed to take forever to rub the sleep from their eyes.

Helmuth took less time to get going, his high energy level reached quickly as he urged Gizella, the family cook, to prepare breakfast.

Helmuth and Hanna had planned to visit her mother Ottilie at her Kitchener nursing home. That was half-way to Toronto and even allowing an hour or two for a visit and another hour for lunch, the Buxbaums still had plenty of time to meet Roy at Pearson International.

Helmuth had planned to leave their home about eight and be on Highway 402 within about five minutes. But by the time he and Hanna got into the Oldsmobile it was nearly 8:40 a.m.

The fog was starting to burn off as they drove the short distance west on County Road 14 and onto the 402. Two kilometres ahead lay the Nova.

The conspirators had left Springbank Park about 6 a.m. at Allen's urging while it was still dark and foggy. He wanted to get to the pre-arranged spot early so there would be no last-minute snags. They pulled the car to the shoulder beside the deep ditch and jacked up the rear to make it look like tire trouble. The hood was opened. The sun made its appearance as they laid their trap. Traffic was light.

Allen fished the weapons out of the trunk, keeping the revolver and giving the KK9 to Spider. Armes remained in the back seat of the car to act as lookout. His job was to watch traffic coming from the east, on the other side of the median. The hood blocked part of his view and he peered around it as best he could. Spider took the submachine gun and walked down into the gulley and part way up the other side where he hid behind a bush. Allen slipped into the front passenger seat of the Nova and watched traffic approaching from behind.

The sun rose steadily, dissipating the last traces of the fog and making Armes squint as he monitored traffic coming from the east. It seemed it was going to be another hot day and the humidity was already high. In the bottom of the ditch, the culvert lay open and ready. A few metres away, the hired hand waited, his index finger resting on the trigger of the KK9.

Anxiously, Allen kept checking his watch and his adrenalin started pumping when it reached eight. He strained his eyes at the traffic that was beginning to build in the morning rush hour taking workers to the factories in the south end of London. Every few minutes he consulted his watch, speed still coursing through his system, keeping him fidgety. Occasionally Spider would peer out from behind the bush and Allen would gesture that everything was fine.

As the minutes ticked toward 8:30, Allen began to worry. He knew from a friend who used to work with the provincial police near the town of Strathroy, about ten kilometres to the west, that there was a regular provincial police patrol that passed this spot every morning at 8:55. The OPP detachment at Strathroy sent one of its officers into London every morning to district headquarters to pick up the mail, he had learned. If Buxbaum didn't soon show, the patrol would come by and the killing would have to be abandoned.

The traffic continued to build and Allen became worried as the time reached 8:35.

"If he doesn't show in another twenty minutes, it's off," he shouted to the gunman in the gully.

Fifteen minutes later Allen got out of the car and shouted to

Spider to forget it, the killing was off. He lowered the jack and was about to return it to the trunk when he saw the Oldsmobile come into view.

"They're here. Get back," Allen hissed at the man with the KK9 who had started up the gully. Spider darted back behind the bush.

Buxbaum was behind the wheel. He pulled the big car up about a metre behind the Nova.

Allen walked back to the wagon, approaching the passenger side window. The window came down and Hanna spoke. "Car trouble? Anything we can do?"

The young man replied the car's fan belt had broken. "Do you have a spare nylon we could use 'til we get to a garage?"

Hanna said he could have hers, just a minute. Allen peered across to the driver and saw Buxbaum.

"Do you know anything about cars?" he asked Helmuth. The older man replied he was no mechanic but he'd have a look. He got out and joined Allen at the front of the Nova, shielded from view by the still-open car hood.

Allen went straight to the point. "You're late. We've been sitting here for hours."

Buxbaum said he was sorry but he and Hanna had slept in. "You've got a gun?" he asked.

Allen patted the front of his jeans. The small revolver was tucked behind his belt.

"But it's too late. The cops come along here about now," he said. "We gotta get outta here."

The conversation was interrupted by the honk of a horn. Hanna was trying to get their attention. She waved her panty-hose out the window. Buxbaum went to his wife and returned with the stockings to the front of the Nova.

"It's too late," Allen repeated. "And there's too much traffic now. We can't do it."

But Buxbaum was insistent. He checked the traffic speeding past and said it wasn't that busy. "Hurry up and get her out of the car and get it over with," he told Allen.

"Look," he said, pointing to the roadway, "there's not that much traffic."

Allen looked back and saw that Helmuth was right. Not a car in sight. "Awright, awright," he hissed and started back toward the Oldsmobile.

Part way down the Nova fender he spotted a black-and-white car approaching. The OPP cruiser was here. Right on time. He froze in his tracks.

"Six," he shouted to Spider who had started moving toward the Oldsmobile. The pre-arranged signal meant the cops had arrived, forget everything.

The cruiser slowed and pulled onto the shoulder, stopping several car lengths in front of the Nova.

Constable Phil Medlyn, in his mid-fifties, a veteran officer with the provincial police, pulled on his hat and began walking back toward the group at the side of the road.

A good-natured officer already planning his retirement, Medlyn wasn't looking for more work this morning than the leisurely pick-up of mail, a coffee with the boys at DHQ, and a drive back to the Strathroy detachment at Hickory Corners.

"Any problems here, fellas?" Medlyn asked.

As he approached, an older, balding man with a white shirt and black mustache started walking back toward the brown station wagon. The older man stood at the driver's side of the bigger car, looking toward the ditch and occasionally glancing at the officer.

It was the bushy-haired man at the front of the Nova who replied: "It was the fan belt. We fixed it. Everything's under control, thanks."

Medlyn agreed that things looked under control. The Nova had Ontario plates, rather than out-of-province markers, no need to look into this further. Thus assured, he returned to the cruiser and drove off. It wasn't the way a younger, more eager officer would have handled the situation. Another officer might have asked more questions and checked the car registrations on the police computer. And he might have died doing it.

Allen heaved a deep sigh as the cruiser pulled away. Buxbaum returned to the front of the Nova and repeated his demand that the killing go ahead. Allen looked at Armes inside the car.

"N-G," Armes said, giving the verbal shorthand for "no good."

Allen said there was no way, now. They'd been spotted by the cops and they'd have to come up with something else.

"OK, forget it," Buxbaum replied. "I'll get back to you."

Buxbaum took the pantyhose and returned to his car and drove away, leaving the would-be killers to figure out what to do now.

Armes was irate. "Buxbaum screwed up," he said. "He owes us. It woulda gone down if he wasn't so fuckin' stupid. Slept in. What an asshole. We were ready to go. He owes us the money."

The frustrated trio drove back to Jan Hicks' apartment. The KK9 was put back in its knapsack and they cracked open several more beer.

Allen telephoned Barrett at the Westbury about 9:30 and gave him the news.

"Buxbaum blew it. We were ready to do the job and he was late. Said he slept in."

Barrett sounded disappointed. He said to call him back about 1:30. He expected Buxbaum would be in touch with him and they'd try to sort things out. Allen said they still expected to get paid. Barrett said not to worry; there would be plenty of money for everyone.

Allen agreed to call back and took Spider and Armes to the parking lot of the Wellington Tavern, dropping them off about 10 a.m. Allen, by now quite weary, decided to return to the South London apartment he shared with his fiancee, Lisa Mattalo.

He was in his robe, brushing his teeth and about to go to bed when she awoke and assumed he had just gotten up after slipping in late the previous night. Allen let her believe that and dressed again, forsaking sleep. The alibi might come in handy, he thought. About an hour later he collected Spider and Armes back at the Wellington and returned to Hicks' apartment where he telephoned Barrett, as arranged, at 1:30 p.m.

Squirrel had been phoned by Buxbaum who told a different version of what had happened that morning along Highway 402.

"He said you guys screwed up," Barrett told a disbelieving Allen. "And he's not going to pay."

Allen protested but Barrett quickly stifled him.

"He says you get paid when you do the work. And he's coming back from Toronto tonight and you get another chance."

Barrett said Buxbaum wanted the killers at the same place on Highway 402, but in the westbound lane this time. He'd be coming back with his nephew and would pass the spot about 7 p.m. He gave explicit instructions that his nephew was not to be harmed.

Allen decided he wanted nothing to do with this plan. The cops had seen his face and the other side of the road was nowhere near the culvert. He needed the money but this was something he wanted no part of. "I was only into being screwed up once," he later explained.

Spider overheard Allen protesting and took the receiver from his companion. He spoke to Barrett and seemed to like the proposal. He and his partner Armes would finish the job, he told Barrett.

Squirrel was relieved. He didn't want another of his schemes coming unglued. He didn't know how he'd explain that to Helmuth.

Allen let Spider talk to Barrett on the bedroom phone and he went to the living room where he shared his misgivings with Armes. Suddenly, Spider appeared and motioned to Allen.

"Squirrel wants to talk to you," Spider said. Allen got on the line and was directed by Barrett to turn over the car and the revolver to Spider. "Don't worry," Barrett assured Allen, "we'll look after you. You'll get money out of this."

Within minutes Spider got both the car and revolver and he and Armes dropped Allen off at his mother's home where he was supposed to fix her refrigerator.

About 3:30 p.m. Allen wandered down to the Wellington. There he found Spider, Armes and a friend of theirs, Terry Kline. The subject of Highway 402 and events of the day were studiously avoided. At some point Spider and Armes left, but Allen had been getting drunk and drowsy and hadn't noticed the time. He went home about 9:30 and collapsed in sleep.

After the aborted roadside episode in the morning, Helmuth and Hanna continued east on Highway 402 to Kitchener, halfway to Toronto. They drove directly to Millwood Manor, the nursing home where Hanna's mother lived.

Buxbaum knew he was barely tolerated by Ottilie Schmidt so he dropped off his wife and drove the two blocks to the home of Heinz and Martha Wagner. Martha, Hanna's older sister, was busy cleaning curtains when Helmuth pulled into the driveway about 10:30. Heinz was sanding and scraping, readying the outside of the house for painting. He expressed surprise at seeing his brother-in-law, thinking the Buxbaums were still in Europe. Wagner didn't much care for Buxbaum but he had learned to be civil after a decade of silence sparked by the nursing home disagreement.

Wagner invited him into the living room for a glass of grape juice and couldn't help but notice how jumpy his brother-in-law seemed. Helmuth explained he had a lot to do this day. He had banking to do in Toronto before he picked up his nephew Roy at the airport. He was pacing back and forth and suddenly asked if Wagner still had fruit trees in his garden.

The two moved into the garden — Buxbaum leading the way — to admire the trees and they pulled up some lawn chairs. They talked about relatives in Europe and nursing homes. Buxbaum startled Wagner at one point by falling out of the chaise lounge he had taken. He explained he was "nervous," Wagner later recalled. The men talked more about the nursing home business and Buxbaum said he'd given up hiring missionaries as administrators. Nurses, he advised Wagner, have better business sense. "They make more money," he declared.

After an hour, Martha phoned Hanna at the nursing home and asked her to come over to the house. The four chatted until about noon when Martha suggested the Buxbaums stay for lunch. Hanna declined, however, explaining "My honey wants to take me out for lunch and I shouldn't refuse it."

Hanna suddenly remembered she'd left her purse at the nursing home and would have to pick it up after they left. Goodbyes were said but in a few minutes Helmuth and Hanna returned with a gift of ornate candleholders they'd bought in Austria.

During a second round of goodbyes Martha kissed her sister. It would be the last time she saw Hanna.

The Wagners compared notes after Helmuth and Hanna left. Heinz said he couldn't get over how uptight Buxbaum was, Martha said she'd thought it strange that Hanna wasn't wearing nylons.

The Buxbaums returned to Highway 401 and a few kilometres east of Kitchener stopped for lunch at a restaurant in Preston. Buxbaum told his wife he had a business call to make. He telephoned Barrett and said the killing try had been botched.

After eating, the couple continued into Toronto, did some banking downtown and arrived at the airport about forty-five minutes before Roy's scheduled 4 p.m. arrival.

Hanna was tired and didn't feel like going into the airport without her nylons, so she rested in the car while Buxbaum went inside to pick up his nephew.

Roy arrived about a half-hour late and easily found his "Oncle" Helmuth. It wasn't his first solo trip to Toronto and he was a good traveller. As he waited for his luggage to appear on the baggage carousel, Roy went to the washroom and his uncle made a business call from a nearby pay phone. Buxbaum was confirming with Barrett that the change in venue and time for the killing was acceptable. He was assured that things would go right this time.

"Remember," Buxbaum told Barrett, "the nephew, he's

not to be hurt.'' Barrett promised the message had gotten through. Look for the same car from the morning, he advised Helmuth.

Roy finally located his bag and the frozen halibut and he and Buxbaum made their way to the Oldsmobile where Hanna was waking from a snooze.

Hanna drove and Roy, glad to be back with his favorite aunt and uncle, chatted happily with them before drifting off to sleep. He awoke when they pulled off the highway near Milton for hamburgers at a McDonald's. The skies had become overcast.

Helmuth took the wheel after McDonald's when Hanna expressed concern about driving in the rain. He switched on the headlights and the car continued west toward Highway 402 and Komoka.

Ahead, Spider and his partner Armes were finishing their last beers at the Wellington. Sometime after 6 p.m. they decided it was time to get on with the job.

Spider was at the wheel of the Nova, Armes beside him, as they drove west from London. The speed was beginning to wear off and they were feeling the effects of lack of sleep. Armes, with a diabetes-like condition related to his blood-sugar, found he was blacking out briefly, a sure sign his body craved rest. At one point, as the car continued westward he turned to the back seat and started to say something to Pat Allen. But Allen wasn't in the car, something he thought strange. Allen had been with them throughout this binge, hadn't he?

Armes turned to Spider and saw he had the revolver beside him on the seat and a nylon stocking was wrapped around the baseball cap he was wearing. Armes suddenly realized what was happening, this was murder try number two. Spider, he thought, looked serious.

Armes would later claim he hadn't intended to get involved in the evening replay, he was merely along for the ride.

As they neared County Road 14, Spider began to pull over. Armes said this wasn't the spot, Spider must be mistaken, it was farther along. He repeated this several times, explaining later he was hoping to get Spider, who was unfamiliar with the highway, to travel past the Komoka exit.

He finally let Spider pull over at the railway overpass just past the exit. Spider got out of the Nova, opened the trunk and placed some green felt over the rear licence plate. He then hid behind a concrete abutment near the shoulder.

Armes took up a position at the rear of the car, looking back at oncoming traffic. He had no masks or weapon. His job was lookout.

Many minutes later, Armes saw the Oldsmobile wagon come into sight. The big car slowed and turned off the highway at the exit ramp to County Road 14 and Komoka, a couple of hundred metres up the road. Armes heaved a deep sigh as it disappeared from sight. Later he would tell a courtroom he was immensely relieved by this turn of events.

His relief was short-lived, he saw something that made his heart sink.

"The car appeared again, on the on-ramp, coming onto the highway."

Hanna's fate was sealed.

9/Suspicion:

"...unusual, to say the least."

The killing had been a messy affair. The last minute change in plans meant the gunmen hadn't been able to make it look like a kidnapping. The culvert where the body was to have been secreted was on the other side of the highway two kilometres to the east. Here in the ditch near the family station wagon lay Hanna Buxbaum. Face down, she was covered with blood and still alive, but her breathing was becoming shallow.

Helmuth and Roy watched the Nova speed off and then jumped from the Oldsmobile and began waving frantically at passing traffic.

Truck driver Colin Lawrence of Toronto was the first driver to come upon the scene. Driving for McKinley Transport, Lawrence was hauling a load of auto parts from Toronto to Sarnia and he didn't hesitate to stop his big rig when he saw two men waving their arms by the railway overpass.

The instant the truck stopped, the older of the two men, a mustachioed man in a long-sleeved white shirt and grey slacks, ran up to the driver's door of the rig.

"My wife's been shot," he blurted out. "Two guys with masks shot my wife."

Lawrence ran to the spot indicated by the man and found a heavy-set woman lying, face down, in the mud. He saw a wound to her temple and blood on her face. He checked her breathing. He could hardly detect it.

"She's in bad shape; we've got to get help," Lawrence said. "Someone with a CB. I don't have one."

He ran back to the roadway with Buxbaum not far behind. There wasn't much traffic although an Esso oil tanker was approaching from the west on the far side of the highway.

"It was a blue car, I don't know what kind," Buxbaum volunteered as he and Lawrence watched the tanker approach. "The licence plate was covered and the two guys had masks."

Lawrence ran off across the median and flagged down trucker Alec Johns who was travelling from Sarnia to Toronto. Helmuth and his nephew followed several paces behind.

Lawrence and Buxbaum breathlessly relayed the information they had and Johns barked it into his radio.

He raised motorists "Lucky Linda" and "Tiny Bubbles" on the CB and asked them to call police and an ambulance. Johns gave his location and was assured by the women that help was on the way. As he was talking, the Esso driver noticed Buxbaum standing beside Lawrence. While Lawrence seemed as agitated, the man with the mustache whose wife had been shot was altogether different.

"He seemed rather calm," Johns recalled later. "Lawrence and me were somewhat hyper and excited. To me, he (Buxbaum) did not seem excited at all. For what had happened he was just standing there."

As he was making this observation a car pulled up in front of Johns' rig followed quickly by a tow truck. A young man got out of the car and asked if anyone was in trouble. The tow truck driver had a two-way radio and Lawrence asked him to raise his base station in London. He couldn't make contact.

The men then ran across the highway toward the Oldsmobile station wagon, the car driver bringing a first aid kit from his trunk. The tow truck driver got blankets. Johns stayed at his CB.

The motorist, Mark Halden, a take-charge guy with training in emergency first aid and cardio-pulmonary resuscitation, was going home to Thorold with a girlfriend travelling from Sault

Ste. Marie in Northern Ontario. He had driven south on Michigan's Interstate 75 and entered Highway 402 at Port Huron-Sarnia. He was still three hours from home.

He rushed to Hanna's side, checked her vital signs and found them reasonably good considering the ugly wounds. He turned her onto her side to keep blood from filling her lungs and found the wound to the side of her head. He placed a compress on it.

Halden knew seconds were precious, he couldn't wait for the CB network to provide help.

He looked back to the shoulder of the road and saw the man with the mustache. He sized him up for a few seconds and asked if it was his station wagon. Buxbaum replied yes, it was.

"Then get going. Go to Strathroy. Get an ambulance and the police. It's just up the road. Go! Go!"

"Stratford?" Buxbaum asked.

"No. No. Strathroy. It's a couple miles up the road. Go!"

Buxbaum shouted to Roy to join him and the pair hopped into the wagon and kicked up gravel as they took off.

Despite having his hands full with his patient, Halden made a quick assessment of the man with the mustache and he would be surprised later at the hospital to learn he was the victim's husband.

Halden noticed the man didn't seem to want to go near the woman, preferring to stay on the shoulder of the road, on the other side of the guard rail.

"I found him to be very cold, somewhat plastic, very artificial, very removed from the events that were occurring. Very stand-offish."

The man had offered little assistance and no information, Halden recalled later. He remembered him because his actions were "unusual, to say the least."

An unmarked provincial police cruiser arrived in minutes followed shortly by an ambulance. More police arrived as Hanna was loaded into the ambulance with Mark Halden remaining at her side. On the fifteen-minute trip to Victoria

Hospital in London, Halden successfully performed cardio-pulmonary resuscitation when Hanna's heart stopped.

Meanwhile, about ten kilometres west, Constable Roger Aisladie was parked in the median. A member of the police force in the town of Strathroy, Aisladie had been dispatched to the highway, just outside the town limits when town police were advised there had been a shooting on 402. He was to look for suspicious-looking westbound vehicles.

After a couple of minutes at the emergency vehicle turn-around, Aisladie noticed a brown station wagon stop suddenly on the shoulder of the westbound lane and screech to a halt. A middle-aged man and a teenaged boy ran to his cruiser. The man said his wife had been shot and she needed medical help. Aisladie advised the man an ambulance was on the way. Then something dawned on the soft-spoken, British-trained Aisladie.

"Are you pursuing the suspects?" he asked.

Buxbaum replied he wasn't, but the robbers had been driving a blue car. He provided descriptions sought by Aisladie for broadcast to other cars. The passenger did the shooting, he said, and wore a baseball cap with crest and casual jacket. The driver had a beige baseball cap over dirty blonde hair and wore a jean jacket. Aisladie relayed the descriptions to the town dispatcher.

The policeman asked Buxbaum for identification. He produced his driver's licence. Aisladie then asked for a statement and wrote carefully as Buxbaum told him the following: "I was driving along the 402. I saw a blue car on the side of the road with the hood up. A man was standing beside the car. He was trying to wave me down. I decided to stop and help. I can tell you that will be the last time I stop to help anyone."

Aisladie was taking particular care to get every word. Policing in a small town like Strathroy, population 8,000, seldom involved anything more than traffic citations and assaults. This was a shooting and he made Buxbaum speak slowly.

Buxbaum continued: "I pulled up behind the blue car and

suddenly the front door opened — no, the back door — and this man points a gun and said to him (Roy), 'stay down'.. I then remember my wife's door was opened. The man said something about money and jewellery... he was shouting and pointing the gun at my wife. He grabbed her and pulled her from the car and shot her.

"I want her to get the best possible hospital treatment," he said, interrupting himself. He mentioned a Toronto hospital unfamiliar to Aisladie.

The policeman asked Buxbaum if he knew what kind of gun it was. Buxbaum said he didn't, but Roy volunteered he thought it was a .38-calibre.

Aisladie checked with his dispatcher and was told to remain with Buxbaum and Roy. As they sat in the median, Roy noticed a westbound blue Nova and drew it to his uncle's attention as being similar to the robbers' car. "Yes, you could be right," Buxbaum said, as he watched the car disappear to the west.

As the three sat in the cruiser awaiting further instructions, Aisladie began jotting down observations of Buxbaum.

In court later, he would report that he'd found Buxbaum "cold, (he) appeared calm. He didn't seem concerned about returning to his wife. He did not appear as upset as I thought for a husband who had seen a violent crime such as this. He was very patient."

Aisladie said he saw no tears and Buxbaum never said there was something he could have done to prevent the shooting, reactions he would have expected.

While Aisladie was watching Helmuth and Roy, Hanna arrived at the emergency entrance at Victoria Hospital. It was 8 p.m.

Dr. Robert Anthony, the surgeon who heads the department examined her quickly and found she was barely breathing. She was deeply unconscious and had little brain and heart activity. X-rays were to show metal fragments in her skull.

After forty minutes of major resuscitation efforts, monitoring equipment failed to detect any brain activity whatsoever.

He pronounced her dead at 8:52 p.m. and walked into the interview room to break the news to her husband who had been brought to the hospital by way of the London OPP detachment.

"I'm sorry, Mr. Buxbaum, your wife has passed away," Anthony reported to Helmuth. "There was nothing we could do. She died from the gunshot wound to her head."

The victim's husband lowered his head and shook it, Anthony recalled. "Why? How could this happen?" he said quietly. "This can't happen."

He then asked for a tranquilizer. Anthony was reluctant, saying he didn't think it would be appropriate. Eventually, at Buxbaum's insistence, he provided a sedative similar to Valium to help him sleep that night.

Anthony found that Buxbaum displayed little emotion upon hearing Hanna was dead, but the doctor wasn't overly surprised at that. As head of emergency he had found that reactions had varied widely to the unpleasant news he sometimes had to deliver.

Buxbaum told Anthony that he and his wife had six children and asked if he were sure there was nothing else the doctor could do. The doctor replied he was sorry. Buxbaum sobbed briefly and asked to see the body. A nurse pulled down the sheet covering Hanna's face and Buxbaum quickly turned away.

"I don't want to remember her like that," he said.

Recording this exchange was provincial police Constable Christopher Lewis who had brought Buxbaum to the police detachment and then to the hospital. Lewis asked if there were someone Helmuth would like him to notify. Buxbaum said he wanted his minister, Reverend Paul Fawcett, and provided the phone number to Lewis.

Buxbaum was asked by Constable Richard Pellarin to provide a formal statement and he complied. About 9:30 p.m. Fawcett arrived and he and Buxbaum embraced. Pellarin gave the men about ten minutes alone and resumed taking down Buxbaum's version of what had happened.

He said that he and his wife had left their Komoka home

about 9 a.m. and visited his mother-in-law in Kitchener. They had stopped for lunch in Preston and had continued on to the Toronto airport, arriving about fifteen minutes before Roy's flight. Returning, they had stopped at the McDonald's in Preston for hamburgers. At the Komoka exit he said that he had seen a man standing beside a car with its hood up farther along the road. The man was waving his arms. Buxbaum said that he had continued past the exit to help the man and as soon as the car was stopped another man opened the right rear door. This man had a gun and a stocking covering his face. He wore a beige ball cap and a jacket over a blue-green tee-shirt. In his right hand he held a gun which looked like a toy. He grabbed Hanna by the hair from behind, demanded her money and jewels and dragged her from the car and shot her. Buxbaum said he was then sent to Strathroy by a man who came upon the scene and began administering first aid.

At 10:10 the statement was completed and at 10:27 Fawcett identified the body of Hanna. Buxbaum was returned to the London OPP detachment, arriving at 10:55. During the short drive he expressed concern about the fish that was in the rear of the car and said he didn't want it melting. He was told he couldn't go near the car, it was impounded as identification experts looked for clues in the killing.

At the request of Detective-Inspector Ron Piers, Pellarin took another statement from Buxbaum at 11:55, completing it at 1:15 a.m.

He took more details from him about the physical description of the men. Buxbaum said the first man was five-foot-six, 150 to 160 pounds with dirty blonde hair. He was about twenty to twenty-three years old and had a beige ball cap with a fishing crest on it. He had a yellow or reddish tee-shirt. The second man, the gunman, was five-foot-ten, with a muscular build. He had a dark brown nylon stocking on his head and wore a brownish jacket and blue tee-shirt. He was a little older and appeared "very rough and very nervous." He had shouted "the jewellery and the money, you fucking bitch,"

Buxbaum recalled, something he repeated several time before shooting Hanna.

He was interrupted briefly for a hand-washing by an identification officer. The washings, routine in murder cases, are used to determine the presence of gunpowder or other chemicals.

Pellarin noticed that Buxbaum showed little outside emotion and was co-operative. He appeared tired and indifferent, initialling the statement without bothering to re-read it. He seemed anxious to get home and break the news to his family.

Before Buxbaum left the detachment, Corporal Leo Sweeney asked the question that was uppermost in the minds of police from the first in this strange robbery: Why had Helmuth driven past the Komoka cutoff? Easy, replied the millionaire. The blue car looked like that of Brian Richardson, his neighbor, and there had appeared to be some breakdown.

It wasn't long before the policemen at the London and Strathroy detachments were talking about their theories of this incident which they described to the press as an "apparent robbery." Suspicious by training and experience, the officers began developing theories that weren't complimentary to Buxbaum.

Meanwhile, in another part of the city, the killers were celebrating, drinking beer and congratulating themselves on their handiwork. And in Toronto, Barrett and his companions were also partying, drinking and injecting speed and cocaine.

Immediately after gunning down Hanna, Spider and Armes continued west on Highway 402, turning off at Middlesex County Road 39 just before Strathroy. The pair drove past the Strathroy OPP detachment on their way back to London by Highway 22. Spider stopped the car and directed Armes to remove the green felt that covered the Nova's licence plate. Armes complied and tossed the felt in the ditch.

About 8 p.m., they arrived back in London and drove to the home of Spider's estranged wife.

Spider and his wife had been separated for nearly three years and were planning to get a divorce. But they kept in touch with each other partly for the sake of their two children. She raised the children at an apartment in a big house on Elmwood Avenue in south London. She was accustomed to seeing her husband show up at all hours of the day and night. She was no stranger to speed and could understand when Spider was on the drug and just wanted someone to rap with. He visited her twice on July 5 and was stoned on speed on both occasions.

The first visit came about 4:30 a.m. when he showed up with the blue Nova and his companions Pat Allen and Terry Lewis. Spider wanted to talk about some rumors he'd heard that his wife was seeing some men. He and his companions were obviously high, she remembered. She rubbed the sleep out of her eyes and made some instant coffee for her early morning visitors. They said nothing about murder, although they said they were wasting time waiting for the sun to rise so they could go out to Highway 402. Spider and his friends stayed for about an hour, then left.

The next time she was to see her husband was about 8 p.m. This time, still driving the blue Nova, he was accompanied only by Armes.

He asked her for some cleaning solvent and rags, saying they wanted to clean out the car. When she fetched them, her husband showed her a revolver he was carrying.

"I really did it this time," he said, replacing the gun in the front of his pants. He turned the cleaning material over to his companion Armes and told him to get the car spotless.

Spider and his wife slipped into the garage at the house and he showed her a large, off-white rectangular purse he fetched from the car. He rummaged around in the purse and after checking the wallet, passed it to her.

She found it contained the driver's licence of someone she did not know: a Hanna Buxbaum of RR 3, Komoka. She found several credit cards all bearing the same name. Spider found some gold earrings with tiny gold hearts on them and some foreign coins. He gave some of the coins to her to give to their daughter, the remainder he gave to Armes who put them in a jar and buried it in the backyard. Spider left the purse in the garage and on a subsequent visit put it into a green garbage bag and threw it into the Thames River a few blocks away.

"Who is this woman?" his wife asked. "What have you done?" Spider, edgy and obviously upset, admitted he had shot the woman along Highway 402. Out of Armes' earshot he complained about his partner and the way the event had unfolded.

"It was supposed to go down in the morning but Pat got cold feet when the cops came up," he said testily. "And Terry, he was supposed to put a bag over the kid's head. The kid probably saw me."

He told his wife he was upset the way things had gone and that he would never forget Hanna's pleading for her life and her begging Helmuth, "Honey, please, don't." He broke down crying and cried on her shoulder as he recounted the incident. He said he'd told Buxbaum it should have been him he was shooting.

After Armes assured him the car was clean, Spider moved it back by the garage, covered it in an orange tarp from the trunk and told his wife he'd be back later that night for it. He left the keys with his wife but told her not to take the Nova out. The car would stay in this spot for three days, until Sunday. On that day, Anita Pitcher came for the car and Spider's wife relayed a message from Armes that she was to run it through the car wash before taking it back to the car rental agency.

Before he left, Spider told his wife that he and Armes were going to go to Toronto to collect their money for the killing. He said they were to get $10,000, an amount that could climb to $30,000.

With that, he and Armes left by cab for the Wellington Tavern. It was just as well as far as his wife was concerned. "I didn't want to listen after awhile," she said later, "I didn't want to know."

She was one of the few Londoners who didn't want to know more about the killing. Within hours of the events along Highway 402 news of the strange death was on the radio and television. It was to be the headline story in the *London Free Press* and appeared in papers across Ontario.

The London area, which records but a handful of murders in a year, was shocked. How could this woman be dragged out of the family car and shot? Why wasn't her husband robbed? Why did the Buxbaums travel past their exit? Something was definitely strange about this murder and the police weren't the only ones looking for answers. And they weren't the only ones who were wondering about Helmuth Buxbaum.

10/The Payoff:

"If I pay these guys off, everything will be fine..."

About a half hour after Hanna was pronounced dead, Pat Allen was roused from his overdue sleep by the ringing of his telephone. Spider was on the line and said that he and Armes had some beer and wanted to come over. Allen said it was fine by him but he was tired and didn't feel much like partying.

Fifteen minutes later, the pair arrived. First in the door of the apartment was Armes who winked at Allen, cocked his head and nodded, making his finger into a gun. "Yes," Armes said, smiling. Allen instantly understood that the killing had taken place.

Spider entered and immediately went to the phone in the kitchen. Allen couldn't overhear what was being said.

After the call, Spider joined Allen and Armes for several beers and tried to convince the bleary-eyed Allen he should join them at a party. But Allen was tired and he wanted nothing to do with it. He agreed to let Spider return to the apartment and stay the night after telling him that his fiancee, Lisa, would be there. Spider said he'd take the couch, thanks. The moment his guests left, Allen returned to bed.

While Allen slept, Spider and Armes found their party after dropping into their base of operations, The Wellington Tavern. Two hundred kilometres away in Toronto, Barrett and his friends kept their own party rolling, consuming prodigious amounts of cocaine, speed and liquor. At the OPP detachment in London, Helmuth Buxbaum was still answering questions.

The next morning, the refreshed Allen got up early and roused Spider from the couch. Allen said he wanted to go to Toronto to pick up Hicks and get their payoff money from Barrett. Armes called and Allen told him to come over; they were going for a train ride to Toronto. The trio dropped off at Spider's wife's so that Allen could pick up a pair of dress pants he'd left there. Allen said they were going to collect for the killing. They caught an early train to Toronto.

Armes was the only one of the three men who had any money. He paid for the cabs and train fares and was promised that Barrett would repay him in Toronto for his expenses. As Armes filled in Allen on the details of the killing, he also stewed because the bar car didn't open until 11:30 a.m. When it opened, Armes made up for lost time, downing eight beers before the train pulled into Union Station. Allen remembered Spider's saying little. He just sat quietly, looking very pale.

Sometime after noon, the trio arrived at Toronto's Westbury Hotel, looking for Barrett. Allen led the threesome to Barrett's room where they found Anita Pitcher putting on makeup at a mirror. Squirrel was sound asleep in bed. Allen shook him roughly and asked where Jan Hicks was. The groggy Barrett told Allen to give him a chance to wake up. His eyes were puffy and he obviously had been partying hard.

Barrett suddenly caught on to what was happening and immediately demanded of Allen: "Did you get the rings? One of them was worth fifteen grand."

Allen replied he didn't; he hadn't been involved and besides, the kidnapping scheme had been bungled. "Where's Jan?" he repeated, his voice betraying his anger at the condition of the murder's mastermind.

Barrett gestured toward the next room where Allen found Hicks drying her hair. D'Iorio, Barrett's partner in drugs, was in bed, sound asleep.

Assured that Hicks was in no trouble, Allen returned to

Barrett's room where Spider and Squirrel were arguing. Barrett seemed confused. Allen joined the discussion immediately.

"Come on Squirrel," he demanded. "Ten grand. You owe us ten grand. That was the deal. These guys did the job and you owe us."

Barrett, still fighting to clear his head, was unclear about who had done what. But he knew one thing. He had no money. He must have spent most of it on drugs, but he wasn't sure. And now these guys wanted $10,000.

When he heard Barrett stall and say he didn't have the money, Armes jumped in. "How about my money? I've been paying for cabs and trains and beer. You owe me."

The wily Squirrel saw a fast solution to the minor annoyance. "You got any receipts?" he challenged Armes. "I don't pay without receipts."

Armes leaped for Barrett's throat and was joined by Spider. A minor scuffle ensued that was broken up by Allen.

Allen, his voice barely controlled, was furious: "Ten grand just like the deal."

Spider took a more direct approach to impress his anger on Barrett. Helped by Armes, he grabbed the slightly built Squirrel by the ankles and dangled him off the balcony of the Westbury, letting Squirrel admire the view of Carlton Street, fourteen floors straight down. Squirrel pleaded with Spider to let him back in. He had an idea.

Back on his feet, the shaken Barrett finally found his tongue and assured the threesome he'd make arrangements and they'd get their money.

Barrett said he had to call London and he'd go back and pick up the money if he could get in touch with Buxbaum. Allen, Spider and Armes were insistent, they weren't leaving until they got their money. Allen directed the ever-compliant Hicks to return to London with Barrett to make sure he lived up to his part of the deal.

Once this arrangement was set, Barrett began making phone

calls to London, while Allen and D'Iorio went off in search of speed at area bars. Armes, Spider, Hicks and Pitcher went drinking at other bars.

Late in the afternoon the London crowd re-convened at the Westbury. Feelings were still running high and at one point, someone, upset at the amount of drugs being ingested by Barrett, threw some cocaine out the window of the room to float into the streets below.

After things settled down, Barrett and Hicks took a cab to the Toronto airport and just missed an Air Ontario scheduled flight to London. Barrett began making a fuss saying he wanted to charter an airplane or helicopter because of a "life or death" situation. He finally settled for another Air Ontario flight an hour later and contacted Hicks' sister, Karen, in London to page Buxbaum at the London airport and inform him that Barrett's flight would arrive at 8:20 p.m. instead of 7:20.

Buxbaum was at the airport with an envelope of money and had nodded off in a chair. A family friend, Calvin Stiller, was returning on a flight from Cleveland at about 8 p.m. when he noticed Buxbaum sitting alone and asleep in the waiting room about twenty-four hours after his wife had been killed.

Stiller, a prominent surgeon pioneering in organ transplantation at London's University Hospital, found it odd that Buxbaum was at the airport and alone. He tapped the millionaire on the shoulder and expressed his sympathies.

"Yes, it was a terrible thing," Buxbaum said. "She deserved a better death than that." Stiller would remember the remark vividly. It was odd that Buxbaum was sitting alone at the airport the day after Hanna's death and it seemed just as odd he'd say a thing like that. He wondered if Buxbaum were well but couldn't linger at the airport to tend to him. After leaving him, Stiller telephoned the Buxbaum family to advise them that Helmuth was alone at the airport and that he might need company.

A few minutes after this encounter, RCMP Constable John Martin received a telephone call at his post at London airport.

The RCMP detachment at the Toronto airport alerted him to a pair of suspicious-looking passengers on Air Ontario Flight 817, due to arrive at 8:25 p.m. A "Mr. and Mrs. Barrett" had drawn attention to themselves when they'd bought tickets with cash and made a fuss about the urgency of getting to London. Martin might want to keep an eye on the couple, the Toronto detachment advised.

A drug deal might be in the works, Toronto said. The man had complained about the lack of seats on scheduled flights and told Air Ontario staff "Charter me a jet. I've got the money to pay for it."

The plane arrived on schedule and Martin saw the slight man and the taller woman with the frizzy hair enter the terminal building. Both were wearing blue jeans unlike the majority of passengers on the flight, mainly businessmen. They stood out from the crowd. The couple went toward the gift shop where Martin was standing and the constable overheard the man tell his companion to "wait here". The man then went over and spoke to a balding, heavy-set man aged from forty to fifty, who had been sitting in the lobby for more than an hour. The two men then went into the washroom with a backward glance at Martin. In a moment they emerged and went outside to a red and white customized van that had been parked at meters outside the terminal door. The older man got into the driver's side, his companion into the passenger's. In about three minutes the younger man emerged and returned to the female. As she went to the telephone, the younger man came up and asked Martin for a light for his cigarette. The van pulled away at this point and in a few moments the couple boarded the same plane for a return flight to Toronto. The total episode lasted about fifteen minutes.

Martin would later identify the balding man as Helmuth Buxbaum, the younger man as Robert Barrett.

As they got onto the plane, Barrett slippped Hicks an inch-thick envelope stuffed with 50- and 100-dollar bills. Hicks hadn't recognized the man Barrett had met. Only later would she learn that it was Helmuth Buxbaum. As soon as they boarded the nearly empty aircraft Barrett went to the washroom and returned to snort several lines of cocaine at his seat.

When Barrett and Hicks arrived in Toronto, they were immediately stopped by the RCMP, taken to another building and searched. Cocaine was found on Barrett and he was charged with possession of the drug and released. As Hicks was searched she placed the envelope on a table. Inexplicably, it wasn't touched and she collected it before being released.

Later that night, back at the hotel, Hicks turned the envelope over to Allen. It contained $13,000. Allen gave $500 to Hicks, $5,000 to Spider, $3,500 to Armes, and Allen retained $1,000. The remainder went to Barrett.

Barrett was annoyed at the contents of the envelope. He had been promised $20,000, but at the London airport Buxbaum had told him that $13,000 was all he could raise on short notice. Barrett consoled himself with $1,500 worth of cocaine he'd also picked up from a contact at the London airport away from the eyes of the watchful Constable Martin. In the next several days Barrett left messages at Buxbaum's office that he hoped would serve as a reminder that he felt he was owed another $7,000.

The killers and their friends spent another night partying in Toronto before drifting back to London on Saturday and Sunday, travelling by bus and train.

It hadn't been easy for Buxbaum to slip out to the airport and make the payoff to Barrett. Swamped by sympathetic friends and members of his church, he had been barely able to get away from his house.

Once Buxbaum's minister, Paul Fawcett, arrived at Victoria Hospital just after Hanna had died, members of his church swung into action. The well-meaning Baptists would try to share Helmuth's grief, to help him over his tragedy. They wanted to shield him from outsiders and the press. Members of the church smothered Buxbaum with their kindness and support. At first it was appreciated, but he soon began to chafe at what he viewed as outside interference and he wanted some time alone to wrap up loose ends in the killing.

Among the Buxbaum's closest family friends were the Conley family. Philip Conley, twenty-nine, a teacher and principal at the Christian Academy of Western Ontario, had known Buxbaum for about eight years. Buxbaum had been a large supporter not only of West Park Baptist, but also of the academy, and had helped Conley through school and afterwards by finding him summer and part-time work at the nursing homes. This summer, in fact, Conley was supervising ground crews at the homes.

The Conleys lived about five kilometres from the Buxbaum home in a house owned by Buxbaum, himself. The Conleys had taken the Buxbaum's adopted daughter Ruthie, now seventeen, into their home nearly two years before when Buxbaum had forced her out.

About 10 p.m. on the night Hanna was killed, Conley was alerted to the death by Fawcett. Conley and his wife, Christine, immediately went to the Komoka nursing home. The Conleys finally saw Buxbaum about 2 a.m. at his house. He was upset and crying.

He talked with the Conleys for awhile then retired for the night to the sanctuary of his bomb shelter. The Conleys stayed up all night talking with the three oldest sons, Paul, Mark and Phillip. The subject of capital punishment for the killer of his mother was much on Paul's mind. About 4 a.m. Friday, Paul drew up a telegram to Canadian Prime Minister John Turner, asking that he reinstate the death penalty for murderers. Paul would talk to the press later in the day and say that he felt "righteous anger" at the killing of his mother. "They deserve to pay the price for what they did."

Paul told reporters: "I'm not bitter. I don't hate, because we're Christian, but we feel we need justice."

"I'd strongly like to say that I truly believe that capital

punishment would deter further killings... If these two people would be executed, further killers would think twice about killing innocent people."

At 6 a.m., the Conleys woke the youngest children, Danny and Esther, and told them of the death of their mother. Early that day Paul called security guards to keep the press and gawkers away from the Buxbaum house. The motive for the killing was still not clear, so the guards would also protect the family. They arrived later in the day.

Conley and his wife were relieved by a minister friend, Kel Trudgin, about 6 p.m. when they went home to get rest. Conley ran errands with Helmuth, but it wasn't until after Conley left that Buxbaum was able to slip away alone and travel to the airport. The Conleys returned the following day, Saturday, to find that Buxbaum and Fawcett were making funeral arrangements. They returned Sunday to join the Buxbaums in devotional prayers and went to the London funeral home in the afternoon and evening.

It didn't take Conley long to notice that Buxbaum was acting strangely. At the funeral home in the afternoon he realized that Buxbaum was dealing with something more than grief. About 3 p.m. the Buxbaums and Conleys were greeting visitors when the funeral director came up to Helmuth and told him there was someone on the phone for him.

Conley and Buxbaum's accountant, Nick Potocska, overheard part of his conversation and Conley advised Potocska to write it down for future reference. Buxbaum seemed annoyed at the caller and his voice rose just before he hung up. "I told you I would see you on Tuesday," Buxbaum said.

Asked by the suspicious Conley and Potocska who the caller was Buxbaum replied that it was "a fellow from Toronto who needed money for food and clothes."

The caller, in fact, was Barrett. Exasperated at not being able to reach Buxbaum through the office, Barrett was determined to collect the remaining $7,000 for the killing. Asked later about the propriety of calling Buxbaum at the funeral

home, Squirrel matter-of-factly replied that he saw no problem:
"He owed me the money."

The funeral was held Monday and more than 800 persons
attended the ceremony at West Park Baptist Church. Some
"mourners" were plainclothes police officers studying those
in attendance, looking for a clue, any clue in the bizarre murder.

The service was trilingual, in German, English and Russian.
The Russian was spoken by Buxbaum's uncle, Georgi Vins,
who'd travelled from Chicago to attend. Vins, whose words
were translated by his daughter, Natasha, said he was heart-
broken at Hanna's death. "Her life was taken because she
wanted to do good for people," he said.

Paul Buxbaum spoke briefly at the service, showing — as
he had to the press — remarkable composure for a son who
was so close to his mother.

"Many people have asked us why this had to happen," Paul
told the hushed crowd. "One reason is that this is not a normal
world — it's a fallen world." Paul said he had praised the
Lord for the time Hanna had with her loved ones and said the
one thing he wanted to do more than anything that sad day
was to kiss his mother. Mourners wept openly as the twenty-
year-old left a message for others. "I'd like to encourage the
young men and young women here today to kiss their moms.
That's one thing I want to do today."

Later at the cemetery, Helmuth became upset when a black
man came out of the crowd to shake his hand and offer
condolences. He later told Conley he was bothered that
security guards hadn't kept the man away because the man was
involved in drugs. "What if that guy had stabbed me?"
Buxbaum demanded to know.

Hanna was buried in the Buxbaum family plot at the wind-
swept Lobo Township cemetery a few hundred metres east of
the family's home, which is tucked behind brick gates proclaiming "God is Love." She was laid to rest beside Helmuth's
parents. The inscription on her headstone read "Their works
do follow them," the completion of the quotation from Revela-

tions 14:13 which was inscribed on the Buxbaum parents' stone, "Blessed are the dead."

Later that same day, Buxbaum began complaining to Conley that he wanted to be alone. Conley said he felt he could be most helpful by staying close. About 8 p.m. Buxbaum tried to shed his unwanted companion.

He told Conley he was going to the bathroom. Conley was looking out toward the circular driveway and saw Buxbaum get into his van and start the engine. Conley ran to the van and expressed his concern that Buxbaum would want to go anywhere.

"I've got to go to the bank," Buxbaum replied. "I need money. I like to carry lots of money with me."

Conley was insistent. Buxbaum didn't need money for anything.

Buxbaum was just as stubborn. "I've got to get out of here. I've got to get money."

Conley reached inside the van, turned off the ignition, took the keys and put them in his pocket.

Buxbaum fumed, "Why did you do that? Come on, Phil. Don't treat me like a kid."

The smooth-talking Conley got Buxbaum out of the truck and cooled him down with a suggestion they walk over to Buxbaum's favorite part of his property, the trout pond. Buxbaum's anger subsided and he confessed to Conley that he was feeling badly about the life he had been leading in recent years. He said he'd been going to bars in London and drinking with people he shouldn't have.

"You just have a drink with them and they get you hooked on cocaine," he told the younger man. Conley wasn't surprised by this admission; he'd had many talks with Hanna and she had confided in him her fears about Helmuth and his use of drugs. In fact, she had sought Conley's help in finding a treatment program for her husband. Buxbaum said he'd continued taking cocaine to help him forget his business and family problems.

As the two men stood beside the pond, hands in pockets,

Buxbaum talked about his drug use. Conley gently suggested that Buxbaum should go to the authorities and tell them about his drug acquaintances. It could be someone in that crowd who killed Hanna, Conley suggested. Buxbaum replied that he couldn't do that; they would come and get him, too. He had to pay someone $2,000 for drugs and that was why he was trying to go to the bank.

Conley told Buxbaum to stay home, not to pay anyone anything and realize he was among friends who would protect him. He again suggested that Buxbaum contact police with his suspicions.

Buxbaum sounded desperate. "I'm supposed to go to the Park Lane Hotel and pay this money. If I don't they will call me here, about nine o'clock tonight. I can't have anyone calling here. Not now."

The call didn't come at nine, but Conley stayed close to the telephone. At about ten o'clock, a man identifying himself as Steve phoned and asked to speak to Helmuth. Conley handled the caller with Buxbaum listening in on an extension. Conley told the man that Helmuth was not available. The man said he was sorry to hear about Hanna and that he'd call back. Conley asked Buxbaum if the man were Rob Barrett, about whom Hanna had spoken. Buxbaum said it wasn't. The man didn't call again.

Conley stayed close to Buxbaum. The following day, Tuesday, July 10, he insisted on accompanying Buxbaum on a trip into London for a visit first to the office and then to Buxbaum's corporate lawyer, Del McLennan, to discuss Hanna's will. Conley drove the van to the office where Buxbaum received condolences on his loss. After checking the mail, Buxbaum took several members of his staff to lunch at a swank nearby restaurant. Conley then drove Buxbaum downtown, but en route to the lawyer's, Conley was abruptly directed to stop the van outside Chris Brooker's coin shop on Stanley Street. Buxbaum didn't wait for Conley to park. He jumped out of the van, saying he wanted to get some money. "If I pay these guys off, everything will be fine.'' He walked briskly across the busy roadway and into the shop. Conley, startled by this action, found a nearby pay-telephone to report Buxbaum's actions to Reverend Fawcett.

It wasn't easy babysitting Buxbaum and Conley sought advice from the minister. Buxbaum's unpredictable behavior was alarming Conley. Perhaps Fawcett could meet with him and Buxbaum downtown at the lawyer's office. As Conley was talking, he saw a cab carrying Buxbaum speed by. It was headed downtown. He hung up and took pursuit, arriving at the lawyer's office shortly after Buxbaum. Fawcett arrived minutes later.

After the lengthy meeting, Fawcett drove Buxbaum to his business office while Conley followed in the van.

If Tuesday was a strange day for Conley it was even stranger for the police investigating Hanna's death. They were becoming increasingly suspicious of Buxbaum and had discussed placing a wiretap on his telephone.

About 8 a.m. police received a tip that there was something unusual at the murder scene. OPP Constable Tony Veenendall was detailed to the site where he found a crude dummy hanging from the railway overpass, immediately above the spot where Hanna had been slain. Stuffed with house insulation, the wood mannequin wore long johns and a shirt. It was suspended by a rope around its neck. A sign calling for the return of the death penalty had blown off before Veenendall arrived at the spot. The bizarre episode could not be explained by police who were stepping up their search for a blue Nova believed involved in Hanna's shooting.

Within ten days police had interviewed 200 persons who had heard something or seen something along Highway 402. By the time the case was brought to preliminary hearing in December, that figure would swell to more than 600 as investigators followed up every lead.

On July 20 the Nova was finally located on the lot of Rent-A-Wreck.

Police suspicions about Buxbaum resulted in their getting permission to place wiretaps on the phones of Buxbaum, Barrett and Allen on July 9. Buxbaum's conversations were meticulously recorded and studied. Police became very interested when Buxbaum seemed to be making arrangements to enroll his children at Black Forest Christian Academy, in Tanden, West Germany, fifteen kilometres from the Swiss border and planned, himself, to move to Switzerland. It was also learned that he had ordered a shoulder holster and ammunition and had talked to a gun dealer about buying a high-powered rifle. Buxbaum was arrested July 23 and charged with first-degree murder and with conspiracy to commit murder. Word of his arrest caused a sensation in the London area and came as a shock to members of the Baptist and Mennonite communities. Barrett was arrested the same day and charged with the same counts. The pair had been asked to come into the London OPP detachment in the afternoon. After answering several more questions, Buxbaum and Barrett were booked. The blue Nova sat in a police garage, a few metres away.

On August 10, Spider was arrested in Toronto. Allen and an acquaintance of his, Terry Kline, a twenty-six-year-old booker of exotic dancers, were arrested the same day; Allen in London, Kline in Calgary where he was visiting his ailing mother. On August 16, Hicks was arrested in London and on August 26, Armes was arrested in Winnipeg where he'd just taken a job selling home renovations. All were charged with first-degree murder and conspiracy to commit murder in the death of Hanna Buxbaum.

11/Building a Case:

"...I thought, my gosh,
there could be no finer man in all of Canada."

The arrest of Helmuth Buxbaum in the murder of his wife came as no great surprise to many people in London. The few exceptions were members of the London Baptist community who didn't know Helmuth well and couldn't believe one of their flock could be under suspicion for such a horrible crime. But they respected law and order and came to feel that perhaps the police couldn't be entirely wrong. Within a few weeks of Buxbaum's arrest, the congregation of West Park began placing distance between themselves and Helmuth Buxbaum. They decided that their adherent was still a member, but was now "under discipline."

Londoners were shocked at the murder, disbelieving that something so bizarre could happen so close by. Many felt it incredible that the "robbers" had demanded money only from Hanna, a person the press had correctly portrayed as a good woman with no enemies.

Why hadn't the robbers gone after Helmuth, the wealthy nursing home operator? Something was fishy here and the finger of suspicion had been pointed directly at Helmuth Buxbaum from the first.

The police, of course, were convinced from the outset that something wasn't right. They had interviewed Buxbaum repeatedly and, several days after Hanna's death, placed wiretaps on phones at his home and office. If they were expecting to hear a confession, however, they were disappointed. It was the prospect of Buxbaum's taking off to Europe with his family that finally prompted police to move, a little sooner than they'd wanted to.

After Buxbaum was arrested, they searched his Komoka home, early in September, and found a few things that made them feel a bit more secure about their suspect — five grams of cocaine and an ounce of hashish. In addition, they discovered a small arms cache in the "bunker", the fallout shelter that had been built under the garage. A .45-calibre Colt semi-automatic handgun, a .22-calibre handgun and numerous long rifles were found, as well as a large supply of ammunition. Although police felt that this cache was significant, they didn't know until later that Howard Ruff's enthusiastic disciple had planned to protect his family from post-holocaust survivors.

Soon after Buxbaum was charged, an old family friend, Douglas Dakin, moved in with his wife, Louise, and four children to look after the Buxbaum children at the Komoka house. Dakin acted as legal guardian for the five Buxbaum children.

Dakin, who had known Helmuth since 1965, had been his minister at West Park Baptist, and had briefly been a business partner with him in two homes for the retarded. The two men were founding board members of the Christian Academy of Western Ontario but a personality clash eventually forced Dakin to sever his ties with the school. Despite their differences and his knowledge of Buxbaum's womanizing, Dakin had remained a close friend. And now that Buxbaum was in trouble, Dakin was not about to forsake him. Now with another London Baptist church, the minister could not believe that Helmuth could be suspected in the death of Hanna.

Dakin was shocked that police had discovered drugs in the Komoka home. Soon after, he made another discomfiting discovery. Secreted in the "bunker" were row upon row of pornographic films. Dakin didn't need to screen the films to know their content; he was aghast at their titles alone. He counted forty-eight films in all and rather than report them to police, burned them. Police later found a few Dakin had missed.

The friend and former minister had known about Buxbaum's adulterous lifestyle for about fourteen years and had attempted to do something about it until he left West Park in 1970. Dakin said later, in court, that he had turned over counselling to his successor, Paul Fawcett, and had hoped for the best.

Meanwhile, police were continuing their intense investigation. They were to leave no stone unturned in their determination to build an air-tight case against their suspects. Provincial police switchboards were swamped with tips in the first few weeks after the killing and investigators painstakingly tracked down every one. With the arrest of each new suspect, more calls came in. And news that Buxbaum had hired Toronto lawyer Eddie Greenspan, a noted legal sharpie, only spurred on their efforts to be thorough. Officers pushed themselves to work twelve- to twenty-hour days to prepare first for bail hearings and then for the preliminary hearing. By the time the preliminary hearing opened on December 5, more than 800 witnesses had been interviewed and scores of official statements taken.

The nature of the police investigation was a reflection of the man behind it.

At the helm of the police effort was Ron Piers, 41, a soft-spoken Ontario Provincial Police detective-inspector with a preference for dark, well-tailored suits. He looked more like a salesman or accountant than a cop and only his clipped speech and street grammar betrayed his calling.

Piers joined the anti-rackets branch of the force in 1979 where he became a detective-sergeant. Anti-rackets investigators spend much time on fraud and it wasn't long before Piers became involved in some major crime investigations. He demonstrated a flair for thoroughness and consummate patience. His investigation of a notorious financial scam resulted in the collapse of two Niagara Falls companies, Re-Mor Investment Management Corp. and Astra Trust Co. Hundreds of small investors had been bilked out of about $6 million and company principal, Carlo Montemurro, was eventually sentenced to six years in prison.

Another Piers case was the $20 million bankruptcy of Windsor Packers. When it was all over, fraud convictions and two-year jail terms were handed down to two principals in that firm.

On May 1, 1984, Piers and another veteran officer, Ron Forsyth, were transferred to the new CIB branch in London and promoted to the $42,000-a-year rank of detective-inspector. Forsyth had been a detective-sergeant in Kenora in Northern Ontario.

Piers and Forsyth were clearing up old cases and still in the process of moving when Hanna Buxbaum was gunned down. The case was immediately assigned to Piers.

The new detective-inspector had organized a team of investigators from the Strathroy, London, St. Thomas, and Woodstock detachments. With patience and the thoroughness that was his trademark, Piers led his team through the sifting of the bizarre and at-times confusing life of Helmuth Buxbaum and his associates.

His right-hand man would prove to be Constable Mel Getty, a beefy and boyish officer with a fine memory and a weakness for a particular wine-colored sport coat that stood in stark contrast to his superior's muted style.

Getty, thirty-two, a father of three, had been a provincial police constable for twelve years when he was called into the Hanna Buxbaum murder investigation. He was given the time-consuming task of taking and compiling statements from the hundreds of witnesses interviewed by police and the job of compiling the 2,000-page Crown brief laying out the prosecution's case.

Once Piers and Getty had amassed their evidence, they turned to a seasoned prosecutor, Middlesex County Crown Attorney, Mike Martin, Q.C., to shepherd the case through he courts.

Martin, fifty-eight, prosecutor in Middlesex for twenty

years, was a formidable opponent for any defence lawyer. This Crown did not like to plea bargain (agree to accept a guilty plea to a lesser charge if an accused person would plead guilty, saving the trouble and expense of a trial). A practising Catholic, who would sometimes take certain prosecutions as a personal crusade against evil, Martin was appalled when he learned of Buxbaum's lifestyle. A father of four, Martin sympathized hugely with Hanna and dedicated himself to putting Buxbaum behind bars. Martin figured that Buxbaum was a bad man, a sinner, and he determined not to let him get away. The prosecutor was delighted with the thorough work of Piers and his investigators. Shoddy police work was the last thing he wanted to encounter on this high-profile case.

Martin, because of his occasional flashes of righteousness and his reluctance to make deals with defence lawyers, had long ago earned the sobriquet of "The White Knight" in London's legal circles. The name also had much to do with his shock of prematurely white hair.

Martin was unimpressed by the affidavits Greenspan had filed on Buxbaum's behalf. The contrast between the information in the affidavits and the sworn evidence of witnesses was so sharp that Mr. Justice A.W. Maloney, was moved to note it. Maloney said he found that the testimonials which he read before hearing the bail request, "made me feel like quite the lesser person by comparison." The affidavits, he said, painted Buxbaum as "a living saint." However, after the first few witnesses, Maloney said he had learned that Buxbaum was a drug addict and adulterer. "I see now a very different man than what I saw sworn in the affidavits." At one point, Maloney confronted Paul Buxbaum about the affidavit he had sworn in support of his father.

"I read that affidavit and I thought, my gosh, there could be no finer man in all of Canada," Maloney said. "Is that

what your father is, or do you agree the picture today is somewhat different than your affidavit?''

Faced with that challenge, Paul Buxbaum could only muster
a weak ''Yes.''

The more Maloney heard, courtesy of the vigorous cross
examinations by Martin, the less he seemed to like Helmuth
Buxbaum, and the less faith he had in Greenspan's affidavits.
Toward the end of the bail hearing, he went so far as to ask
Greenspan not to refer to the affidavits and added, ''I'm glad
my name isn't on the back of them.'' He made reference to
the ''grave incongruity'' in Helmuth Buxbaum, who like Iran's
leader Ayatollah Khomeini, ''prays to God and then shoots
people at sunrise.''

Needless to say, Buxbaum was denied bail. Mike Martin
had won his first skirmish with Greenspan.

The Middlesex crown had seen much in his career and he
had a knack for dropping a street crime-colloquialism into his
language without batting an eye. He would talk about Buxbaum
and say that only an innately bad man would ''waste'' his
wife at the side of a highway. A listener unaccustomed to his
colorful turns of phrases would think it odd to hear such language peppering the speech of the stern, sometimes glacial,
local prosecutor.

Martin came to Middlesex in 1963 as an assistant crown
attorney after a seven-year stint in private practice in St.
Catharines. His seriousness and his unbending approach to
prosecutions in the county earned him the respect of defence
lawyers, although some would grumble that he sometimes
overstepped the bounds of fairness in his pursuit of a conviction.

During a murder trial in the early 80s, Martin re-enacted a
roadside throat-slitting for a supreme court jury. Taking the
blood-hardened clothing of the female victim, Martin laid it
out on the floor in front of the jury as though the victim were

still in the clothing. Then, for impact, he repeatedly slashed at where the throat would have been, driving home the enormity of the crime. His theatrics, although they won a conviction, were later criticized by defence lawyers who viewed them as needlessly inflammatory.

The prosecutor liked to explain that his approach was merely to balance opposing forces. To counter the thrust of a defence lawyer he would dig in his heels harder. A crown attorney must ensure that justice is being done, he would remind critics, even if justice might mean acquitting an accused person. "But we are not doormats for the defence," he would add quickly.

Martin assembled his own team for the exhaustive job of prosecuting Buxbaum and his co-accused. He selected his senior prosecutor, Alasdair (Al) MacDonald, to be his right-hand man and also chose a junior crown, Brendan Evans, to be part of his team.

MacDonald, forty-three, an air force brat who had completed half of his degree in medicine before switching gears and pursuing law, began his career in a large Toronto law firm where he discovered that criminal law was his favorite sort of practice. He joined Martin's office in 1977, fed up with the administrative chores of private practice.

Evans, thirty-four, a father of three, would have the painstaking, but important, task of comparing and analyzing witness statements and performing much of the drudgery in the case. His father, Gregory, a respected lawyer from Timmins, had been appointed to the Supreme Court of Ontario and was chief justice of the court at the time of Hanna Buxbaum's killing.

Greenspan, forty-one when the preliminary hearing began, would find the prosecution trio humorless for the most part. With his irrepressible sense of humor, Greenspan almost took delight in "giving the gears" to Martin, who would respond with a stony stare straight ahead.

A bright man with a passion for hard work and cigarettes (Belmont Milds), Greenspan was always fretting about his waistline and in the months before the preliminary hearing had gained back about thirty hard-lost pounds.

Eddie Greenspan was lured to Toronto because of his early love for criminal law and Toronto was where the action was. The father of two girls was a devoted family man and he would try to have them join him downtown for dinner a couple of times a week when he was working late (which was frequently).

Greenspan, a Q.C., was a familiar face at the Supreme Court of Ontario and the Ontario Court of Appeal. He could dazzle with his knowledge of Canada's criminal code.

He and Toronto author George Jonas produced a series of CBC radio programs called Scales of Justice, dealing with interesting Canadian criminal cases. Greenspan's association with Jonas was a long one, dating back about a decade to one of Canada's most celebrated criminal cases, a case in which Greenspan served as junior defence counsel.

Greenspan assisted Joe Pomerant in the defence of Peter Demeter, a wealthy Mississauga, Ontario builder charged with murder for arranging the death of his Viennese-born model wife, Christine. Jonas covered the trial — which ironically was held in London in 1974 — and went on to write the best-selling *By Persons Unknown* with his then-wife, Barbara Amiel.

Demeter, forty at the time of his trial, was eventually convicted and sentenced to life imprisonment. His conviction was unsuccessfully appealed by Greenspan. Some observers of the lengthy London trial insisted later that Greenspan might have won acquittal for the builder if he'd been conducting the defence rather than assisting the sometimes unpredictable Pomerant.

Demeter had had three classic motives for hiring someone to kill his wife: a bad marriage, another woman, and $1 million life insurance on his wife of more than five years.

Asked early in Helmuth Buxbaum's preliminary hearing if there were many similarities between the Demeter and Buxbaum murder cases, Greenspan told a reporter that Demeter was worth about $400,000 while his new client had a gross worth of about $28 million. "And this would make a much better book," added the always-glib Greenspan.

From early on in the bail and preliminary hearings, Greenspan seemed more concerned with weighing prosecution evidence than with discussing its implications with his client. Bob Sheppard, Greenspan's lanky articling student, was left to deal with Buxbaum during recesses, leaving many regular spectators to conclude early that Greenspan didn't particularly care for the man he was defending. Sheppard, a former carpenter who had returned to school as a mature student and family man, was also given the task of chauffeur and strongman to carry around the heavy briefcase full of defence documents.

Greenspan is one of the most high-profile of Canada's defence lawyers and he hasn't earned his reputation by resting on his laurels. Greenspan and his young assistant worked late every night on the case, meticulously comparing statements and transcripts, looking for some raw material with which to construct a defence. He earned his big fee in the defence of Helmuth Buxbaum, understood to exceed $1.1 million, with another $250,000 bonus if he could get an acquittal.

Greenspan doesn't like people without a sense of humor and he found Mike Martin to be that sort of person.

Greenspan tried to bait Martin, to get him angry, to tease a smile from the snowy-haired prosecutor. But Martin seldom cracked. Greenspan had to settle for the occasional grin from Martin's juniors, MacDonald or Evans.

At the preliminary hearing, Greenspan would draw sympathetic words from the presiding judge, but little else.

In the early days of the prosecution of Helmuth Buxbaum, the score was slightly in favor of the prosecutor. The big test would be the trial but that was a long way off. Much would happen in the meantime.

12/Preliminaries:

"...there's no lack of money..."

Helmuth Buxbaum and Robert Barrett were led into cavernous Courtroom Number Two at London's Middlesex County courthouse shortly before noon on Tuesday, July 24.

More than a hundred spectators were on hand to catch a glimpse of the millionaire and the drug dealer at their first court appearance before Justice of the Peace Len Obokata.

The two men wore handcuffs and were kept at opposite ends of the oak prisoner's box. They stared straight ahead impassively during the brief proceedings. Buxbaum, looking haggard, was wearing a blue-grey suit and matching striped tie; Barrett wore a white cotton shirt and blue jeans.

They were charged with first-degree murder and with conspiring "the one with the other and with persons unknown to murder Hanna Buxbaum." It was nineteen days since Hanna had been gunned down. Five more arrests were to follow.

The pair were in court for just two minutes during which time they were remanded in custody to re-appear in court in three weeks, August 14. Greenspan, represented in court by an agent from his office, indicated from Toronto that he would seek a bail hearing for Buxbaum before that date. In Ontario murder cases, only the province's supreme court can grant bail and the court wouldn't be sitting in London again until September. Greenspan wanted a quick bail hearing and was willing to expedite the matter in Toronto.

Under continuing tight security (other arrests were expected soon and police were edgy that Buxbaum and Barrett might be in some danger or, possibly, part of an escape attempt) Helmuth and Squirrel were returned to Elgin-Middlesex Detention Centre to await developments.

Buxbaum, who hadn't liked the publicity surrounding his promotion of political friend Gordon Walker and the insertion of religious tracts in pay envelopes, was deeply upset with the attention he was getting. He told anyone who would listen that he was innocent. Just to be safe, however, he'd hired one of the most prominent criminal lawyers in Canada.

The successful nursing home operator, now prisoner 1362, maximum security wing, chafed at the humiliation of being thrown in jail. He was angry at the newspapers and felt they weren't being fair. This was all a mistake, he tried to explain to other prisoners and to anyone else who would listen.

His stress level was raised several notches when he saw the front page of the *London Free Press* on the morning of August 2. The paper had sent a reporter to a Wednesday night prayer meeting at West Park Baptist at which the subject of Buxbaum was discussed. Fawcett urged about a hundred members of the well-to-do church to demonstrate they were a caring community by being bondsmen for their prominent member who was in trouble.

Fawcett said that members of the congregation felt the arrest of Buxbaum had tarnished the good name of the church. In fact, the minister said, he'd received a call from someone outside the church claiming that "we must be an awful bunch of hypocrites to have a man like that in our congregation." Fawcett urged church members to rally around brother Helmuth.

The reporter quite legitimately understood Fawcett to be looking for members willing to put up bail money, but the day the story appeared, Fawcett angrily called him up and complained.

"That's ludicrous," he said testily. "Why ask people to put up money when there's no lack of money for bail?"

The clergyman said he was merely seeking to drum up "moral support" for Buxbaum. "There was no mention of bail money," he insisted.

Fawcett, strong on matters of faith and naive in those of law, had inadvertently caused considerable distress to his wealthiest parishioner.

Public interest in the case was intense. The London and Toronto media and large numbers of spectators followed the appearances of Buxbaum, Barrett and, late in August, Hicks, Spider, Allen, Armes and Kline. Courtrooms were jammed and security was tight as the seven appeared for brief remands, usually handcuffed together. London hadn't seen a case like the Buxbaum murder since Peter Demeter's trial a decade before. But this was even more sensational. Here was a local man, a millionaire, charged in the brutal slaying of his wife, a good Christian woman. Better stuff than Demeter. Much better. Interest in his co-accused was minimal. It was Helmuth Buxbaum the spectators craned their necks to see.

Buxbaum's bail hearing hadn't been as easy to arrange as Greenspan had hoped. It began September 6 in Toronto before Mr. Justice A.W. Maloney of the Ontario supreme court. It continued September 17 and 18 in London and resulted in Maloney's rejecting Greenspan's bid to free Buxbaum.

At the hearing, evidence from which could not be published, an attempt was made to have Buxbaum's comptroller, Howard Johnson, act as surety. If Buxbaum were to fail to comply with the terms of his release, Johnson would have to pay $15,000 to the court. The arrangement sounded good, until Johnson revealed he had just been given a raise by his boss that would easily cover the $15,000. Maloney was not impressed with this bit of footwork. Buxbaum tried another route to buy his freedom. He filed a $1 million letter of credit with a London bank, an amount he would forfeit should he flee the country. Having already heard evidence that the net worth of the nursing home chain was about $14 million, Maloney was equally unimpressed with this offer.

Not surprisingly, on September 18, the supreme court judge directed that Buxbaum be kept in custody. As the decision was rendered Buxbaum bowed his head in the prisoner's box and slumped forward. He had been in custody now for nearly two months and there was little prospect of an early trial date. In court that day were his eldest son, Paul, and several family friends. They seemed upset.

Other bail hearings were held for Hicks and Kline and they, too, were kept in custody.

In the meantime, a date of December 5 was chosen for the start of a preliminary hearing into the charges against Buxbaum, Barrett, Allen, Armes, Hicks, Kline and Spider. When that day arrived, the prosecution severed the charges against Spider and set a December 18 date for his preliminary. He appeared briefly with the six others on December 5 and was remanded to December 18. The prosecutors wanted to be able to use testimony from Spider's wife, but they couldn't if the gunman were still charged jointly with the other six. In common law, a wife or husband — even if estranged — cannot testify against her or his spouse. By severing Spider, the crown could use his wife's evidence against Buxbaum and the others.

Buxbaum didn't like jail and he was trying to do everything he could to get out. His wealth had saved him from trouble before and he was sure it would get him out of this jam. He'd hired one of the most prominent lawyers in the country to defend him and the millionaire was crushed when Greenspan was unable to get him back out onto the street. He was paying good money, believed to be $50,000 just for a retainer, and he expected results. Now that he was denied bail, Buxbaum had to live with the fact that Greenspan was a busy man and a speedy preliminary hearing and trial was out of the question: Greenspan had a full plate of current cases.

With three months until his preliminary hearing, Buxbaum was becoming annoyed at the delay. He got wind of a breakout attempt and approached Barrett and Allen who he'd heard were behind it. He offered Allen $10,000 to be included in the scheme and promised he'd look after the speed dealer for the rest of his life. Nothing came of the escape try and when the authorities heard of it, security was stepped up. When the seven accused went to court from now on, handcuffs and leg irons were the rule.

It was typical of Buxbaum to hire Greenspan, an expensive lawyer, to buy his way out of jail. He then tried to buy his bail through the comptroller and when that failed, attempted to be included in a breakout. He'd learned that money could buy just about everything he wanted: prestige, church and people. Why should he feel any differently just because he was in jail? Money remained his real God.

In the maximum security wing, Buxbaum stood out. He was about twice as old as the average prisoner kept at the Elgin-Middlesex Detention Centre. The other prisoners knew him and he had instant status because of his age and the seriousness of the crime he was charged with. An informal pecking order exists in all jails and the deepest respect is reserved for those prisoners facing the most serious charges. And Buxbaum, a millionaire who could be comfortable with politicians, corporate lawyers and other businessmen, and who was a pillar of the Baptist Church, found he could be surprisingly comfortable in jail. His chameleon-like quality of blending in with the crowd he was with stood him in good stead. He was used to dealing with drug dealers, pimps and other denizens of London's underworld, so that, in jail, he saw many familiar faces. Guards who had been concerned about how their celebrated prisoner might fit in were amazed to see how well Buxbaum coped. When he was sent to segregation briefly, it was not for protection; it was because he had violated rules governing the borrowing of books from the jail library. Buxbaum was treated as just "one of the boys" by the other prisoners.

He was despondent, however, at the thought of how his incarceration must look to outsiders. And he was particularly upset at the impact the situation would have on his children. He spoke longingly of them to anyone who would listen and he hoped they wouldn't hate him. He never spoke of Hanna, however, although other women were on his mind. "I need a woman," he would complain to counsellors and others who would drop in to ask about his welfare. In six months the depression would take its physical toll and he would shed more than fifty pounds from his two-hundred-pound frame.

His inner turmoil was reflected in two acts of self-mutilation before the preliminary hearing began. In September, he slashed the veins in his left arm with a paper clip he had somehow acquired. He was taken to hospital and sewed up in what was classified as a suicide attempt. The second act had far deeper overtones. On November 30, six days before the preliminary hearing was to start, he was discovered by guards, blood covering his groin. He had stuffed three paper clips up his penis. He was rushed to the jail infirmary to have them removed and given treatment and drugs to combat infection. This latter, bizarre act, wasn't life-threatening but it was the act of a man who realized that his penis was one of the reasons he was in this place. He may have been trying to punish the offending appendage to ease his guilt. From now on, he would be more closely watched.

After the preliminary concluded and he was awaiting trial, Buxbaum was briefly moved to segregation for his library offences and his few visitors were amazed at what they found in his cell: a small library of his own — a German language Bible, a German-language concordance for the Bible, an English-language Bible, some Reader's Digest magazines, and a couple of explicitly pornographic magazines. Ordinarily, the latter material would not have been permitted in jail, but he was allowed to keep it by sympathetic guards. Jail had not dulled the millionaire's interest in feminine flesh.

On December 5, the preliminary hearing got off to a rocky start. Spectators had lined up for nearly two hours and by the 10 a.m. scheduled start of proceedings, more than a hundred of them were vying for the fewer than sixty seats available in Courtroom Seven at London's courthouse.

The hearing was before London's senior provincial court Judge Alan Baker, formerly a top local defence lawyer and before that, prosecutor. Because of cramped conditions in the prisoners' box, the six accused were forced to sit in the jury box, a situation which caused many double-takes among the lucky few spectators who squeezed in late.

After several days, the hearing was returned to the second floor provincial Courtroom Three where Baker normally sits and spectators who weren't in time had to be turned away.

Evidence unfolded slowly in the first days of the preliminary hearing. The initial witnesses were trucker Colin Lawrence who was the first upon the murder scene, the Esso driver, Alec Johns and first-aid man, Mark Halden. Halden told of finding Buxbaum very ''plastic'' and lacking emotion in their brief encounter.

Another witness was Constable Phil Medlyn, the OPP officer who'd stumbled across the morning murder try. Medlyn told a tale that had overtones of a Keystone Cop reel, but revealed the routine lived by a provincial police officer in a rural area. He testified that he hadn't thought the roadside meeting was much at the time and had carried on to district headquarters to collect the mail. The incident slipped from his mind until two days later and he recounted for Greenspan how he'd spent his time in the interim.

Medlyn said that when he'd returned to the Strathroy detachment he took firearms training, lunched at 1:15 p.m., tested the detachment's radar unit in the afternoon and checked a car alongside a county road before booking off duty at 4 p.m. He didn't see television news that night or the radio stations which were reporting the murder and said he didn't read the morning newspaper.

The officer testified that he reported back for duty the following morning at 8 a.m. and then learned of the murder. He was immediately directed to take a raincoat to an officer at the murder scene. His logbook recorded that he had then gone to a two-car crash and spent the rest of the morning looking for a blue vehicle, believed to be a Nova, that all detachment officers were directed to watch for. At 12:30 p.m. he was detailed to the Buxbaum home in Komoka to get information about some credit cards on behalf of another officer. Medlyn spoke to a woman there and was directed to the Buxbaum's business office on Hyde Park Road in London where he got the information from the office manager.

Back at the detachment, Medlyn provided the information he'd gleaned about the credit cards to Corporal Leo Sweeney and heard other officers talking about the case. Medlyn said he then had lunch and in the afternoon checked a report of a car damaging a hedge west of Komoka. He then cruised through a conservation area campground performing what he described as "criminal enforcement."

Asked by Greenspan what criminal enforcement was, Medlyn replied succinctly: "driving around." He booked off duty at 4 p.m. Still nothing had twigged in his mind about the morning incident along the 402.

The next day, July 7, Medlyn said he reported for duty at 8 a.m. and was sent to an Adelaide Township address to look into some damage done to a lawn and then returned to the detachment to check the radar unit again. He was involved in traffic control and at about 10:25 a.m. noticed a blue Nova in Strathroy that seemed to match the description issued by his office. He checked it out but it wasn't the car. Medlyn then returned to the conservation area and went back to the detachment just before noon.

At the detachment, he and another officer started chatting about the strange murder of Hanna Buxbaum. Medlyn recalled that at one point his companion mentioned that "it could be a Demeter-type occurrence." Medlyn booked off for lunch and went home, thinking about his colleague's words. Something was nagging him. He sat down for lunch and in mid-sandwich it occurred to him: he'd seen the Nova and the station wagon on the morning of the killing, two days ago. It struck him like a thunderbolt and he immediately ran outside to the cruiser in the driveway, jumped inside and began scribbling down every-thing he could remember of the morning confrontation. Later that afternoon he would recognize Buxbaum at the cell area of the London OPP detachment as he told his story to investigator Ron Piers.

Other early witnesses included police officers who had arrived at the scene as well as Strathroy Constable Roger Aisladie who was parked in the median when Buxbaum and his nephew sped up. Dr. Robert Anthony related how he had broken the news of Hanna's death to Helmuth; the Buxbaum's neighbor testified that he owned a big blue Chrysler which his neighbors might be familiar with, but that he had been in Florida at the time of the shooting. Other witnesses included Rent-a-Wreck staff who had rented the blue Nova, the limou-sine driver who took Barrett's party to Toronto, and RCMP Constable John Martin who had observed Barrett, Hicks and Buxbaum at the London airport the day after the shooting.

But talk was going on behind the scenes. Since early in the case, the prosecution had been talking to Armes, trying to see if he could give them the evidence they needed to convict Buxbaum of deliberately planning and paying for the killing of Hanna. Armes had been kept in protective custody at the jail because it was known he was talking to police. Armes was a logical candidate to approach. He had witnessed the killing, but had no weapon and insisted he was only along for the ride. If necessary, the Crown figured, they could let Armes plead guilty to a lesser charge in exchange for his testimony against the others. But Armes was unable to adequately link Barrett, Hicks and Allen to Buxbaum, so the talks went nowhere.

Before the third week of the preliminary hearing, talks were going on behind the scenes between the prosecution and law-yers for Allen, Barrett and Hicks. A deal was being discussed. The Crown didn't get evidence as damning about Buxbaum's on-scene reactions as it had hoped from its first twenty-seven witnesses and was willing to negotiate. Lawyers Wally Libis, Fletcher Dawson and Mike Epstein, representing Barrett, Allen and Hicks respectively, made a pact. If the prosecution were willing to deal with one of them, it had to be all three. Martin wasn't overjoyed at losing three first-degree murder counts and wrestled with his problem. Finally, he decided it was necessary to deal in order to convict the man he most desperately wanted, the architect of the killing, Helmuth Buxbaum. But details hadn't been worked out on the weekend while Greenspan, unaware of the negotiations, was home in Toronto.

Monday, December 17, was the ninth day of the hearing and Anita Pitcher took the stand to face her cross-examination by Greenspan. She related how she'd given conflicting statements to police about her involvement in helping Pat Allen rent the Nova. Pitcher said she'd been threatened by police that she would be charged with being an accessory if she didn't co-operate and tell the truth. Greenspan, who had just pried from prosecutor Martin two statements Pitcher had given to police, sought an adjournment after about an hour of evidence to study them. In the break, he got wind of what was going on. After an adjournment of nearly an hour, court resumed and prosecutor Martin sought an adjournment to 2:30 p.m. to "consider the Crown's position."

At the afternoon resumption, Martin sought a further adjournment to the next day because of "procedural problems." He added there were "some arrangements I must make." Greenspan said he didn't want "to spoil the party" that was going on around him and didn't object to the further adjournment. The lawyers and Judge Baker went into chambers where the situation was revealed.

Court recessed quickly, leaving spectators puzzled. Before meeting the judge, Greenspan, his brow deeply furrowed, pulled out one of his Belmont Milds and scowled that he had a migraine headache. A worried Helmuth Buxbaum pulled Greenspan aside.

"What does this mean, Eddie?" he asked, seeking comfort from his high-priced lawyer.

"It means, Helmuth," Greenspan replied, "you're fucked."

13/The Deals:

"I don't think it is in my best
interests to give evidence."

The deal was worked out that night.

Prosecutor Martin would accept guilty pleas from Barrett and Allen to charges of conspiracy to commit murder, from Hicks to being accessory after the fact of murder. All other charges would be dropped. In exchange, the three would testify for the prosecution against Buxbaum and Armes and also against Spider. Kline would testify against Spider and all charges would be dropped against him.

Despite the dangers inherent in "turning rat" against their former co-accused, the lure of co-operating with the prosecution had distinct advantages for Barrett, Allen and Hicks. A conviction for first-degree murder carried with it a life sentence with no eligibility for parole for twenty-five years. And while they had varying involvement in the murder, they all ran the risk of conviction on first-degree murder charges. The maximum sentence for conspiracy to commit murder was fourteen years and parole could be applied for after a third of the sentence were served. Accessory, strangely, had a maximum of life imprisonment, longer than a conspiracy sentence. However, unlike murder with its life sentence, parole could be applied for after a third of whatever sentence were imposed.

Given their co-operation, the Crown would not seek the maximum terms for Barrett, Allen and Hicks. The three were assured by their lawyers that they could be back on the street in a few years.

Early on December 18, 1984, Barrett, Allen and Hicks entered their guilty pleas before Mr. Justice Horace Krever of the Supreme Court of Ontario. Krever, who had been sitting in London for two weeks, made room on his busy docket by accepting the pleas an hour before court normally opened for the day.

Although his client wasn't involved in the pleas, Eddie Greenspan received permission to make a submission to Krever. Greenspan asked the judge to ban the publication of the fact that Barrett and Allen had pleaded guilty to conspiring *with* Helmuth Buxbaum to murder Hanna. He pointed out that to have that fact reported in the press would imply that Buxbaum had been part of the conspiracy.

"This is a case that has received a great deal of local attention, and suffers from a great deal of notoriety," Greenspan said, adding that he already believed that the venue of the trial would have to be changed to another community. Linking the names would harm Buxbaum's chance for a fair trial, he argued.

Greenspan asked Krever to ban publication of any reference to Helmuth Buxbaum's name in the charges to which Allen and Barrett had pleaded guilty.

The judge said he doubted he had authority to impose such a ban but permitted Greenspan some time to look up legal precedents for his request. In fifteen minutes Greenspan found two: one involving a publication ban on a change of venue application and another banning the use of names of witnesses who were inmates at a prison. Greenspan's knowledge of the law proved once again to be formidable.

Krever was persuaded by the experienced defence counsel and agreed to the ban, "in the interests of a fair trial" for Buxbaum. He also banned publication of the fact that Greenspan had sought the order.

Allen, Barrett and Hicks were remanded in custody for preparation of pre-sentence reports and sentencing on January 17.

The preliminary hearing for Buxbaum and Armes resumed downstairs in Judge Baker's court and in the first order of business the first-degree murder counts were withdrawn against Allen, Barrett and Hicks.

After interviews with the Crown lawyers, the trio was then trotted into Spider's preliminary hearing, which had started the same day that Allen, Barrett and Hicks entered their guilty pleas.

Probation officers then began the task of compiling pre-sentence reports on Allen, Barrett and Hicks in preparation for the January 17 sentencing of the trio.

They would find the case of Jan Hicks to be particularly tragic.

Janet Hicks was one of three children, all girls, born to Weston Beverly Hicks and Willena Hicks. Her father was an ill-humored and violent man, a frequently unemployed laborer who abused his wife and girls. On November 9, 1967, the forty-seven-year-old Weston Hicks, who lived apart from his family in the downstairs of a two-storey house while his wife and girls lived upstairs, flew into a violent rage. He wanted to use a new car that his wife, a registered nurse, had just pur-chased after many months of saving, but she denied his request. In the course of a dispute with his fourteen-year-old daughter, Janet, he struggled over a lamp cord then stomped into his wife's bedroom, looped the cord around her neck and strangled her to death. Willena had been sleeping after working an all-night shift at the Ontario Hospital in London. The attack occurred at dinner-time. Janet's younger sister, Karen, then six, ran screaming into the street in front of their modest home, alerting the neighbors that her daddy had killed her mommy.

The following April, Weston Hicks received a life sentence after a Supreme Court of Ontario jury convicted him of non-capital murder in his wife's death. That conviction was set aside and a new trial ordered by an appeal court that ruled the trial judge had failed to adequately outline the defence theory. A year later, Hicks was convicted again and imprisoned for life. In both trials, Janet Hicks had to testify against her father. In 1972, while reading a letter from his daughter Janet, Hicks suffered a heart seizure in Kingston penitentiary and died.

Despite this background, Hicks, by the age of thirty-one, had become a solid member of the London community. Some of her friends would prove poor choices, but Janet Hicks and sisters Karen and Judy would overcome their past. At the time of Hanna's murder, Janet Hicks had worked at an east London biscuit-manufacturing firm for fourteen years. Her work was considered so exemplary, her employer told court that a job would be waiting for her once her jail sentence were completed.

Hicks' defence lawyer and even Crown Attorney Martin, who, ironically, twice successfully prosecuted Weston Hicks, would be moved by the tragic background of Janet Hicks and they would ask Mr. Justice Krever to give her a modest sentence.

Terry Kline had been another story. The twenty-six-year-old dropout from Grade nine and product of a broken home had bounced around a number of jobs before latching onto a small business of painting and decorating. He began supplementing his income by arranging bookings for exotic dancers and other good-looking girls who had decided they could earn money with their bodies more easily than with their minds. The slim, handsome Kline moved easily with the crowd that frequented the Wellington, Kelly's and the Park Lane and his nickname of "Sunshine" was well known. He knew many of the principals charged in the Buxbaum murder. He didn't know Helmuth very well at first, thinking — like many of his friends — that Buxbaum was an undercover cop.

Kline had been a heavy user of cocaine but had switched to LSD and was drinking heavily by early 1984. He was a mess, he would admit. His food intake consisted of one raw egg per day. His mind was scrambled from the hallucinogen and alcohol and it took him several months to figure where he'd been at the time Hanna was shot. He was to learn he'd been visiting a lady and was in her bathtub at the time of the killing. As talk circulated after the murder, some of his acquaintances began asking Kline about the mask he'd worn at the scene of the crime. He began to panic, believing he may have had something to do with Hanna's death. He talked openly about having heard of murder plans, hoping that someone could assure him he hadn't been involved.

The name "Terry" would turn up in wiretaps placed on Buxbaum's telephone and others, but the callers were speaking of another Terry, Terry Armes. But police became suspicious of Kline after interviewing people he'd spoken to. On August 10 he'd been arrested. Sixteen days later, the real Terry — Armes — was arrested. Police would insist for some time that it wasn't a case of mistaken identity. Kline, they argued, was involved. He knew of a plot, was part of this crowd, and had left London for Calgary (where he was actually visiting his mother in hospital). And most of all, this guy with the scrambled brains, couldn't prove that he hadn't been involved. He didn't have a clue where he'd been at the time of the murder. At Kline's bail hearing, a supreme court judge reviewed the evidence police had against Kline and ruled he should be kept in custody. Any mistake of identity should have been uncovered at the bail hearing.

A few days before Christmas, Kline was released from jail after four months in custody. The media reported his release but could not report how Kline had been mistaken for Armes. To do so would have prejudiced Armes' right to a fair trial. Crown Attorney Martin announced simply that Kline had been released as soon as it became apparent that there was not enough evidence against him to take him to trial.

For his part, Kline enjoyed the limelight of press attention. He'd been a suspect in the biggest murder case to hit London and found he could get his name and picture in the newspaper and on television very easily. He was a godsend to the press which couldn't report the bizarre evidence unfolding in the two preliminary hearings. Kline began calling reporters and eventually conducted mini-press conferences as he launched a bid to get compensation for the time he spent in jail in this case of mistaken identity.

"I just wish the police had listened," he would tell reporters. "I am innocent. It's been a bad nightmare."

The barely literate Kline revealed that he was planning a

book on the Buxbaum case. He said he had already written 2,000 pages longhand and expected it would sell well.

As he tried to decide how to proceed with his case against the authorities, Kline tried to pick up where he'd left off, but discovered he was no longer welcome at some of his old haunts. A visit to the Wellington Tavern got him a police ticket for trespassing. At another bar he was called a "stool pigeon" and received a split lip in the resulting fist fight.

In February, Kline wrote to the Ontario attorney general Roy McMurtry, seeking compensation for loss of income and respect because of being thrown in jail.

In his awkward prose, Kline complained that he had spent "143 days (in jail) wondering and worrying of the death penalty or 25 years in prison." Some of his former friends, he wrote, had been "ignorant and unfair" toward him, but the same fate might await them if they were to "stumble."

"I think I should be repaid for the life I have lost."

McMurtry never saw the letter. As Kline was composing his plea, the attorney general was being appointed Canada's High Commissioner to Great Britain. Weeks later, a reply came from the director of Ontario crown attorneys, turning down any government compensation. Richard Challoner, writing on behalf of the attorney general's office, advised Kline that the laying of murder charges against him was proper and that the charges were dropped when the prosecution determined there wasn't enough evidence to warrant a trial. Challoner noted that at the bail hearing, the supreme court had assessed the case against Kline and, considering his lack of employment and residence, decided he was best kept in jail.

"Bearing in mind all of those factors," Challoner concluded, "any request for compensation cannot be granted."

While awaiting word from the provincial government, Kline had circulated a petition in support of his bid for redress. Because of the notoriety of the case, he easily drew several hundred names, most culled from the downtown bars in which he was still permitted entry. Kline also went onto a radio talk show and had a lawyer sit in with him to ensure that he didn't say anything to jeopardize the rights of Buxbaum, Armes and Spider. His story drew a large number of sympathetic callers.

Compensation denied, Kline's only hope was to sue the government. He found a lawyer in Toronto willing to take the case despite its slim chance of success. The case is expected to take some time to reach court.

The preliminary hearing for Buxbaum and Armes resumed in early January, 1985. Among the first witnesses were Pat Allen and Rob Barrett. After several days of evidence, the hearing was adjourned to April 1.

January 17 was the day set for sentencing Allen, Barrett and Hicks. When asked by Mr. Justice Krever if they had anything to say before he passed sentence, all three apologized for the pain they had caused others by their actions.

The prosecution and defence lawyers had agreed to a statement of facts in the case and on sentences. Crown Attorney Mike Martin read to Krever a five-page set of facts in the case, outlining the involvement of the three who had pleaded guilty. The facts showed the setting of the stage for the crime and showed that the Buxbaum marriage "was an unhappy one. Although Hanna Buxbaum was a virtuous, religious, wife and mother, Helmuth Buxbaum frequently, during their marriage, had sexual relations with other women, including numerous prostitutes. He also abused illicit drugs including cocaine and marijuana..."

Greenspan's sought-after ban on making a link between the three in court and Buxbaum, Armes and Spider was still in effect. The press chafed at this restriction and implied its own suspect. One example: "The killing of Hanna Buxbaum was a $25,000 contract job and came about twelve hours after a first bid to murder her was foiled by an unsuspecting policeman..." It wasn't hard to imagine who in the cast of characters originally charged might have $25,000 on hand and a desire to kill Hanna.

Krever found the facts shocking and said it was "difficult to think of a more reprehensible act...(than) to agree for money to take the life of another human being.''

Barrett was sentenced to ten years in prison for the murder conspiracy, Allen to eight years, and Hicks to fifteen months in jail for accessory after the fact of murder.

Words of sympathy were expressed for Janet Hicks. Krever was moved to remark: "I don't think I have ever come across such a case where an accused person has had such a tragic existence prior to the offence.''

Her lawyer, Mike Epstein, insisted Hicks' involvement was only peripheral although she now felt she might have thwarted the killing if she had known about it beforehand.

The three were led back to their cells to await transfer to widely disparate jails and rely on the grapevine and press accounts to see how their co-accused fared.

The sentencings received wide publicity. By far the most avid reader of newspaper reports was an inmate at the Elgin-Middlesex Detention Centre: Helmuth Buxbaum.

Buxbaum was angry at the account of the event in the *London Free Press*, which had been following events closely since the killing. The *Free Press*, with a circulation of about 130,000, had recently appointed an ombudsman, former managing editor Jack Briglia, to field reader complaints about the paper's coverage.

It was to Briglia that Buxbaum expressed his displeasure:

Mr. Jack Briglia
Ombudsman for
The London Free Press,
London, Ont.

Jan. 29/85

Dear Mr. Briglia,

The newspaper article about the sentencing of Mr. Allan (sic) and Barrett on Jan. 18/85 was a grave injustice to me for the following reasons:

1. Mr. Justice (sic) Baker had clearly forbidden any publication of any presented "evidence" during the preliminary hearings.

2. Your article clearly implied that I was involved in the murder of my wife.

3. Your article has caused incredible agony and pain to my children.

4. Your premature article has irreversably (sic) damaged my reputation because most people have a tendency to believe the newspaper and are incapable to distinguish between the incredible and credible news writers.

I wish you a very successful carrier (sic) as London's *Free Press* first ombudsman.

Yours sincerely,
H.T. Buxbaum

P.S. Could you print your correct address, so that subscribers would be better informed and encouraged.

The neatly penned letter was mailed from the jail. It raised several eyebrows in addition to those of Briglia. Because Buxbaum was a man on trial for murder and the trial hadn't yet taken place, the paper could not print the letter. Buxbaum would have a chance to explain his side of the story at his trial.

He got an unexpected chance to speak a few weeks later, but turned it down.

The gunman's lawyer, John Drake, had spent considerable time trying to decide if he should call Buxbaum and Armes to testify. If anyone were going to deny that Spider had been involved, it would have to be his co-accused. The two had most to gain by denying any link.

The fourth day of Spider's preliminary hearing was February 25 and Drake announced that he would be calling Buxbaum and Armes because "I'm very interested in hearing what they have to say."

Armes was called first but late in the afternoon came the

moment spectators had been waiting for. John Drake called his next defence witness: Helmuth Buxbaum.

Buxbaum, wearing a dark blue suit and matching dark blue tie, was escorted into the courtroom from a side door in the prisoner's box and onto the stand. When the court clerk attempted to swear him in, Buxbaum said quietly that he didn't want to be sworn in. Judge Walker asked Buxbaum his reason.

''I'm innocent and I don't want to give evidence until my trial,'' Buxbaum replied.

Walker must have expected something like this. He immediately flipped to the relevant section of the Criminal Code and told Buxbaum that pursuant to its provisions, he was directing that he be jailed for eight days and that he return to court at the end of that time. Had this been a trial, rather than a preliminary hearing, Buxbaum could have been found in contempt of court and subject to a harsher penalty. The rules governing preliminary hearings are different.

Eight days later the story was the same. Again Buxbaum wore a blue suit and was prepared with an explanation. ''I'm innocent. I was wrongfully charged. Wrongfully arrested and wrongfully put in prison for 250 days. I don't think it is in my best interests to give evidence.''

Another eight days and Buxbaum again refused to testify. After discussing the situation with the prosecution and defence, Walker decided to commit Spider for trial without having the benefit of Buxbaum's testimony.

''It's fairly clear from Mr. Buxbaum's three appearances before me that he will not change his position,'' the judge said in sending Spider to his supreme court trial. He added that he would take no more action against Buxbaum.

The other preliminary, that of Buxbaum and Armes, would resume April 1 and conclude April 23.

Spectators in April heard of Buxbaum's bid to poison Hanna, his joining the dating service and hiring prostitutes, and his offers of money to two of them to bear children for him.

After several prostitutes had testified to Buxbaum's voracious sexual appetites, an older gentleman who had been sitting in the hearing every day collared a newspaper reporter and asked how much longer the hearing would take. Told the proceeding wasn't soon likely to wind up, the spectator, a man in his late seventies, who wore both eyeglasses and hearing aid, immediately changed the subject. His face still flushed from the sometimes-steamy testimony, he winked at the reporter and offered his view of Buxbaum: "He deserves a medal. The old stud."

As the month of April dragged on and spring came to southwestern Ontario, Eddie Greenspan and his assistant Bob Sheppard decided to take a first-hand look at some of the bars featured in the evidence.

One night the two hopped into a cab, Greenspan taking the rear seat. He was convinced the trial had to be moved out of town because of the intense publicity surrounding it but wanted to test the local waters. "So what do you think of this Buxbaum business?" he asked the cabbie. The driver, like cabbies everywhere, had heard all the stories, some of them only remotely resembling the truth. "She had it comin'," he opined. "What?" an amazed Greenspan inquired. "Yeah," came the reply. "She was screwin' around with men and he knocked her off." The subject was dropped.

Another night, Greenspan and George Jonas were sampling beverages and the ambience at the Abbey Hotel, a low-budget watering hole popular with truckers, chiefly because of the strippers. It was here that Buxbaum had met Susan Ambrose, the one-time-maid turned stripper he tried to have poison Hanna. Greenspan, pugnacious in court as well as on the street, got into an altercation with a customer. One of Canada's top defence lawyers was getting ready to put up his dukes when his friend Jonas dragged him out of the establishment.

On April 23, after twenty-nine days of sittings, Helmuth Buxbaum and Terry Armes were committed for trial. There had been seventy-three witnesses, of which seven had been called by the defence. The transcripts of the hearing would fill several volumes and could not be carried by one person.

The next month, Greenspan took a change of venue application to the Supreme Court of Ontario, arguing that the publicity in the London area had prejudiced Buxbaum's right to a fair trial. He wanted the trial to be in the Toronto area. The prosecution didn't oppose the application and Ontario's chief justice, Gregory Evans, agreed to the move. A month later Evans decided the trial would be held October 15 at the Supreme Court assizes in St. Catharines, about 200 kilometres east of London.

About a month before the trial started, Terry Armes appeared before Mr. Justice Gregory T. Evans of the Supreme Court of Ontario, who was sitting in London. Armes pleaded guilty to second-degree murder. First-degree murder and conspiracy-to-commit-murder counts were withdrawn.

His long discussions with the Crown's office had finally borne fruit.

The prosecution would now be able to concentrate its efforts on Buxbaum while Armes, a bit player in the episode, would be sent off to prison.

Second-degree murder is defined in the Criminal Code as murder where the planning and deliberation required to make out first-degree murder is absent. For some time, the Crown had been concerned whether Armes' tenuous grasp on his sobriety had meant he'd actively participated in the planning and carrying out of the murder.

For his part, Armes ran the risk of being convicted for first-degree murder — like Barrett, Allen and Hicks before him — a conviction for which would mean a life sentence with no eligibility for parole for twenty-five years. A conviction for second-degree murder meant he wouldn't be eligible for parole for ten years.

Armes sat quietly throughout his brief appearance in court September 13, a Friday. He was resigned to his fate. He'd confessed all to the police and it was time to get on with taking his medicine. Ironically, he was to be kept off the street for a full decade, while Barrett and Allen, prime architects of the killing, would be back in circulation by the end of 1986 if they could win parole for good behavior.

Even the judge was moved to remark that the unfortunate Armes was "probably at the wrong place at the wrong time."

Four persons had now been jailed in the killing, another was set free. Only Helmuth Buxbaum and the gunman were left.

Their day in court was fast approaching as Terry Armes was led off to penitentiary.

14/The Trial. Prosecution Phase:

"...there never has been a perfect trial."

Tuesday, October 15, 1985 was a foggy, grey day in St. Catharines, the Niagara Peninsula city of 125,000 where the trial was to be held.

About 300 residents of the judicial district of Niagara North trod along leaf-strewn streets to the angular three-year-old fourteen-million-dollar courthouse at the intersection of Church and James streets. They were part of the jury panel from which four juries would be chosen. Twelve of them would be selected to hear a district court fraud trial, two other groups of six would hear civil trials and twelve would hear the case against Helmuth Treugott Buxbaum.

Few of the Niagara North jurors had heard about the Buxbaum case. The local media had long before carried snippets about the death of Hanna Buxbaum. It was precisely because of this lack of publicity that the case had been moved into their midst from London, 200 kilometres to the west.

It had been fifteen months since Hanna Buxbaum died but the St. Catharines area would soon shed its ignorance. There were few spectators in court this first day, the day after Thanksgiving.

Twenty-two members of the media, from London, Toronto and St. Catharines were on hand for opening day proceedings. If the good folk of St. Catharines didn't know what to expect from the Buxbaum trial, the press certainly did. Their reports would soon be front-page news and seen on the national newcasts.

The fourth-floor courtroom in which Helmuth Buxbaum's fate was to be determined was a strange mixture of grey-white concrete, blonde-oak spectator seats and judge's dais and counsel tables salvaged from the old King Street courthouse a block away. The century-old, dark-stained wood and ancient chandelier clashed with the stark, modern surroundings. The sharp juxtaposition was perhaps fitting given the strange contrasts in Helmuth Buxbaum's life.

The trial was before Mr. Justice John Gerald Joseph O'Driscoll, fifty-four, a judge of the Supreme Court of Ontario for fourteen years. O'Driscoll, a native of Sault Ste. Marie, was a Roman Catholic who had articled and then practiced under legendary Toronto criminal lawyer Arthur Maloney. Slight, bespectacled and heavy-jawed, he had the reputation of a tough, humorless judge who had little sympathy for those he viewed as wasting his time. He was also considered one of Ontario's most experienced criminal court judges.

Proceedings didn't get underway until the afternoon of the first day. Buxbaum was led into court and he moved quickly into the prisoner's box. His appearance had changed markedly since his committal for trial. He seemed trim and fit. He wore a new navy blue suit that gave him a crisp, tailored look. At his preliminary, his suits had been ill-fitting, not having been modified to accommodate his weight loss. He wore glasses, wire-rimmed, for the first time, to correct failing eyesight he blamed on poor lighting conditions in jail. He smiled readily and seemed to be in good spirits.

Buxbaum had been moved from London to the detention centre in nearby Thorold on July 5, ironically, the first anniversary of Hanna's death. It was a move intended to get him closer to the scene of his trial and closer to Toronto, the home of his lawyer, Eddie Greenspan.

The millionaire was looking all business and seemed eager to get the trial underway.

O'Driscoll had barely taken his seat when Greenspan was on his feet with two pre-trial motions. He said he had learned that star crown witnesses Rob Barrett and Pat Allen had been under police drug squad surveillance during the time they were supposedly plotting murder with Buxbaum. Greenspan wanted copies of all wiretap transcripts. He argued that the wiretaps must be helpful to the defence because the prosecution hadn't told him about them and apparently wasn't planning to intro- duce them as evidence. In addition, Greenspan said he'd heard at the last minute that Barrett, the "linch-pin" witness for the crown, was to be the first witness. Greenspan said the prosecu- tion, which earlier had indicated its first witnesses were to relate to Buxbaum's "motive", was wrong to give him so little warning of the appearance of such a crucial witness. He asked the judge to prevent the prosecution from calling Barrett for several days so he could prepare.

In support of his motion on the wiretaps, Greenspan pro- duced a London private investigator and the manager of the Lamplighter Inn who both said that early in 1984 police had been watching a room which had been occupied by Barrett and others.

Greenspan argued into the next day when prosecutor Martin replied that the wiretaps were not connected to the Buxbaum case.

O'Driscoll didn't mince words when he ruled out Green- span's lengthy arguments. He said there was no evidence to warrant the proferring of wiretap records and that he did not want "to embark on a foray into the wild blue yonder."

He went on to reject Greenspan's argument that evidence from Barrett should be delayed. He was not impressed with Greenspan's "moving recitation" about the hardship Barrett's appearance would create, but he didn't intend to direct the prosecution how to conduct its case and call its witnesses. He said he was not impressed with Greenspan's allegations that the crown was being unfair. "I don't want to hear any more comments about whether the Crown is being fair. I don't want any interminable whining."

Greenspan had been shot down; the jury selection began.

Buxbaum's lawyer then challenged the jurors for cause, a motion aimed at weeding out jurors for potential bias. The crown did not oppose the move and the court embarked on a lengthy process of interviewing potential jurors with a series of carefully chosen questions.

Greenspan sought and won the right to ask jurors if they'd be unable to give Buxbaum a fair hearing if evidence were to disclose he'd taken cocaine and had been unfaithful to his wife.

He and Crown Attorney Mike Martin canvassed fifty-four jurors before they agreed on twelve. Two women and ten men were selected by the end of the week. And before hearing any evidence they had already received strong hints that both cocaine and adultery were involved in the case they were about to hear. They were also warned that the case could last until Christmas or early into January.

The two female jurors were a young housewife and a middle-aged inspector at a General Motors plant. Three of the ten men also worked at General Motors plants in the area, one man ran a cake-decorating shop, two were teachers, one a professional engineer, another an electrician, another a paper company millwright, and one a corporate vice-president for a food-processing firm. A stationary engineer, chosen early in the week, begged off jury duty with a sore foot aggravated by sitting in court. He was excused after producing a note from his doctor.

Jurors in the case were provided with school-type black notebooks and pens to record evidence in the lengthy trial, over the objections of Greenspan who said the practice was rarely used and might mean that the best note-takers in the jury would have their opinions prevail. He was again overruled.

The following Monday, October 22, prosecutor Martin outlined his case in a forty-minute recitation. In his low-key style, the white-haired prosecutor described how Buxbaum had wanted out of a bad marriage and had approached three persons to seek their help in having Hanna killed: hookers Dawn Watson, Susan Ambrose and his pusher, Rob "Squirrel" Barrett. He described Barrett's supplying of cocaine and women to Buxbaum and how the millionaire and Squirrel had agreed to a $25,000 contract on Hanna's life. He went on to explain how the businessman had provided money and pictures of his wife to Barrett who, in turn, had attempted to interest John and Brigitte in Florida and finally found Pat Allen. Allen, in turn, had conscripted the gunman and Armes. He told how Barrett had collected $13,000 from Buxbaum at London airport the day after the killing and how the gunman had received $5,000, Armes, $3,500, Allen, $1,000, Hicks, $500 and Barrett himself, $3,000.

"Helmuth Buxbaum did not pull the trigger," Martin told the jurors. "He paid the killers to do so and he drove her to the place of her death."

The prosecution's first witness was its star, Rob Barrett. During the afternoon and the next morning, assistant prosecutor Al MacDonald led Squirrel through his evidence from the time he met Buxbaum with Collette Vandenberg to the day after the killing.

Barrett described his dealings with Buxbaum in which he supplied cocaine and women from their first meeting.

"Almost immediately he was saying she (Hanna) was being like a pain in the ass," Barrett said in a line that captivated newspaper reporters and their headline writers.

He testified that Buxbaum had told him that he couldn't divorce Hanna because she would win the children and that he couldn't bear to lose them.

Squirrel said he had left for Florida shortly after Paul Buxbaum had fired him from his landscaping job on May 23 and that he still had had no firm plans for murder, even though Buxbaum had given him pictures of Hanna and $5,000 to help him find killers.

"I hadn't planned on doing the murder," Barrett told the jury. "It was more or less a scam for me to make some money."

When he left the country, Barrett made sure he left Buxbaum with the impression that the killing would take place while he was away.

Barrett told of having offered Jean $15,000 to kill Hanna and of how the Quebecker and his girlfriend had vanished with the pictures, $500 and directions to the Buxbaum house. He hadn't seen him again until encountering him at Laval prison where Barrett was serving his sentence. At that time, they exchanged a few words in the prison kitchen, Barrett said.

He expressed his fear of testifying: "I'm a material witness in this case. Mr. Buxbaum got his wife killed and so I don't think he'd lose any sleep over getting me killed."

Greenspan jumped to his feet and asked that the jury be excused. In their absence, he argued that Barrett's unexpected assertion was inflammatory. O'Driscoll agreed. When the jury returned, the judge cautioned the jurors that Squirrel's fears were those shared by all prisoners who testify for the prosecution and that there was no evidence to suggest they were based on anything beyond that.

Barrett's evidence concluded and a well-prepared Greenspan began a cross-examination that would last for two-and-a-half days. The lawyer began by attacking the credibility of this important prosecution witness.

He reminded Barrett that he'd admitted earlier he could lie when necessary, that he had a lengthy criminal record, that he'd pushed drugs since he was sixteen, that he had a $700-a-day cocaine habit and that he'd been described in his presentence report as manipulative.

Greenspan suggested that Barrett had pleaded guilty to murder conspiracy in exchange for a promise of leniency. Barrett denied it and said he did so as part of a deal to get a light sentence for Jan Hicks and the release of Terry Kline, who, respectively, had little, and nothing, to do with Hanna Buxbaum's death.

He admitted to providing Buxbaum with only half the cocaine the millionaire was paying for and reluctantly agreed with Greenspan who suggested that Barrett viewed Buxbaum as "the sucker of all time."

"I'm going to suggest to you that you developed a game plan," the lawyer continued. "Helmuth Buxbaum was a man who you saw had these unusual appetites for sex and drugs and you, seeing that, for the first time in your life became a pimp."

"Correct," said Squirrel.

The lawyer pressed on.

"You saw this particular weakness of his and you were going to take advantage of him to get even closer to him and make him more dependent on Rob Barrett."

"You're dreaming, Mr. Greenspan," Barrett replied.

When Greenspan suggested that Barrett had been determined to sink his "claws" into his millionaire-mark, Barrett replied that he had only been trying to make money and prevent others from taking advantage of Buxbaum. Greenspan accused Barrett of having introduced Buxbaum to the needle by injecting him with cocaine on their first meeting. Barrett denied it and said that Buxbaum had already been injecting cocaine with Collette Vandenberg.

The lawyer and the star witness began jousting, Greenspan complaining that Barrett was taking "cheap shots" at him, and Squirrel countering that the lawyer was trying to intimidate him by calling him a street-wise pimp.

Barrett insisted he was not angry at Hanna for his firing from the nursing home. He said he knew at the time that Hanna was attempting to get Helmuth treatment for his cocaine problem.

Greenspan pressed Barrett for times and dates but Barrett said he was unable to give precise answers because his memory had been fogged by drugs.

The exchanges frequently turned into arguments. O'Driscoll lost patience and repeatedly warned the aggressive lawyer to stop arguing with the witness.

Throughout the vigorous questioning, Greenspan was planting a seed, the defence theory.

The lawyer was suggesting that Barrett had been antagonized by Hanna who'd threatened to take away his best customer. He presented a scenario in which Barrett had orchestrated the killing without Buxbaum's knowledge and had conscripted Allen and others to carry out the killing with the assurance it had been sought by Buxbaum, who was going to pay big money for it. Buxbaum, it was suggested, was being manipulated to think that the trip to Florida, the Westbury and even the stop along 402 were related to drug deals.

But Barrett was adamant. It wasn't that way at all. Buxbaum wanted the killing. He'd sought it from the first and had provided pictures of his wife and money to get the job done.

Barrett said his accomplices had all been paid and debts settled with the $10,000 he'd distributed to the gunman, Allen, Armes and Hicks.

Greenspan said he doubted that and toward the end of his gruelling examination of Barrett played recordings of police wiretaps on Barrett's telephone from July 10, 1984, five days after Hanna's murder.

In one call, an insistent Allen asked for a meeting with Barrett at 6 p.m. He called back later and asked why Squirrel had missed the meeting. Squirrel replied he'd slept through it. Allen then said he was sending a cab for Barrett and that he had to talk to him. Barrett, sounding concerned, asked who was with Allen and was told no one.

Sometime later, Barrett's wife, Kelly, called Allen to tell him her husband had just been picked up by the cab and that Barrett and Allen should go for a walk. She added, however, that she would be calling back every fifteen minutes to speak to Rob.

Greenspan asked if this didn't indicate that Barrett was afraid of Allen and the others, particularly the gunman. And how could that be, the lawyer asked, if everyone were paid up and happy?

"You were afraid these guys were going to kill you, weren't you?" Greenspan demanded.

"No, sir," Barrett replied.

The lawyer suggested that Allen and company were looking for more money for the murder and that Barrett was afraid because he didn't have it since Buxbaum had only paid up on the understanding it was for drugs. Barrett replied he was paranoid, or "skitsy" from the drugs and the fact he had been involved in a murder.

Then Greenspan began building toward a bombshell with which to conclude his cross-examination.

He asked Barrett if he knew a man in prison named Daniel Borland. Barrett admitted the two were acquaintances and had exercised together in the gym.

Greenspan then produced a photograph of Barrett and Borland standing together in the prison gym.

The lawyer then revealed that Borland had given a sworn affidavit in August relating to a conversation Borland had had with Barrett in the prison kitchen.

Slowly, Greenspan read the affidavit to an obviously ill-at-ease Barrett.

The affidavit read:

"Barrett told me that he had told the police and had already given evidence that Buxbaum had asked Barrett to kill Buxbaum's wife and that it was a contract killing.

"Barrett also told me that he (Barrett) had told Allen that Buxbaum had issued a contract for the murder of Buxbaum's wife.

"Barrett then told me that what he had told Allen and the police was not true and that, instead, what had in fact happened, was that Buxbaum's wife had found out that Barrett was supplying cocaine to Buxbaum and had threatened to report Barrett to the police.

"Barrett told me that as a result, he (Barrett) had arranged for the murder himself and only told Allen and others that the murder was at Buxbaum's request. Barrett told me that, in fact, Buxbaum had never requested the murder.

"...I then asked Barrett why he would not now tell the truth in court about what had actually happened and he told me that he was afraid that he would receive an increased sentence or would be charged with a further offence if he did."

The affidavit concluded with Borland's claim that Barrett had said his nerves were "shot" because of what he was going to have to say at Buxbaum's trial and that he (Barrett) had even lost weight because of it.

Greenspan asked for Barrett's reaction to the affidavit. Barrett replied firmly: "I don't know how Danny got that information. It's all lies."

O'Driscoll jumped into the fray and asked Greenspan about the author of the affidavit.

"I assume at some time in this trial, Mr. Borland will be produced," he asked Greenspan.

"Absolutely correct," the lawyer assured.

But Greenspan knew that would not be until the defence phase of the trial and even if Borland were heard from and not believed, the legal maneuvre had sown some doubts.

It was a nice piece of work and Greenspan didn't seem to be overly upset moments later when O'Driscoll forbade him from summarizing his cross-examination by calling Barrett a liar.

The defence's hand was tipped to prosecutor Martin and it made for an interesting alternative scenario.

Barrett was led out of court after Greenspan had finished with him and the man known as Squirrel passed within two metres of his antagonist Greenspan. He looked daggers at Buxbaum's lawyer. Greenspan returned the glare.

The prosecution had been caught by surprise but it would have several days to try to recoup. Court reconvened three days later, on Monday, and then it was time for assistant prosecutor MacDonald to see if he could undo some of the damage Greenspan had inflicted on Squirrel.

The prosecution's working weekend had proved successful. It now had some surprises of its own for the wily Greenspan.

Before the jury was brought into court MacDonald produced two letters, one of which sharply undermined the Borland affidavit. The first was a letter Barrett had sent to chief investigator Ron Piers early in May just before he went into segregation at Laval. In the letter, Barrett said that his fellow inmates had found out why he was in prison and who he was going to testify against; he asked for a transfer to another prison because he said he feared for his life.

Attached to the letter to Piers was a letter Barrett had received in his cell from fellow inmate Ray Cantin.

Cantin proposed in the letter that he tell Buxbaum's lawyer some "bullshit" about something Squirrel had told him in jail. That would mean he could become a witness for the millionaire and take some money from his lawyer for the testimony. Cantin added it would get him into a jail in Ontario. He planned to escape, he wrote, because "no city bucket will hold me."

The defence argued that the letters shouldn't be introduced to the jury until the prosecution's formal reply to the defence case at the end of the trial.

O'Driscoll agreed, but permitted the crown to question Barrett about a conversation he had had with Borland in which the inmate had offered to take the stand and discredit Barrett to please the millionaire and get money from him for the story.

Barrett had a simple explanation.

"Money changes people," he told Greenspan.

When Barrett left the witness stand after four-and-a-half days of evidence, he was scarred but intact. The defence had hammered him hard and he had partly recovered. But seeds of doubt had been sown in the minds of the jury and they would be particularly careful to scrutinize the evidence of anyone who had been relying on the information of Barrett.

The next witnesses were the Jean and Brigitte, back from Florida.

It turned out that "Jean" was a convict named Paul Ringuette and Brigitte, his young girlfriend, Brigitte McCurdy. Police had found a picture of the shirtless Ringuette standing with Barrett outside the Orlando motel's swimming pool and had worked hard to find the man who had ripped off Squirrel for blood money and the picture of Hanna. Ringuette was covered in tattoos. The tattoos were the only clue to finding him.

A police artist reproduced the drawings and, in conjunction with the Quebec police force, the owner of the body artwork was located in Laval prison — ironically the same prison to which Barrett had been transferred.

Ringuette, about age thirty, a man with close ties to the Hell's Angels motorcycle club of Laval, a Montreal suburb, was currently serving seventeen years for convictions for robbery and manslaughter. He had a record dating back to 1970 that revealed a series of increasingly serious crimes. By 1977 he had graduated to armed robbery, was convicted on four counts and got five years concurrent on each. Two years later, he stabbed a fellow inmate to death during a fight and was given another twelve years for manslaughter. He received day parole in February of 1984 and had chosen not to return to prison. Instead, he moved in with the nineteen-year-old Brigitte McCurdy, whom he'd met through the young woman's brother-in-law while both were in prison.

In June, McCurdy suffered a drug overdose and her fugitive boyfriend Ringuette promptly decided it was time for a holiday. From June 9 to June 16 they stayed at the Gateway Inn in Orlando, Florida, where they had registered as Gilles Hébart and M. Bouchard. A couple of days later they met Rob and Kelly Barrett and not long after Barrett broached the subject of murder when he found out about "Jean's" criminal record.

After Brigitte's testimony, Ringuette came to the stand, speaking through an interpreter because of his limited grasp of English.

"He (Barrett) told me it was the husband of Hanna Buxbaum who paid him to find somebody...to kill the woman," Ringuette testified.

The convict said that although he had accepted $500, pictures of Hanna and of the family station wagon, and a hand-drawn map with directions to the Buxbaum house, he had wanted much more money for the job. Barrett, he said, had talked of as much as $60,000 for the killing. "It was never my intention to kill anybody," said Ringuette. "It was just my intention to get some money to return to Montreal."

A few witnesses later, Nafisha Somani, the former prostitute, came to the stand. Her testimony about Buxbaum's offer of $30,000 if she'd bear him a child proved sensational. The press photographers climbed over each other in a bid to get her photograph, but Somani, embarrassed by a part of her life she wished had never been, evaded capture on film with the help of sympathetic police officers.

Following her to the witness stand was London sex-and-marital therapist Dr. Noam Chernick who'd seen Hanna and Helmuth in 1975 and recommended counselling, but the Buxbaums, he said, hadn't followed up on the suggestion. He told of an appointment Hanna had got for the couple in February, 1984, but said that only Hanna had showed up. Helmuth, he said, appeared later that day and seemed anxious to talk; Chernick saw him early the next morning.

"He noted he was drifting apart from his wife and had been doing so for years," Chernick told the jury.

Helmuth admitted it had been "easy and natural" to drift off toward the "cocaine crowd," Chernick said.

The businessman said he'd been looking for an aphrodisiac because his wife "didn't turn him on," although he was sexually active with other women.

"He said he would enjoy starting his life over again," Chernick said, leafing through notes of the February 17 interview.

"He said he had grown emotionally since marriage, but she hadn't," Chernick told the jury. "He did not think Hanna wanted to change. She got stuck at age four, he complained."

Buxbaum wanted to unburden himself, Chernick said, and all the counsellor could do was "write as fast as I could."

The millionaire said he would like to get off cocaine, a drug to which he had reverted through "silliness and loneliness."

Chernick testified he suggested the couple receive marital counselling and that Helmuth receive special, immediate counselling for his particular problems.

"The offers were made along with time to think about it," the therapist said. "I didn't hear back."

Susan Ambrose took to the stand to relate her month-long experience with Buxbaum during January, 1984, and told of his pressuring her to find poison for his wife.

Greenspan worked her over and got her to admit it was she — not Buxbaum — who first mentioned poison as a means of disposing of his wife. Ambrose insisted, however, that she hadn't been serious when she mentioned it and had become alarmed and fled when Buxbaum caused her to fear for her safety.

Greenspan accused her of fleeing instead because Ambrose had hoped to use the millionaire to help her dreams of a good future and that these dreams had been shattered when she realized Buxbaum was seeing other women. He charged she was humiliated by Buxbaum because he had turned her into a prostitute. Ambrose, a petite but determined witness, firmly denied the suggestions.

The next evidence came from maids at the Golden Pheasant Motel who had overheard a late January discussion between Ambrose and Buxbaum about putting poison into a woman's food.

Then it was on to the pretty, black Dawn Watson, who had received money for going to bed with Buxbaum in early 1984 and told the jury about her sex partner's talk of poisoning, drowning, shooting or kidnapping Hanna. She also told of the trip to Europe in late May in which she had become so disgusted with the millionaire's pursuit of drugs and women that she split from him for her return to Canada.

A few days later, Greenspan asked O'Driscoll to declare a mistrial.

On November 12, at the outset of the fifth week of trial,

Greenspan rose to make his request. The previous Friday the trial had embarked on a *voir dire*, a hearing within the trial in the absence of the jury, to determine the admissibility of evidence that Buxbaum had arranged for $1 million (U.S.) in life insurance on Hanna five months before her death. The defence wanted that evidence kept out of the trial because it was extremely prejudicial and there was some indication that Buxbaum had taken out the insurance on his wife/business partner at the suggestion of his accountant. The prosecution argued that jurors should make up their own minds about whether conclusions could be drawn from it.

The jury is not supposed to know what is being discussed in their absence, otherwise they may be prejudiced in their deliberations. But a CBC reporter made a slip, breaching the ban on reporting such material. Veteran journalist Ted Bissland, of CBLT-TV, Toronto, reported late Friday that the next evidence the jury would hear was about the life insurance. He explained later he was unaware that this was the subject of the *voir dire*, because he had left Friday's proceedings once the jury was dismissed for the weekend. Bissland, fifty-one, who'd demonstrated the unfortunate habit of arriving in court late and leaving early, had checked with the prosecution about the upcoming evidence and was told that the crown intended to call the insurance evidence.

Greenspan, a long-time personal friend of Bissland, said he was convinced the reporter's action was inadvertent, but that the mistake was too important to be overlooked. He said that if O'Driscoll were to rule that evidence of the insurance was admissible, outsiders might think he had been pressured into the decision by the broadcast. Greenspan said he was not criticizing O'Driscoll, but was concerned about the "appearance" of justice in the case. On the other hand, he argued, if the insurance evidence were ruled inadmissible, then the jurors would already have been prejudiced by the news report and a fair trial could no longer be held.

Assistant prosecutor Brendan Evans replied for the crown,

citing several cases, particularly from British Columbia, in which requests for mistrials had been turned down. Those decisions indicated basically that jurors don't believe everything they read or see in the media. Evans suggested that O'Driscoll might urge the jurors to base their verdict strictly on courtroom evidence.

O'Driscoll didn't even bother with this caution as he ruled against Greenspan's request.

"There never has been a perfect trial," he said, adding that the prevailing judicial opinion was that "the accused has a right to a fair trial, not a perfect trial." He didn't think anything unfair had happened. The judge said there was nothing in the late-night news report "that is going to scuttle the trial about to start its fifth week." He warned reporters that the episode demonstrated how easy it was for them to be "led into error." Just to be safe, however, he reminded the media that the request for mistrial had been held in the absence of the jury and could not be reported.

It was then back to argument about the insurance. Assistant defence counsel Chris Buhr argued for its exclusion as extremely prejudicial and indicated it had been taken out at the suggestion of accountant Duncan Findlay. Martin countered that the evidence was important, because Findlay now estimated Buxbaum's net personal worth at about $4 million and that a $1 million windfall from insurance would be welcomed by the millionaire in the event of Hanna's death.

O'Driscoll said the evidence should be tendered in court because it was "capable of being some evidence of motive" but that was for the jury to decide. It was the second major setback for the defence in one morning.

Eugene High, an insurance agent from Boca Raton, Florida, took to the stand and described how his long-time friend Helmuth Buxbaum had paid a surprise visit to his home February 7, 1984 and asked about insurance for Hanna.

High was originally requested to get a quote on $300,000 of one-year term insurance for Hanna, but Buxbaum later increased that to $1 million (U.S.) after learning that the rate per $1,000 of coverage was better. That day, Buxbaum gave High a cheque for $1,659. After her physical examination the following day in the Buxbaum's motel room, Hanna gave High another cheque for $2,341 for the balance owing on the premium for one-year coverage. The policy, High explained, was with Christian Mutual Life Insurance Company, a firm which sells only to "born-again believers in Christ." He knew that Helmuth and Hanna were believers. He'd met them sixteen years before at a religious conference and they attended the same church in Florida. High said he had insured other business partners of Buxbaum during the 1970s. Those policies, usually for $250,000 on Buxbaum and the same on his associate, had been allowed to lapse after a year or two. (Buxbaum's preliminary hearing was told that no claim had ever been made on the $1 million insurance on Hanna.)

As an afterthought, High said, Buxbaum asked about $500,000 of life insurance on himself. High said he knew that Helmuth might have difficulty in getting insurance because of his poor medical history, including his stroke. Many weeks later, Christian Mutual said it would insure Buxbaum, but it wanted a one-year premium of $13,250.

"He was accepted...but he turned it down and said the rate was too high," the underwriter said.

High said that Buxbaum had told him his accountant had recommended the insurance on Hanna as a business protection, and High said he eventually confirmed this with Findlay.

Next on the stand was a tiny brunette from Toronto named Corinne Willoughby. The prosecution called her to refute Greenspan's suggestion that Barrett was the first to inject Buxbaum with cocaine.

Willoughby said she had "dated" Buxbaum from August, 1982 until September 1983 and that he had injected cocaine on that last date. She said she saw the millionaire about twenty times and was paid $200 for sex and usually was given dinner afterward. The twenty-one-year-old who looked about fifteen, said the meetings were at Toronto hotels when Buxbaum was in town, or at London hotels after she started taking the train to join him.

She told of being taken to a Club Med in the Bahamas with another girl in late October, 1982, but said she had decided against a trip to yet another Club Med, in Mexico, with Buxbaum who had planned to bring along two other women. "I wasn't into that," she told the jury which was specifically forbidden from hearing any evidence concerning lesbian performances.

On November 13, nearly a month into the trial, another key Crown witness, Patrick Allen came to the stand.

Allen testified that he had become interested in the murder contract when his old pal Rob Barrett mentioned it to the 300-pound "Big Jim." At Thames Park a few days before the killing, Allen said he was told it was a $10,000 contract. He said that on July 4 he and Barrett met Buxbaum near the McDonald's in west London and they began looking for murder sites. Allen testified he didn't like the spot Buxbaum selected because it was too busy so he led the millionaire to the spot along Highway 402 with the deep ditch and the culvert at the bottom.

He told of having collected his modified submachine gun and the ancient revolver he knew to be "on its last legs." The weapons technician said he had squirted some 3-in-1 Oil into the gun's mechanism and hoped for the best.

Allen related how he had found the gunman and Terry Armes at the Wellington Hotel and enlisted them in the contract.

The former speed addict described the aborted morning killing try and how, after deciding the murder "wasn't meant to be," he had pulled out and turned over the contract to the gunman and Armes.

He said he had gladly turned over the revolver and the blue Nova when told to by Barrett, "because, by rights, Mr. Buxbaum had paid for it."

Allen testified that, exhausted, he went home the afternoon of July 5. "I went home to sleep and watch Star Trek."

He said he went to Toronto the next day with the gunman and Armes, but Barrett didn't have any money for the killers. Allen said he was trying to retrieve his friend Janet Hicks from the group at the Westbury and eventually received $1,000 from Barrett "for my trouble."

Allen said that after his August 10 arrest he met Buxbaum at the London jail and told the older man about an escape effort for which he would need $10,000.

"I told him I was escaping...he replied to me if I could break him out it would be worth another $10,000 and he would look after me for the rest of my life."

With that, Allen was turned over to Eddie Greenspan for cross-examination.

For two days the lawyer hammered away at Allen about his speed habit and his apparent eagerness to take a contract on someone's life when he had never killed before.

"I'm going to suggest to you that killing someone in cold blood, Mr. Allen, was no problem for you at all," the lawyer said.

"When you're a speeder, sir, no it isn't," came the reply.

Allen readily admitted to "scamming" Barrett for money for ammunition for his weapons and to later "scamming" Buxbaum for money for what he insisted was a real escape plan.

The bushy-haired witness said he'd only heard of Barrett's kidnapping scheme several days after Hanna Buxbaum's death.

Greenspan then began attacking Allen for the deal in which he had pleaded guilty to conspiracy in the murder and been given an eight-year sentence. He accused Allen of having opted for the deal only after Anita Pitcher told the preliminary hearing she had seen three persons in Buxbaum's car at the McDonald's and K-Mart the day before the killing.

The suggestion implied that a tale carefully concocted by Barrett and the others was falling apart. The lawyer implied that Allen and Barrett had decided to bail out and take Janet Hicks with them in a deal. Allen denied it and said that Pitcher was "a bit backwards...a typical blonde."

Greenspan then played a series of wiretapped conversations between Allen and Barrett after the killing.

Allen said he had been trying to get more money from Barrett because Spider had been pressuring him to do so. "I was starting to feel pressured," he admitted.

But Allen insisted that his own $10,000 was all he had expected and rejected Greenspan's suggestions that it was merely a down payment on a much larger payoff.

Greenspan had difficulty making much headway with Allen, whose spotty memory resulted in many "I don't remember, sir," responses. Claiming his memory was affected by his drug habit, Allen wasn't giving the lawyer much ammunition to turn back onto him.

It was up to Assistant Crown Attorney Al MacDonald to patch the little damage Greenspan had inflicted on Allen.

MacDonald asked why Allen had pleaded guilty to murder conspiracy.

"I felt in my bones I was guilty of conspiracy...(but) I was not guilty of first-degree murder because I walked (away). I left it. No matter what I did I felt that contract would be carried out. If not that day then a week later."

Allen said he had also pleaded out to save Terry Kline and Janet Hicks, two people he claimed had had little to do with the killing. Worrying about their fate, he said, had caused him to break out in "cold sweats" at night.

The jury then heard from OPP Constable Phil Medlyn who had interrupted the morning murder plan but hadn't remembered the incident until two days later.

Debbie Barber testified that Rob Barrett had lived with her sporadically through 1983 and 1984 at her Ridout Street apartment and that Barrett, always planning for his "deal of the day," was nevertheless chronically broke.

"He was eating my groceries and smoking my cigarettes. I assumed he had no finances at the time."

She told of seeing Barrett and Buxbaum drop into the apartment the day before the killing and how Barrett suddenly seemed to have several hundred dollars. She also told of a July 12 phone call in which Buxbaum called, looking for Barrett and used the name "Andy" to identify himself.

Barber said Barrett bragged that Buxbaum had treated him like a son. Barrett, she said, was proud of his millionaire mark. But she turned back suggestions from assistant defence counsel Chris Buhr that Barrett was angry at his firing from the land-scaping job at the nursing home — a plank in the defence theory. "I remember Rob shrugging it off," she said of the confrontation with Paul Buxbaum in which the millionaire's son ordered Barrett to stay away from his father.

Heinz Wagner then told of seeing a very nervous brother-in-law Helmuth about noon on the day of the killing. Greenspan hammered Wagner for his long-standing dislike of Helmuth because of their one-time bad blood as competitors in the nursing home business.

"I don't hate Helmuth Buxbaum," the Mennonite, Wagner insisted. "I just hate his doings."

Not long afterward, the jury heard from Roy Buxbaum, the back seat passenger in the Buxbaum car.

Now sixteen, the youth had matured considerably since the day of the murder and was a full year older than when he had testified at the preliminary hearing.

His memory had improved considerably as he recalled the murder scene. His father Isbrandt, Helmuth's brother, sat in a front row seat of the St. Catharines courtroom.

Roy told of the telephone call Uncle Helmuth had made while he was still collecting his luggage; how Helmuth had taken over the driving after they had stopped at a McDonald's en route to Komoka; how Helmuth had spotted what he said was the neighbors' car up ahead on Highway 402 and suggested they stop.

He told of the gunman's opening his door and placing the revolver within an inch of his eye and ordering him to stay down.

He remembered his uncle's advising him to comply with

the gunman and for the first time Roy told of Aunt Hanna's pleading for her life.

"Please, I have five children at home," he quoted his aunt as begging before he heard three shots.

He added that his uncle said "Oh, my God, they shot her," as Roy clambered over the guardrail after the blue car sped off. But he said that Buxbaum never ventured near his wife, remaining on the roadside.

The next morning, Thursday, November 21, before the next witness, the defence was making yet another request that Mr. Justice O'Driscoll warn jurors not to read or watch any news reports of the trial.

The defence cited several small factual errors and an artist's rendering of the roadside struggle between Hanna and the gunman as reasons the jury should be warned.

O'Driscoll, as he had on several earlier occasions, remained unsympathetic. He said he had already asked the jury to pay attention to the evidence in court and to be wary of outside information.

"So far the press has been very responsible as to reporting what has happened in this courtroom," and he went on to suggest the motion was sour grapes from the defence because the evidence wasn't coming out the way it might like.

Unfazed, the defence then attempted to keep out the "No, honey, please not this way," quote from Hanna that the next witness, Terry Armes, was expected to deliver.

Assistant defence counsel Chris Buhr argued in a *voir dire* hearing that the quotation only revealed Hanna's "opinion" and was not based on fact. He added there was no suggestion that Helmuth did anything at the scene to help kill her, so the phrase was dangerous evidence. It also wasn't like a "dying declaration" which courts have permitted as evidence believing a person facing imminent death will speak the truth.

O'Driscoll ruled for the prosecution again. He said that while it wasn't like a dying declaration, it seemed to be based on observable evidence and should be brought to the jury.

Armes revealed himself to be a bitter man. He said he still didn't feel guilty of murder, even though he'd pleaded guilty to second-degree murder and had received a life sentence under which he would not be eligible for parole for ten years.

"I was drunk and in the wrong place at the wrong time, but I didn't feel I was guilty of murder."

He admitted he had tried to make a deal with the police after his arrest late in August, 1984, but had been unable to "give them" Helmuth Buxbaum. He couldn't produce evidence damning enough against the millionaire, so the authorities began talking deal with Barrett, Allen and Hicks. Armes had been passed by. He would serve ten years of his life behind bars while Barrett got ten years but could be paroled after about six, Allen got eight years and would be out in about five, Hicks got fifteen months and was already paroled.

Fighting back tears, the slender, fidgety Armes told Greenspan he didn't think he had got much of a deal.

"I wasn't guilty of murder in my heart. I didn't want that woman dead. I got to do a fucking life sentence because I'm a drunk."

The former alcoholic nearly broke down and as he tried to compose himself, Mr. Justice O'Driscoll warned him to watch his language in court.

Armes tried to minimize his role in the killing: yes, he remembered having met with the gunman and Allen the day before the murder; he remembered bits of the morning killing try and said that, next thing he knew, he was westbound with the gunman on the 402, aware that murder was imminent. He said he had managed to get the gunman past the Komoka cut-off and had then watched as the Buxbaum car turned off at the exit before re-entering the highway and pulling up behind the Rent-a-Wreck Nova.

He said his memory was affected by blackouts triggered by his heavy drinking and his hypoglycemia, a blood sugar disorder. He conceded to having been "hammered" the day Hanna died.

Armes said he had watched as the gunman, revolver in hand, went up to the Buxbaum car and dragged Hanna away.

"I buried my head in my hands. I couldn't believe it."

"No, honey, please not this way," he said he heard Hanna beg as she was dragged out of the car and looked to Helmuth for help. But Buxbaum only slipped out his driver's door and stood watching. Armes said he suddenly spotted Roy's head pop up from the back seat of the wagon and a leg stick out of the door as if the boy were trying to escape.

"If he had got out of the car, (the gunman) would have killed him," Armes said. He claimed he had saved the teenager's life by running to the car and sprawling on Roy to keep him down as three shots rang out.

Armes said he looked out of the car to see Buxbaum: "He didn't blink an eye, he just stood there . . . he didn't even flinch."

The some-time home improvements salesman said he saw Buxbaum get up on tip-toes to look over the wagon at his wife as the third shot was fired.

Armes spoke of having returned to the south London home of Spider's wife, and of cleaning the car to remove fingerprints while she and her husband went through Hanna's white purse.

Sometime later, he said that he and the gunman had left the car covered by a tarp and walked to the Wellington Tavern. On the way, the hit-man had tossed the revolver into the Thames River at the Ridout Street bridge.

Armes said that his only reason for pleading guilty to second degree murder was his acceptance of $3,000 the day after travelling by train to Toronto with the gunman and Allen.

He said he had been drinking heavily on the train to Toronto and that when there he had nearly overdosed on cocaine after the confrontation with Barrett. He denied having helped hang Squirrel out the fourteenth floor window of the hotel room and said he was satisfied with his take in the murder.

Armes denied he was a lookout in the morning murder try and that he had waved down the Buxbaum car in the evening.

Greenspan challenged him. "You were a full partner in the

murder plan of the evening of July 5 and you know it.''

"That's not true, sir,'' said the continually flinching Armes, who among many medical problems admitted to having cirrhosis of the liver.

He did agree he had lived in an "alcoholic haze" throughout July 4 to 7.

He also agreed it wasn't until the trigger-man's preliminary hearing in February that he remembered the "No, honey, please…'' quote from Hanna.

Greenspan pointed out that in earlier statements to police, Armes quoted her as saying "Helmuth, please Helmuth… please not this way.''

The lawyer suggested this was what was actually said and that the plea had been directed at two persons, not one. Greenspan said that the first three words had been directed at her husband, but the last four at the gunman as he dragged her from the car.

Armes denied the proposal. He conceded, however, that it wasn't until an investigating police officer, Constable Mel Getty, had mentioned the word, "honey", that he remembered it.

Greenspan suddenly stopped himself as he was building toward his concluding questions for Armes. He asked O'Driscoll to excuse the jury.

Greenspan was furious at his opponent Mike Martin and he looked to the judge for help. Bad blood between the prosecution and defence had continued since the bail hearing and Greenspan lashed out angrily at Martin.

"Mr. Martin yawns loudly all the time,'' he complained, adding that it had been going on for some time. "It is a bad tactic and it is wrong.''

Greenspan complained he'd found it distracting during his cross-examination, adding, "if it is tiredness and he is not involved (in questioning) he should not be in the courtroom.''

When asked by O'Driscoll if he had anything to say about the yawning question, Martin declined. "I will not dignify the complaint with a response.''

O'Driscoll seemed satisfied with that and noted that a number of questionable tactics had been employed in the twenty-seven days of the trial.

"Things have been going on like throwing down transcripts of evidence when you get an answer you don't like," he said in reference to one of Greenspan's familiar petulant gestures.

The justice said that lawyers and judges alike should "develop a bit of a hide and move on."

He ignored the complaint and recalled the jury.

Greenspan had been thrown off stride in a sometimes-effective cross-examination by the simmering animosity between prosecution and defence.

He pressed on gamely and told Armes that Roy Buxbaum had no recollection of the "No, honey please..." quote which Armes had said was delivered as Hanna was being pulled from the car.

"I don't give a shit what Roy Buxbaum said," Armes replied.

On re-examination, Armes was asked just one question by assistant prosecutor MacDonald; if his alcoholic "fog" had affected his memory of Hanna's last moments.

"It's something I'll remember for the rest of my life, that scene," Armes replied. "Her being killed is something I'll remember for the rest of my life."

When Armes left the stand to return to prison, he left behind a chilling story that had remained largely intact.

Before he left court, Mr. Justice O'Driscoll had a question for Armes, the answer to which must have pleased the prosecution.

O'Driscoll wanted to know if the several statements Armes had given to police before testifying at the gunman's hearing were given under oath. (Such statements are not generally sworn.) Those statements had no reference to the "honey" quote from Hanna.

Armes replied that he had not given the earlier statements under oath.

The jury was given a clue as to which statements the judge considered more truthful.

Buxbaum made no bones about whom he considered truthful. As the jurors listened closely, so did Buxbaum. He kept a score card and every time he heard what he felt was a lie, he methodically marked single slashes and joined groups of five together with horizontal lines. By the end of Armes' evidence, Buxbaum's score card had masses of such marks.

The following Monday, November 25, Buxbaum's trial became the subject of comment in the Ontario legislature.

In an unusual move, Bob Rae, the leader of the province's New Democratic Party, cited Helmuth Buxbaum as an example of what the province shouldn't permit: millionaire nursing home operators.

Rae demanded that the government tighten financial account-ability of private nursing home operators to ensure that such operations would be non-profit. He argued that the government should be "appalled" that "individuals performing a public service, heavily subsidized by the government of Ontario are self-described millionaires."

Rae later told reporters he hadn't minded mentioning Bux-baum by name, because his comments had had little to do with the trial. He went on to add that Buxbaum had received six million dollars of the $250 million in subsidies the govern-ment had given to Ontario nursing home operators in 1984.

"It had to do with his lifestyle . . . I keep hearing this phrase 'millionaire nursing home operator'. I find it incredibly offen-sive. Millionaire nursing home operators are, in my opinion, a species that should be extinct."

They were extraordinary remarks for a Canadian politician in the midst of a sensational murder trial, particularly from one trained as a lawyer.

Rae's remarks were carried on the wire services and early the following morning, Greenspan moved to try to minimize the damage.

Greenspan asked O'Driscoll to direct the jurors not to read, listen to or watch any media accounts relating to Helmuth Buxbaum or the trial. Greenspan said the remarks were preju-dicial and might affect a jury that "could have seven members of the NDP."

But O'Driscoll was unmoved. He remained adamant that he wouldn't treat the jurors like school kids. He did, however, have some advice for the jury that morning.

He referred to some comments the jurors might have heard that had been attributed to the provincial NDP leader.

"What I wanted to do at this time is simply underline and reaffirm what I said to you before," he said.

"You have been sworn...to try this case on what you hear in open court in this courtroom. You are to disregard all comments regardless of where or when they emanate. I have not told you not to listen to the radio or not read newspapers and not watch television because you are adults. You are sensible, fair-minded people who can separate the 'wheat from the chaff'. You are not a 'bunch of sheep' that follow the ringing of a bell. I am treating you as fair-minded adults, because if I did otherwise I would be simply insulting your intelligence.

"As far as this trial is concerned, what the leader of any party, or what the leader of every political party may think of Helmuth Buxbaum, and how he does or doesn't operate a nursing home is totally, totally irrelevant.

"The fact that the comment comes, as it does, in the seventh week of this trial, is indeed lamentable. However, I am sure you will toss it aside, the same as you would when you read about this trial and you come across a typographical error."

In the next few days police officers who dealt with Buxbaum immediately following the murder were brought to the stand.

Constable Richard Pellarin who had taken the first two statements from Buxbaum on the night of the killing described the millionaire as calm throughout much of the night and said that it wasn't until two days later, on Saturday, July 7, that he mentioned stopping for a blue car in the morning of the day Hanna was slain. Before that, he had suggested police might want to talk to a man named Croft, who had broken into the Buxbaum house and stolen Hanna's purse on an earlier occasion. When pressed, Buxbaum admitted that the break-in had taken place five years before.

Tellers from two banks were brought to the stand to talk

about some of Buxbaum's transactions the day after Hanna's death.

Cosy Clarke, a teller at a west-end London branch of Canada Trust, testified that at about 2 p.m. on July 6, Buxbaum had showed up with a cheque made out to Hanna and had signed for her in the amount of $8,496.41. Buxbaum had endorsed it and asked for $2,500 in cash with the rest deposited into his account. She had complied with his request, put the money into an envelope and watched as the businessman tried to stuff it into the inside breast pocket of his suit coat which already contained several other envelopes. Buxbaum, she noted, appearing "quite nervous," gave up and carried the envelope in his hand.

The teller conceded under questioning from Greenspan that Buxbaum could have taken the entire $8,496.41 in cash, but had asked for only $2,500.

Another teller told how he had removed $3,000 from the Toronto-Dominion bank at Oxford Street and Wharncliffe Road and attempted to get more money from the bank's *Green Machine*, money machine. Jennifer Flatman, said that she too, had found Buxbaum "very nervous" during his transactions.

London coin merchant Chris Brooker told how Buxbaum had visited him later the same afternoon and how his regular customer, who was usually very price conscious, appeared anxious to sell a five-ounce bar of gold bullion. "He didn't want to quibble," Brooker testified and readily accepted the merchant's offer of $2,100. But Brooker said he could only give Buxbaum $700 that day and promised the remaining $1,400 for the following day.

The prosecution was speeding through witnesses at this point in the trial, calling Leonard Peltier who had delivered a half-ounce of cocaine to London airport for Robert Barrett on July 6; RCMP Constable John Martin who had seen Buxbaum meet Barrett at about 8 p.m. the same night; Dr. Calvin Stiller who had run into his acquaintance Helmuth asleep in the airport lobby; stewardesses who had seen Barrett and Jan

Hicks on the return Air Ontario flight from London to Toronto and had noted a large amount of money and some white powder on a small mirror.

The hit-man's wife spoke of seeing her husband show up in the blue Nova at about 7:30 on the night of the killing and of having watched as he went through a white purse containing identification of a Hanna Buxbaum from Komoka while his companion Armes cleaned the car out.

Philip Conley, Buxbaum's long-time friend then testified and talked of comforting Buxbaum and helping him to break the news of their mother's death to the Buxbaum children.

Conley told how Buxbaum had seemed tired and upset when he saw him at about 1 a.m. at the Buxbaum home, about eight hours after Hanna's murder. He related how Buxbaum had said he couldn't sleep in the bed he used to share with his wife and had opted instead to spend the night in the basement fallout shelter.

He told of his concerns that Buxbaum might be blackmailed by the drug pushers he'd admitted to being associated with and said he suggested they go to the police. Buxbaum, he said, insisted he wasn't being blackmailed but needed to raise money to get the pushers "off his back."

Greenspan got Conley to say he'd never seen a fight between Helmuth and Hanna and that there had been a lot of love expressed in the large family.

But when the lawyer asked if he had detected tension in the Buxbaum household in the eight years he had known the Buxbaums, Conley replied "that's a difficult question." Greenspan didn't let him elaborate.

Another friend and business associate, Nick Potocska, was called to the stand. Potocska, who had been hired by Buxbaum in 1981 as office manager and had risen to corporate controller and eventually, treasurer, described Buxbaum's uncontrolled spending of corporate funds in 1983 and 1984.

Potocska told of the bankers for the nursing home becoming annoyed that the Buxbaum group of companies was exceeding its $1.1 million line of credit, primarily owing to Buxbaum's heavy spending of cash reserves.

The controller said that when he brought the situation to the attention of his boss in August, 1983, Buxbaum promised he'd curtail his spending — some of which he was making on precious metals. But that same month, Potocska said, Buxbaum went on to spend $70,000 more.

Buxbaum had accused his money manager of "trying to control him as opposed to trying to control the company," Potocska said.

He told of having again mentioned the situation to Buxbaum at a fall health conference in Florida and having at the millionaire's request explained the situation again in front of Hanna.

Potocska said he had advised the Buxbaums that a "liquidity crisis" was looming on the horizon and that unless Buxbaum curtailed his expenditures the companies — despite good profitability — would be forced into insolvency in a matter of a couple of years.

"She (Hanna) expressed surprise that there was such a problem that existed and asked for some clarification from Mr. Buxbaum as to what I was referring to," he testified.

Buxbaum assured his wife the matter was under control, Potocska said, and she sought no further details from the controller.

Potocska said company accountants studied the situation further and discovered Buxbaum had taken $2 million from the companies in 1983 and 1984 and could not track down $1.1 million of it.

He described 1983 as the companies' most profitable year in history. As an aside, he noted that Buxbaum had claimed $1 million in income on his 1984 income tax.

The crown case was beginning to wind down by the end of the first week in December, the eighth in the trial. It was time to clean up a few details.

The prosecution brought to the stand Toronto forensic

accountant Gary Moulton who had analyzed Buxbaum's cash transactions before and after the murder. His evidence was called to reinforce evidence from Barrett about Buxbaum's distribution of large amounts of cash to get his wife killed.

Moulton said he found that in the week ending May 26, 1984 Buxbaum had raised $16,652, in the week ending July 7, another $18,094 and the next week, ending July 14, another $10,500. The rest of the weeks surveyed showed he had raised $4,000 to $5,000 in each, he said.

The accountant testified that on July 4, the day before Hanna's death, Buxbaum had raised $5,496 and on July 6, another $11,198 from seven separate sources.

It wouldn't be long until the jury was reminded that Barrett had testified that Buxbaum gave him $5,000 on May 24 for his trip to Florida where he'd promised to find a killer; another $5,000 on July 4 and the $13,000 payment at London airport on July 6.

The crown's last witness, its sixtieth, was the man who headed the investigation into Hanna Buxbaum's slaying. Detective Inspector Ron Piers came to the witness stand in the ninth week of the trial. He told of re-enacting the scene confronting Hanna and Helmuth as they approached the Komoka turnoff on Highway 402.

He said from the last possible spot at which the Buxbaums could have pulled off, he could neither identify the make nor color of cars he put at the spot where the blue Nova had been located. He said he was only barely able to make out the figure of a policeman he had stationed beside the ''killers' '' car.

Piers said he re-enacted the scene twice, once with a dark blue car, another time with a silver-grey car.

He told of contacting Buxbaum shortly after police had seized the blue Nova on July 19, two weeks after Hanna's death and inviting him to come down to the London OPP detachment to see if he could positively identify the car.

Piers said that Buxbaum had agreed to come about noon the following Monday, July 23.

After Buxbaum viewed the car, Piers said that he asked the millionaire if it were the same car the Buxbaums had stopped for both in the morning and evening of July 5. Buxbaum agreed it was.

The inspector then invited Buxbaum to a downstairs boardroom to answer a few questions. The interview was tape recorded, unknown to Buxbaum, he said.

Greenspan, who initially fought having the recording go to the jury, relented when the prosecution agreed to delete the portion from the point toward the end of the ninety-minute tape where Buxbaum advised Piers he didn't want to say anymore without his lawyers present.

In that conversation, Piers asked a stammering Buxbaum a series of questions about his return from Europe and details about the events of July 5. It was when he started quizzing Buxbaum about his telephone calls to Florida and his appearance at London airport the day after Hanna's death that Buxbaum began to realize this investigator possessed some unsettling information.

Buxbaum insisted his wife had decided to join him on the trip to Toronto to pick up Roy.

"I was planning to go by myself, but my wife said no, she wanted, she said I'm going to visit mother, anyway. Might as well come along."

Buxbaum said he had stopped behind the blue car shortly after entering Highway 402 and said that he had found the request for Hanna's stockings "strange."

At one point, Buxbaum reminded the officer that his memory wasn't very good because he'd suffered a stroke, but he offered to undergo hypnosis to assist police.

Pressed by Piers to detail the morning incident, Buxbaum gave sketchy details of the "muscular" fellow he spoke to with a flat nose like that of a boxer.

"I walked up to the front to his car, to see if I could help him, which is ridiculous because I don't know anything about cars. So, in the meantime, my wife took off her stockings. I didn't realize that and I went back to the car and, ah, she said why don't you give them these stockings, they've got holes in them anyway. So, so I took the stockings and went back to the car and gave 'em the stockings . . . and then after the OPP officer stopped and took off again, ya know, I was ready to leave and this guy came back to the car and gave the stockings to my wife an said I don't, I don't need them, thanks.''

Asked if he made any phone calls during the day, Buxbaum volunteered he'd made a call at a pay phone at the Toronto airport as he picked up Roy. Pressed by Piers again, Buxbaum cleared his throat and said he had been trying to reach a girl named Lucy whom he'd met on an earlier flight and who had just arrived in Canada. Buxbaum said he had just wanted to know how she was getting along.

No, he apologized to Piers, he didn't have her phone number or address. He said both would probably be in his personal calendar and he didn't have it with him.

Piers went over the evening approach to the blue car. Buxbaum explained: ''I was ready for the turnoff. It was at the Komoka turnoff when I saw this man waving, ah, on the side of the car.''

He said he had assumed it was out of gas because both its hood and truck were open. He said he had intended to stop and then back up the entrance ramp to get into Komoka.

Piers was curious if Hanna had said anything about the car ahead.

''Was there any conversation between the two a ya about going up to assist this motorist, or to help this motorist, or anything like that?'' the investigator wanted to know.

Buxbaum replied: ''Yeah. I, just said to her, I think I'll, I'll stop and see what, if I can help them.''

''Did she make any comment?,'' Piers asked.

''And she didn't want me to. She said, no, no, don't, don't stop,'' the millionaire said.

"But you went along?" Piers continued.

"But I, I went anyway, yeah, so the rest is, ya know," Buxbaum said, his voice trailing off.

He complained about having to go over the events again but Piers insisted he had to know the sequence of things so he could find Hanna's killers. Buxbaum seemed to appreciate that and permitted the questioning to continue.

When he was led through the evening shooting, Buxbaum insisted he had slipped out of his door and had moved onto the highway pavement to wave for help. When he was doing this, he said, he heard three shots. He expressed amazement he hadn't been shot.

After the shooting was reviewed again, Piers abruptly changed gears and wanted to know about some calls Buxbaum had made from Treugott Management to Orlando, Florida.

Piers: "There was a call on the fifth of June, 1984, for four minutes. Can you tell me who you were calling down there?"

Buxbaum: "Yeah. I think that was, um (long pause) Oh, what was his name? (pause) I think it was Bartlett. Yeah."

Piers: "Who?"

Buxbaum: "Bartlett, ah, something like that."

Piers: "An who, who is he?"

Buxbaum: "Oh, he's a guy that I met, met sometime ago."

Piers: "Bartlett?"

Buxbaum: "Bartlett, yeah."

Piers: "B-A-R-T-"

Buxbaum: "Oh, Barrett, pardon me, Barrett. Not Bartlett. Barrett."

Piers: "Okay. And what would you be talking to him in, ah, Florida for?"

Buxbaum: "Ho boy. (pause) You, you know him. He's a, he's a cocaine dealer."

Buxbaum insisted he was merely returning a call to Barrett, who was attempting to bring some "real good coke" to Canada.

Piers told Buxbaum about several more calls to Orlando and his now-wary interviewee insisted that Barrett had been "badgering" him about a job and about cocaine. But Buxbaum said he'd gotten off the drug by that time.

Piers homed in on Buxbaum's visit to London airport and Buxbaum agreed he'd met Barrett there.

Piers: "For what reason?"

Buxbaum: "I don't know. I think that he probably had some coke on him or somethin'. I didn't wanna buy any more but he kept badgering me for more for, to buy more from him."

Piers: "Why did you go to the airport in the beginning, on, on a Friday, July 6?"

Buxbaum: "You know, I think you're trying to put me into something here that —"

Piers: "Mr. Buxbaum, all I'm trying to do is get the answers to some questions."

Buxbaum: "Yeah, I know, and I, I don't think, I wanna talk to a lawyer before I answer any more questions here."

The jury wasn't permitted to hear the last quotation from Buxbaum, since the right to a lawyer is one guaranteed in law and such a request shouldn't be admitted as evidence because it might be construed as being prejudicial.

In the long wait for his lawyer, Buxbaum accused his interrogator of implying things and of trying to "frame" him in a cocaine investigation. Buxbaum seemed so preoccupied with talk of cocaine that Piers was moved to remind him that this was a *murder* investigation.

Piers testified that when Buxbaum's lawyers Del McLennan and Tim Price asked if Buxbaum were free to leave, the veteran officer said he quickly assessed the situation and the quality of answers he'd received and announced that Buxbaum couldn't. He was under arrest and charged with first-degree murder.

Mike Martin wanted to close his case at the end of Piers' evidence but the defence wanted to hear three more prosecution witnesses so it could cross-examine them.

Eddie Greenspan launched an unsuccessful bid to force the prosecution to call Janet Hicks, Terry Kline and a man named Andy Anderson who Barrett said he'd talked to of murder.

After the motion was rejected, Mike Martin rose on Thursday, December 12 to announce to the jury he'd closed his case. It was the fortieth day of the trial.

Eddie Greenspan then rose and said he planned to call a defence. He'd start to do so the following Monday, December 16.

Court took a three-day weekend.

The jurors could be excused if in the midst of their Christmas shopping they turned their thoughts back to the case.

And wonder what Eddie Greenspan could possibly have up his sleeve.

15/The Trial. Defence:

"... frailties ... exposed to public gaze."

A light snow was falling and slush filled the streets of St. Catharines Monday morning as Eddie Greenspan rose to outline the defence case.

The jurors, who'd sat through the mass of prosecution evidence, were anxious to hear how the defence lawyer would counter the sheer weight of the crown case.

Greenspan was ready. Quickly and forcefully he laid out the defence and immediately answered the pressing question: would his client testify?

"The right to remain silent is the fundamental right of every accused person," he reminded the jury.

"Mr. Buxbaum has told me he wants to testify at this trial ... to tell he did not hire Rob Barrett to kill his wife," Greenspan announced.

"He had nothing to do with her death, whatsoever." It was Greenspan's keynote and the jury was all ears.

Reading rapidly from his typewritten opening, the chubby defence lawyer warmed to his task, glancing up only briefly to ensure he had the attention of the jurors. He did. He outlined a series of witnesses he planned to call to debunk the major elements of the crown case.

"The crown's case," he said, "centered to a great extent on the life and times of Helmuth Buxbaum. His frailties and his weaknesses, including his appetites for women and cocaine, have been exposed to public gaze.

"He has sat here for nine weeks listening to his private life being exposed before you. It will finally be his turn to speak."

The packed courtroom was following every word.

But Greenspan conceded that Buxbaum had had problems with his wife.

"As important as Hanna was to him, their sexual relationship was not everything he wanted it to be." Buxbaum had complained he was impotent with her after the 1982 stroke and had sought out other women. Yes, Buxbaum had used cocaine occasionally before the stroke. But it was Barrett who started injecting him with the drug, he said, getting the older man "psychologically addicted."

The reason Buxbaum's friend Barrett had travelled to Florida a month before the killing was to set up a "wholesale" supply of cocaine, and nothing else. Greenspan sounded sure of what he was saying.

At the shooting scene, Buxbaum was "never so afraid in his entire life. He followed the events in shock and disbelief."

The next day at the airport, Greenspan continued, Buxbaum gave money to Barrett for a cocaine deal because Barrett was in fear of his life. He needed fast money. (Greenspan had said that Hicks would describe the trip to London from Toronto as a "life or death" situation.)

Buxbaum was on tranquilizers the day after his wife died and still cannot account for many of his actions that day, the lawyer concluded.

"There is no question he gave money to Rob Barrett. The reasons had nothing to do with murder."

It was a strong opening. In just sixty-eight minutes, Eddie Greenspan had laid out the defence case and the answers to so many questions. The opening address was the result of hard work. It had gone through five major revisions before the defence counsel was satisfied with it.

When he sat down, the perspiring Greenspan knew there was

some even harder work ahead of him — getting his witnesses to say what he'd promised.

Things went quickly downhill. Greenspan ran into problems from the first as he attempted to poke holes in the credibility of Susan Ambrose. O'Driscoll agreed with prosecutor Martin who objected to Greenspan's calling as witnesses the neighbors of Ambrose because her housekeeping was a collateral issue and, therefore, not admissible. For the same reason, O'Driscoll refused to hear evidence Greenspan planned to call showing that Ambrose had listed her employment with a Vancouver agency for strippers when she applied for hydro service.

The first witness Greenspan finally managed to get to the stand was Lucan car dealer Glen Nevin who performed $300 in repairs on Ron and Susan Ambrose's car on January 4 and 9, 1984. This figure was far below Ambrose's estimate of $1,500 that she claimed had kept her selling sex to Buxbaum.

Another early witness was Findlay, the London chartered accountant. He had recommended life insurance coverage for Helmuth and Hanna because of concerns in 1984 about the implications of capital gains taxes. The Buxbaum children would be liable for heavy taxes if both their parents were to die, he said, about $2.25 million.

"I knew because of his (Buxbaum's) health situation he might not be insurable," Findlay said, but nevertheless he recommended that they should both apply for coverage.

Findlay remembered a phone call he received in early 1984 from insurance agent Eugene High in Florida. Findlay said he told the agent that it was he who had recommended insurance to the Buxbaums.

Mike Martin was brief on cross-examination, going directly to the point.

He got Findlay to agree that if either Helmuth or Hanna died, the surviving spouse could continue operating the company and no capital gains taxes would be due. The accountant also agreed that the large tax bill would be due only upon the death of the second Buxbaum parent.

It was clear that there was no sense having only the husband or wife insured. Findlay agreed that no taxes had been payable on the death of Hanna.

The jury would no doubt be wondering why Buxbaum kept the policy on his wife if there were no reason in business to do so.

A couple of witnesses later was fifty-four-year-old Ken Surette, a London resident and former army warrant officer who acts as handyman around the Buxbaum house and the Komoka nursing home.

Surette said Barrett joined him on the grounds crew for about three weeks in May, 1984. Surette said that he and Barrett were regularly invited into the Buxbaum kitchen for coffee with Hanna, and that the mother of six talked ''constantly'' to the new helper.

He said there was one particular day when Hanna insisted that Barrett stay and talk longer. About ninety minutes later, the new employee emerged from the house, somewhat shaken.

'' 'I have never been spoken to like that before in my life. She was very blunt. She knows everything that Helmuth and I have done. Helmuth must be telling her everything!' ''

Barrett said he'd never met a woman like Hanna before and that she knew about his supplying her husband with drugs, Surette testified. ''Can you imagine that?'' he quoted Barrett as exclaiming. ''She accused me of giving dope to her husband.''

The jury now knew that Hanna had been wise to Robert Barrett. But try as he might, Greenspan could not get Surette to say Barrett was angry at Hanna's discovery.

Once again, Martin took straight aim. Had Barrett been upset about Hanna's words?, he asked.

''I had heard him say nothing bad about Hanna Buxbaum,'' Surette answered. He agreed she had always been ''charitable and decent'' to Barrett.

Surette said that although it was sometimes difficult to read the emotions of the immature and always-grinning Barrett, his reaction to Hanna's talk had been ''more surprise'' than anger.

Reverend Donald Launstein, the next witness, the senior pastor of Wortley Baptist Church in London, had known the Buxbaums since 1982.

Launstein said he accompanied the Buxbaum family on the 1984 trip to Europe and found Helmuth and Hanna to be a loving couple.

"They seemed to be more affectionate than the normal couple of that age, holding hands and enjoying each other's company. Quite often when people have been married that long they don't walk around holding hands."

On cross-examination, Martin asked Launstein if Helmuth and Hanna used pet names for each other like " 'Honey,' and that sort of stuff?"

Launstein readily agreed: "Yes, that sort of stuff."

In the prisoner's box, Buxbaum smiled broadly and shook his head, seemingly in disbelief at the prosecutor's determination to get him.

Tall Janet Hicks, thirty-two, wearing a bright blue dress, several dangling ear-rings, and rings on all her fingers came to the stand on December 18. She told court she'd spent five months in jail and another five months in a half-way house in Hamilton before being released on parole a month before. Sentenced to fifteen months in jail the previous January 17, after admitting her role in Hanna's murder, Hicks was already a free woman. Hicks, nervously recounting her role in the affair, told how she was sent by Pat Allen to Toronto. She was to keep an eye on Barrett "to make sure he didn't get into any trouble...so he wouldn't blow the deal."

The former cookie maker said she was promised $1,000 for this "babysitting" job. Hicks insisted she didn't know the nature of the "deal". It wasn't until July 7 that she learned from a newspaper photo that Helmuth Buxbaum was the man she and Barrett had met at London airport.

She disappointed Greenspan in not saying that Barrett had considered it a "life or death" situation to get money from Buxbaum in London.

But she did please the defence lawyer when she contradicted evidence from Armes. Armes had told the jury his head was in his hands during the shooting. Hicks remembered his bragging to the crowd at the Westbury that he watched the shooting and didn't even bother to wear a mask.

Far from court, that same day, December 18, Buxbaum's nursing home chain was sold for $19 million to a London architect. Everything but a small home in Charlottetown, P.E.I. was liquidated.

From the sale, Buxbaum would realize a net personal after-tax profit of about $4.5 million. It meant, however, that he was virtually out of the nursing home business, an empire founded with the abandoned old farm he'd bought for $17,000 about twenty years before.

Observers felt that the trial had adversely affected the sale price. It was thought worth another $3 million to $4 million had it not been for the notoriety of the murder trial.

The St. Catharines jury was not told of the sale. Instead, for the next two days they would learn about the defendant's health...warts and all.

A London neurologist testified he believed that Buxbaum's April, 1982 stroke resulted from some neck manipulation he underwent about two hours before he was stricken. Dr. Thomas Feasby said a neck artery had been damaged and a blood clot formed, cutting off the blood supply to the right side of Buxbaum's brain. He told of the two related epileptic seizures Buxbaum suffered a few days later in hospital.

Then it was on to the Buxbaum family doctor, Gary Nance-kievill. He discussed the effects of the stroke on his patient and Buxbaum's complaints of impotence later in 1982 and in 1983. The physician also related how in May, 1984, Buxbaum had wanted treatment at a Michigan clinic for what another doctor had called his "cyclothymic personality" — exaggerated mood swings.

The soft-spoken Nancekievill, a practitioner from Komoka,

brought along the records of Buxbaum's visits from 1976 to 1984.

The records would be a disaster to the defence and a bonanza for the prosecution. Mike Martin sought an early recess once he got his hands on the doctor's notes.

The jury soon discovered that on fourteen occasions, between late 1977 and 1981, Buxbaum had been treated for "urethritis", a painful burning in his penis caused by a venereal-type disease. At one point, in February, 1978, he exhibited a wart on the end of his penis, unquestionably of venereal origin. It had to be surgically removed, the doctor said.

The doctor's notes also disclosed that late in 1979 Nancekievill thought his wealthy patient was having marital problems.

Nancekievill read from his note of a November 8, 1979 appointment in which Buxbaum "superficially" discussed his wife and complained that she had had a hysterectomy, meaning he couldn't have sexual relations for eight weeks.

"It is very obvious that the marital situation is not in harmony," Nancekievill said, quoting his handwritten notation.

The doctor was directed toward a note he had made during Buxbaum's recovery from his stroke. Nancekievill said that on May 11, 1982, Buxbaum complained that his family had placed too many controls over him during his recovery.

"They were dictating to him what to do and he didn't like that," the doctor said.

The witness for the defence was becoming a witness for the prosecution. The jury had been told that Buxbaum was indulging in extramarital affairs before his stroke and had also complained about his sex life with Hanna.

Eddie Greenspan had unsuccessfully fought to keep the jury from hearing about Buxbaum's penis problems. In re-examination he did what he could to undo the damage of the unwelcome admissions. He had Nancekievill agree to two things: urethritis has been known to be caused by chemicals, such as chlorine (the Buxbaums had a swimming pool), and that while Buxbaum's physical recovery from the stroke was fine, the doctor had undertaken no psychological testing.

Court broke December 20 for a two-week Christmas recess.

The defence camp was dispirited. For the most part, their first week of evidence had fizzled.

The prosecution team was jubilant. They'd got a couple of major defence witnesses to bolster the crown case — an unexpected bonus.

Helmuth Buxbaum and his family were despondent. He had expected to be home for Christmas. His children had been told it was a sure thing. Esther, now sixteen, was home from school in Saskatchewan; Mark and Phillip, now nineteen and eighteen, had returned from college in Florida. The family believed in their father. They hated his being in jail. It was a sombre Christmas in Komoka.

At his cell in Thorold, south of St. Catharines, Buxbaum would have a lonely Christmas, punctuated by visits from family members.

Other visitors were Greenspan's law students, Bob Sheppard and Howard Rubel, who began the task of preparing Buxbaum for the most important days of his life.

The time was fast approaching when he would have to answer the volley of questions a determined prosecutor would fire at him.

After the Christmas break, the trial resumed January 6 for its forty-sixth day.

The defence brought forward Patricia Pearce, a London travel agent who Greenspan hoped would cast doubt on Corinne Willoughby's evidence about when she last saw Buxbaum. Willoughby had testified that she stopped seeing Buxbaum in September, 1983, when he was trying to convince her to join him for a December trip to a Club Med in Mexico. She'd testified that he was injecting cocaine at the time — months before Barrett arrived on the scene. Pearce said, however, that the trip to Mexico wasn't booked until November. She conceded in cross-examination that anyone can informally arrange with others to take such a trip before making a formal reservation. The defence bid to discredit Willoughby's evidence was blunted.

The next witness was an eye-popper. Terry Gallagher, dyed blonde and a shapely twenty-five, was wearing her new New Year's Eve dress. The pink, knit shift was backless, exposing a vast expanse of skin — another of Helmuth's women.

The London student-nurse was upset about being called to court and Greenspan was permitted to cross-examine his own witness when her answers appeared unhelpful to him. Gallagher admitted she'd had sex with Buxbaum in 1984 after meeting him through his regular companion, Dawn Watson. Greenspan hadn't told the jury why he was presenting Gallagher. He soon gave up trying to extract information from her when she couldn't remember Dawn Watson saying anything about Buxbaum's wanting to get rid of his wife. She denied that Watson had ever mentioned Buxbaum and murder at the preliminary hearing.

Under cross-examination, Gallagher agreed that Buxbaum was unhappy with his wife and had been seeing her in June of 1984. She said he wanted to see her upon his return from Europe.

The defence was still having its difficulties.

Next to take the stand was a witness who had been sitting outside court for several days and causing Greenspan and his team several sleepless nights.

John Barrett, twenty-seven, the older brother of Rob Barrett, had been waiting to testify since Greenspan opened the case for the defence on December 16. The defence lawyer told the jury that the older Barrett, with whom Rob lived early in 1984, would say how upset his younger brother had been with his firing from the landscaping job at the nursing home and how Rob had blamed Hanna for it. He was also to say that the trip to Florida, shortly thereafter, was taken so that his brother could arrange a cocaine connection and that it had nothing to do with finding killers.

But John Barrett would prove to be a problem. The morning after Greenspan talked about what this witness would say, OPP constables Mel Getty and Paul Edwards paid a visit to Barrett in his St. Catharines motel room and took from him a twenty-four-page statement. The statement would prove to be a nightmare for Greenspan.

Barrett told the officers of travelling to Detroit with Buxbaum and the millionaire's corporate treasurer, Nick Potocska. It was on a day in April, 1984, shortly after Barrett had been introduced to Buxbaum by his brother, Rob. John said that Buxbaum had talked of travelling to Detroit for a real estate convention about buying real estate with ''no money down'' and that John had asked for a lift so that he could visit relatives in that city. He said that he couldn't connect with his cousins, so he accepted Buxbaum's offer to share the millionaire's motel room.

During the five-hour interview, John Barrett told Getty and Edwards about some bizarre behavior on the part of his new friend. Barrett said that Buxbaum had pumped him about his connections in Detroit for ''cocaine, women, and, or, boys for sex.'' Barrett said he had found cocaine for Buxbaum and spent much of the next two days being introduced to the drug by the nursing home operator. He also spoke of cruising Woodward Avenue in Detroit looking for prostitutes.

John said that Buxbaum injected him for the first time and that there was a heavy session of injections in which Buxbaum injected himself — and his new friend — in the arm, ankle and penis. He told how Buxbaum had pulled his own pants down, masturbated himself and asked John to apply cold towels to his groin. At one point, Barrett said, Buxbaum lay down on a bed with him, assuring him everything was going to be fine.

He then told of the return to London a couple of days later with Potocska and Buxbaum.

''We stopped at one place on the way back to get a coke and something to eat. Helmuth got sweet and sour chicken to eat. Nick was there and Nick went to the washroom and returned. Helmuth asked me if I wanted to do some more coke but I said no, I had had enough. I went to the washroom. Helmuth followed. I went into a cubicle and Helmuth stood at the urinal. Helmuth had brought a container of plum sauce with him.

"Helmuth injected himself with cocaine, then he stood in front of the mirror and dipped his penis in the plum sauce. I went out and sat beside Nick. Helmuth came out with the container of plum sauce. Nick had also ordered sweet and sour chicken and Helmuth handed Nick the plum sauce he had taken into the washroom and Nick ate it with his chicken. Helmuth didn't eat the plum sauce and I didn't eat."

The police were delighted with the new and damning material. The prosecution initially felt it would try to bring all this bizarre behavior to the attention of the jury.

The defence was demoralized. They needed John Barrett's evidence about his brother's being upset at the firing and his blaming Hanna. Otherwise the defence theory about Rob Barrett having his own motive to kill Hanna would fall flat. Greenspan and his team agonized over the new information (the prosecution brought the statement to the defence shortly after it was made), believing the plum sauce revelation was a product of John Barrett's imagination.

Greenspan finally decided that, regardless, he had to call John Barrett and fight to keep the jury from hearing about the suggestions of homosexuality, the penis injections and the plum sauce.

On the witness stand, Greenspan got Barrett to say his brother was "down in the dumps because he'd lost his job," but Barrett added, unhelpfully for the defence, "Like any normal person would be."

In the absence of the jury, Greenspan then argued that the incidents in Detroit John Barrett had described were highly prejudicial. They had demonstrated bad character on the part of the accused man with no relevance to the murder allegation.

Prosecutor Martin said that while he wouldn't press for the details of where cocaine was injected and anything about the plum sauce, he wanted to show that Buxbaum knew how to find and take cocaine without Rob Barrett. Buxbaum, he said, was anything but Rob Barrett's "client Baptist in a three-piece suit." Instead, the prosecutor said it was important to show that Buxbaum was "really self-sufficient in this cruel world of drug abuse."

So the jury didn't hear about the penis injections or the plum sauce, but they did hear about the Detroit trip, the finding and taking of cocaine and the cruising for prostitutes. Barrett told how Buxbaum also directed him to visit a pharmacy, pretend he was a diabetic and get syringes for the cocaine injections.

He also told of Buxbaum's complaining about his wife's "fat buttocks" and how he preferred "slim, attractive women" aged sixteen and seventeen. "He said they were naive."

Martin got Barrett to say he knew about the contract to kill Hanna Buxbaum when he asked his brother about the money he took to Florida in May.

And Barrett said that he remembered Buxbaum complaining a month later that he was "sick and tired of his wife pestering him about his drug use." This was not what Greenspan had told the jury they were to hear. Yet another defence witness had helped the prosecution.

The next day, January 7, a defence witness actually helped Buxbaum.

It was time for Daniel Borland to tell his story about how Rob Barrett had confessed to setting up the murder without Buxbaum's knowledge and how Buxbaum was innocent. Much of the defence was built on what he had to say.

Borland was chained to the witness chair for his testimony. The inmate had escaped prison several times and police believed he would use the St. Catharines court appearance for another freedom bid.

The convict dutifully recited his conversations with Rob Barrett when they were fellow inmates at Laval prison near Montreal.

Borland, dark-haired and handsome in a rogue-ish way, and with a trim physique from weightlifting, easily smiled as he recited some of the crimes that had kept him behind bars for most of his adult life. He was serving fifteen years and seven months for a combination of escapes, armed robberies and other crimes. He didn't mind bragging about some of his deeds.

He told of "cleaning out the till and serving customers" during one milk store robbery while his accomplice held a female clerk at knife-point. He also related one lucky jail escape in which he had scaled a wall enclosing an exercise yard by using a rope that had been thrown over the wall for another prisoner. "As far as I knew, someone else in the yard planned it and I beat them to the wall," he explained with a wide grin.

Borland admitted to the prosecution that Rob Barrett was a "rat" for helping the police to prosecute Buxbaum. "But he didn't hide it," Borland said of Barrett. "He's very up-front. You know where you stand with him."

Borland insisted, however, that while he wouldn't commit crime with Barrett, he didn't dislike him.

Martin then challenged Borland's motive for testifying for the defence.

"You're just a public-spirited citizen?" the white-haired prosecutor demanded to know, hands on his hips, his voice betraying a tinge of sarcasm.

"No, sir," Borland shot back. "I'm not a public-spirited citizen at all. Barrett said this man was innocent. I wouldn't want to see him go to prison."

The jury was left to assess the credibility of this habitual criminal. He had told the story Greenspan had promised and hadn't helped the prosecutors.

But things were soon to go downhill again.

Phillip Buxbaum came to the stand. He would help his father by talking about the loving relationship he'd witnessed between his parents. The good-looking, dark-haired eighteen-year-old, bore a strong physical resemblance to his father. He was Buxbaum's third-oldest son after Paul, 22, and Mark, 19.

Among the first questions Greenspan asked Phillip were if he loved his father and mother. "Very much," he replied softly in the hushed courtroom.

Phillip said his parents demonstrated much affection for each other and that his father had once advised him to find a wife like his mother, calling her "a precious thing."

Phillip said he knew by April, 1984, that his father was seeing women and using cocaine, but he said he'd had suspicions about his father for a long time.

"I could tell that my father had something in the back of his mind. At age twelve, I could tell there was something bothering him. Something secretive about his life. I confirmed later... it was (his) seeing females."

Phillip said he had noticed bruising and needle marks on his father after talking to his mother.

He said that in May of 1984, the family banded together and confronted Buxbaum about the drug use.

"We exhorted my father to go ahead and try to seek help for his problem and to rehabilitate himself so we could once again be a unit as a whole family."

Phillip said that his mother had been aware of Robert Barrett and his cocaine sales to Helmuth. "She didn't hate him, she hated what he was doing to our family," he said of the pusher.

About the same time, Phillip said his mother found some white powder in one of his father's magazines.

" 'This is what has been going on,' " he quoted his mother as saying. " 'I'm going to put a stop to it.' "

Phillip said that his mother was "angry, upset" when she took Buxbaum to the London apartment where the surprised Chris Browne identified the powder as baking soda.

Greenspan wanted to know how Phillip's mother had reacted to her husband's seeing other women.

"She accepted the fact that it was going on," the teenager said.

"She didn't like it at all, naturally. She loved her husband unconditionally. She was not going to leave him. They were married for life, that was it. To her, she would forgive him for anything he would do and continue on trying to make the best of the marriage.''

The jury had paid close attention to this insider's view of the relationship between Hanna and Helmuth. The defence was willing to admit involvement with drugs and women, so the evidence about that wasn't dangerous. Phillip had helped his father's case.

A surprise was in store for the jury before Phillip left the stand.

On cross-examination, prosecutor Martin drew Phillip's attention to visits he'd made to his father at the Elgin-Middlesex Detention Centre. The visits, in early July, 1985, came nearly a year after Helmuth's arrest and shortly before his transfer to the St. Catharines area.

"He said to me, 'I'm getting out of here, I need your help,' '' Phillip said.

The defence witness said his father spoke of planning to escape from the jail with another inmate who was going to use explosives to blast a hole in the wall. Helmuth was planning to flee to Brazil and wanted his son to fetch his passport and get some money. Phillip said his father sent him to another inmate's girlfriend to retrieve an $8,500 cheque he'd endorsed to her. The teenager said he visited the woman but she didn't have the money. His father then gave him $5,000.

Greenspan had lost his battle to keep the jury from hearing this evidence. It was prejudicial, he argued, because it indicated a "consciousness of guilt" on the part of Buxbaum. O'Driscoll, once again ruled the jury should hear the evidence and make up its own mind about it.

In his re-examination, the defence lawyer attempted to minimize the damage about the escape bid.

He asked Phillip why his father had wanted out of jail.

"Because of the unusual harsh treatment he had received... and he wanted to be with his family," Phillip replied.

He quoted his father as saying, "Martin's (prosecutor Mike

Martin) out to get me. He's going to get me any way he can."

"The press had made a bad situation for him. The public was basically against him before the trial started."

Phillip said his father complained that people inside the jail were "leaning on him...people who wanted money from him."

The witness said that he, at first, agreed to help his father because he thought other inmates might hurt him, but thought about it and reported it to the police instead. He claimed credit for talking his father out of the escape bid.

"Dad, let's fight this one through — let's be men," Phillip said he told the family head.

"He said 'Yes, let's try to win this battle. I know I'm innocent. I should prove it in a court of law.' "

Phillip testified that his father agreed to abandon the plot and converted the $5,000 into a graduation present for his son.

Greenspan then produced two lawyers who specialize in insurance law. They agreed that any claim on Hanna's life would have to be made in the home state of Christian Mutual Life Insurance, New Hampshire. If Hanna had been kidnapped as in one plan, she would have to be missing for seven years before Buxbaum could claim the insurance, they told court. Greenspan was trying to put to rest, for once and for all, the insurance as any sort of supporting motive.

Mark Buxbaum took the stand briefly to recount how his parents shared a "deep common respect" for each other and said his father insisted that his children treat Hanna with the utmost respect.

The defence then explored the damage caused to Buxbaum by his 1982 stroke in order to try to explain some of the millionaire's apparently strange behavior before and after Hanna's death.

Toronto psychologist Ruth Bray said that she had interviewed Buxbaum for six hours and reviewed his medical history.

She said that Buxbaum had reported much less ambition and drive to succeed in life after the stroke and that he was anxious to catch up on things he'd missed: among those things were sex, group sex and the viewing of lesbian performances. Bray said she was convinced that Buxbaum had been "highly intelligent" before the stroke but that his intellect had been dulled.

Paul Buxbaum followed Bray to the witness stand and said that his mother had always been patient with and forgiving of her adulterous husband.

The tall, bespectacled and soft-spoken twenty-two-year-old admitted that he was sixteen when he learned of his father's affair with the woman he housed not far from Komoka.

"I was upset with my father's lifestyle that he chose...I had known about his adultery at that time...I was a teenager. I was very hurt by that."

He compared his father with the biblical prodigal son and said that his mother patiently awaited his return.

He revealed how he came to fire Squirrel from the nursing home job in May, 1984:

"My mother and I had decided to fire Rob Barrett because we felt he was being an extremely negative influence on my father."

Sometime before the firing, Paul said, Barrett called the Buxbaum home late at night looking for Helmuth. Hanna answered the phone because Helmuth wasn't in.

"My mother was very upset with Rob Barrett. She told him to leave us alone, to never talk to my father again. If he did she would phone the police. She was very upset."

Paul said he warned the pusher that he would "get" him by phoning the police if Barrett had anything to do with his father.

The oldest Buxbaum son said he already knew that his father was taking drugs. "You could see needle marks and the blood where he had just injected himself. That wasn't discreet at all."

Asked by prosecutor Martin if the family had insisted that Buxbaum take drug treatment at the Michigan clinic, a more-than-slightly exasperated Paul replied: "How can you tell your father what to do? We were begging him."

Paul said that his father had delayed his treatment, claiming that he was too busy. "He wasn't exactly thrilled about going down there. It's not exactly a nice experience that you have that (drug) problem."

Asked about his father's June trip to Florida, Paul said that he had insisted that his father come to that state to help him — Paul was attending school there — look into some real estate ventures.

Before Paul left the stand he was asked to recall the night of the shooting when his father came home exhausted and wanted to go to the bomb shelter for the night. Paul agreed with Martin that he'd tried to stop his father. "We were afraid he possibly might kill himself or something like that. He was depressed. We were afraid he might take some more cocaine or do something foolish."

When Toronto psychiatrist Dr. Andrew Malcolm entered the witness box, he said it was clear that Buxbaum suffered "organic personality syndrome." The slight, fast-talking and intense psychiatrist said that the stroke had disturbed Buxbaum's frontal lobe and had changed his personality.

Malcolm said that while Buxbaum had a strong sex drive before the trauma of the stroke, he began to demonstrate "sexual disinhibition" afterward . . . "seeking pleasures without restraint."

"There may have been an exaggeration of pre-existing personality traits," he told the rapt jurors. He added that Buxbaum now showed a flattening of his emotional responses.

"This was a man who for many years showed a number of personality traits . . . conscientiousness . . . attention to detail . . . a workaholic . . . and he also had a considerable sexual drive."

Malcolm said he was convinced that as a cure for impotence, Buxbaum thought he could find a sex therapist who would provide a surrogate partner to help him. Then, Buxbaum reasoned (according to Malcolm's theory), that he might as well eliminate the "middleman" and deal with surrogates directly: so he joined an escort service.

"In the course of time he got into a great deal of trouble around that," Malcolm said, with splendid 20/20 hindsight.

The expert in drug dependence said he viewed Buxbaum as "psychologically addicted" to cocaine and said that his drug-seeking and sex-seeking drives were "inextricably mixed up together."

Greenspan wanted the jury to know that the personality change had affected his client, producing the apparently unemotional reactions some witnesses found strange after the shooting.

"I think it (the killing) was an intensely emotional experience for Mr. Buxbaum," Malcolm testified. "I think he was overwhelmed by the course of events. I think he was shocked by his experience on that road."

Prosecutor Martin didn't have much luck shaking Malcolm. During his questioning, Martin continued a habit he'd used throughout the trial. Whenever he mentioned the name "Buxbaum" he would stab his left thumb back toward the man he was prosecuting, without bothering to turn toward the accused multi-millionaire. The jury could clearly see Martin's contempt for Buxbaum.

Finally, the time had come.

Crowds had been building in anticipation of hearing Greenspan's last witness and many spectators were turned away as the St. Catharines courtroom was filled to capacity.

At 2:35 p.m. on January 15, the fifty-third day of the trial, Eddie Greenspan rose to announce his twenty-ninth and final witness.

"My Lord," he said, slowly and deliberately, addressing Mr. Justice O'Driscoll. "My next witness is Helmuth Buxbaum."

The blue-suited businessman strode quickly from his wooden seat in the glassed-in prisoner's box to the padded seat of the witness box. Buxbaum was anxious.

At last, he could face his accusers and tell his version of events. It had been eighteen months since his wife had died and almost that long that he'd been in jail. It was exactly three months since this trial had started. In the next several days he would bow deeply to the judge and carefully study the faces of the jurors as they walked into court and left for recess.

Helmuth Buxbaum was nervous. He'd dreamed of this moment for a long time. And now it was his time to speak. Everything in his world rode on this appearance.

Greenspan began by getting him to talk about his background. This would get him accustomed to answering questions and build up his confidence. There was no need to rush things.

Buxbaum told of his life of deprivation in post-war Europe and how he had decided at age fourteen to emigrate to a new land "to build up my life and my future and my family."

He then traced his life from his arrival at Quebec City by boat, penniless, exactly one week before Christmas, 1958.

He talked of finding work in Elliot Lake and of meeting Hanna Schmidt in 1960, whom his mother "felt would be a very good wife for her son, Helmuth."

Greenspan interrupted Buxbaum's talk of Hanna with a blunt — but very pointed — question.

"Did you hire Rob Barrett to kill your wife, Hanna Buxbaum?"

"No," he replied quietly, pausing, "no."

After Helmuth talked about his wedding, Greenspan asked another important question for the benefit of the jury.

"Where you in love with your wife, Hanna, throughout your marriage?"

"Yes, I was in love with her," he replied, his voice growing stronger, more confident.

He told of being determined to become a success, by learning English, by improving his education and by working many long hours.

"I didn't want my children to go through what I went through. They were never going to go hungry. I was determined to be successful in business."

As Helmuth spoke, his sons Paul, Mark and Phillip watched from a front-row seat. They were going through an ordeal from which their father had been unable to protect them. It would grow worse in the coming days as Helmuth described his sexual adventures outside marriage.

The defendant, in his flat monotone, described his wife as

"a very wise woman...the best friend I had" and how she at first took a strong role in business until their expanding family took most of her attention.

He talked about his first visit to a prostitute in 1967; impregnating a staff member at Komoka Nursing Home in 1970 and agreeing to pay her $60-a-week child support until the woman could find a husband; the affair with his secretary the next year; another in the middle of the decade with a woman who introduced him to marijuana (which he didn't like) and cocaine snorting; to the nurse he housed in 1980, getting son Paul upset.

He said he eventually told his wife about his affairs and she inevitably forgave him.

The 1980 affair Paul uncovered had caused Hanna considerable grief, he conceded to Greenspan.

"She was crying and she was hurt. She reminded me this wasn't the first time it had happened. I had to agree with her on that. But eventually she forgave me for it."

He credited Hanna with helping him get over the physical effects of the stroke. "She nursed me, she helped me get my strength back again...When I needed her help the most she came through really strong."

Greenspan wanted Buxbaum to talk freely about all his indiscretions and feelings to minimize the damage. It would be far worse to have him admit his activities only under Martin's cross-examination.

But hearing about the millionaire's lifestyle and repeated disregard for his wife, the jurors couldn't help but begin to wonder even more about Buxbaum's character. How could he be such a rat?

Buxbaum said that he recovered from the stroke but went on to join Taurus Escort Service. "There were things happening in my life that I couldn't understand and others around me couldn't understand, either," he offered in explanation.

He said that his relationships with the prostitutes was purely sexual and that he still loved his wife. By 1983, he said, he was no longer sexually interested in Hanna.

He said he had met Rob Barrett at Kelly's bar and had seen

Squirrel as "a very likeable sort of a fellow... he sort of knew everybody in the place."

Barrett, he said, badgered him to try cocaine. Barrett injected him with cocaine in an upstairs washroom used by strippers. But the first experience, he said, made him feel ill.

"I thought if that's what coke is like, I don't want to have it again."

He said he returned to Kelly's a week later, in search of strippers, and again ran into Barrett. "I was willing to try it (cocaine) again... another shot. But I should have known better."

Greenspan steered him onto the subject of prostitutes and the witness admitted he'd offered money to two of the "healthier" ones to bear his baby if they got pregnant. He was opposed to abortion and he didn't like the hooker's birth-control methods. He said he was sure that Hanna would have agreed to adopt any such children because she had agreed to pay support to the one extramarital child he had already fathered.

The defence lawyer got him to direct his attention to Susan Ambrose and Dawn Watson, two prostitutes from early 1984 who had testified that Buxbaum told them he wanted his wife dead.

Buxbaum insisted it was Ambrose who suddenly suggested one day at the Golden Pheasant Motel that she could move in with the Buxbaums as a family cook. "My wife was no problem," he quoted Ambrose as assuring him.

"She told me she was a herbologist. She knew about herbs... she could take care of my wife. I just sat there. I shook my head and said 'What are you talking about?'"

He claimed that Ambrose said she'd administered a poisonous herb to a man who had then had a heart attack and that no one had found out.

"'I've done it before. The police haven't caught on to me,'" he quoted the tiny prostitute as telling him.

He then denied outright that he'd ever mentioned murder to Dawn Watson.

He recalled that during their trip to Europe in late May, 1984, Watson had grown angry with him for not taking her home when she wanted. "You'll be sorry for this," she said at one point.

He was asked about his relationship with Rob Barrett at the time he have him the landscaping job. "He had become my friend. I was more or less dependent on his supply of cocaine and wanted to help him out."

When Hanna first discovered his cocaine habit, Buxbaum said he'd told his wife that Chris Browne was his supplier. Later, he said, he'd admitted to her that it was Barrett.

"Hanna was very upset about finding cocaine on me and discovering that I was using cocaine," Helmuth allowed. "She was also getting rather upset at Rob Barrett."

He said he'd agreed with his family to take treatment for his cocaine dependency. "I knew I had to stop the cocaine habit... on the other hand I enjoyed cocaine and I really didn't want to give it up."

Still maintaining the soft monotone, he said he only discovered afterward that his son had fired Barrett at Hanna's request.

"He (Barrett) was very angry at being fired. He went as far as to say if he had a knife he would have stabbed Paul."

During a talk with Barrett late the day he was fired, Buxbaum said that the question of finding a secure supply of good quality cocaine came up and that Barrett suggested he needed $5,000 to establish a better connection. He said that he gave Barrett the money and that by early June Barrett called him from Florida to say that he was working on a cocaine supply in that state.

"I just happened to go to Florida the next day, that was coincidence." He said that he and his son Paul were looking into some real estate ventures and that he dropped in on Barrett at the Orlando motel. At that meeting, he said, he gave Barrett another $1,000 for expenses relating to the cocaine deal.

About a week later, he wired Barrett another $1,500 for

continuing expenses related to the supply situation and because Barrett needed money to return to London, he said.

Following the family's return from Europe, he said that after Hanna had fallen asleep he went to his bunker to inject cocaine. He got no sleep because of the drug.

He said that on July 4 Barrett got in touch with him at his office and asked for money. When Buxbaum balked, Barrett suggested that he give back the stolen mink coat Barrett had sold him for $600 several months before. Barrett proposed to sell it and split the proceeds with Buxbaum. Buxbaum said that he agreed to meet Barrett at the McDonald's restaurant on Oxford Street at about 4:30 p.m.

He said that Barrett showed up at the McDonald's driving a white van and led him to Komoka where he suddenly pulled over. Barrett told him to go fetch the coat and some cocaine.

Buxbaum said that he retrieved the coat from his garage and gave it to Barrett, but decided against sharing the cocaine he'd purchased earlier in the day from a man named "Rick."

After Buxbaum got the coat, Barrett suggested that he follow him west toward Highway 402, but Buxbaum said he refused to go.

"He wanted me to follow him. I said 'No, I promised my wife I would be home for dinner.' " he said he then left Barrett.

He said that Squirrel had persisted about meeting him the following morning. But, according to his own testimony, Buxbaum held his ground; he'd be travelling with his wife to Toronto airport the next morning to pick up his nephew and wouldn't have time.

Greenspan, seldom straying from his detailed notes, carefully led the beleagured millionaire through the events of the next day, starting with the large, happy breakfast the family had shared.

Buxbaum said that he stopped for a blue car just after he and Hanna entered Highway 402 and that the motorist asked for a pair of stockings. He said the OPP cruiser, which had happened along, pulled away after being assured by the "curly-haired'' man and he (Buxbaum) returned to his wife. Hanna, to whom he had just returned the pantyhose, said '' 'This guy gives me the creeps,' I said, 'Me, too,' so we drove off.''

He said that enroute to Toronto he visited Heinz Wagner while Hanna bathed her mother at the Kitchener nursing home. After picking up Roy at the airport, and while they were driving home along Highway 402, at the Komoka cutoff Buxbaum said that he saw the dark car head with a man beside it, ''frantically waving.''

He said that Hanna agreed it looked like the Richardson's car and they pulled up behind it.

''Everything happened very quickly. Everything happened very fast,'' he told the hushed courtroom.

''As soon as I stopped the car I heard the right rear door opening of my station wagon. When I turned around I looked into a masked face and I realized the man had a gun in his hand that he was holding against my wife's head.''

The man demanded money and jewels and was very excited, Buxbaum said.

Although the man had a stocking covering his face, eye holes were cut in it, revealing a pair of ''sky blue'' eyes.

''Do you remember those eyes,'' Greenspan asked.

''I sure do,'' came the reply.

He said that as he was attempting to wave down help after Hanna was dragged from the car, he suddenly heard three shots and then saw the man and a companion running toward the Nova with his wife's purse. They sped off.

His first thought upon seeing Hanna in the ditch was to put her into the station wagon and take her to hospital, he said, but that a truck driver, on the scene within seconds, suggested that she be left undisturbed while police and an ambulance were summoned.

He said that he assisted police as much as possible that night, even though he was falling asleep from fatigue.

But he said that back home in Komoka, still later than night, he couldn't sleep and heard the voices of others in the house.

"I wanted to go downstairs and inject some cocaine."

"Why?" Greenspan wanted to know.

"Because I knew it would make me feel better. . . eventually it did."

Greenspan continued slowly through two volumes of questions contained in black, three-ring binders. He drew Buxbaum's attention to the phone call from Barrett at the funeral home the day after the killing as well as his meeting Barrett at London airport.

He said that Barrett was "in a panic" and said he needed $20,000. If Squirrel didn't come up with the money for a cocaine deal "he would be killed. . . he begged me to help him."

This was the Florida cocaine, Buxbaum said, and he wasn't about to let his friend down.

"I just lost my wife," he explained. "I didn't want to get Robert Barrett killed, he was my friend,"

When he met Barrett at the airport with the money, Squirrel looked "tired and drawn out. He looked scared. I'd never seen him like this before."

It was a full two days after Hanna's murder that he told police about the car he stopped for in the morning, he said, because it was only by then that he felt it might have been significant.

He spoke of enrolling his two youngest children, Danny and Esther, at Black Forest Christian Academy in Germany. He said that he and Hanna had discussed it and that he had to hurry to make arrangements in time for the fall term.

He said he hated being at the Elgin-Middlesex detention centre after his arrest and that a series of fellow inmates, starting with Patrick Allen, began coming forward with proposals for a breakout.

He said he soon became convinced he would never get a fair trial. He expected the prosecution to place "emphasis on the women I had associated with, the prostitutes and the cocaine usage. I thought that would prejudice the public, and probably the jurors, against me."

He outlined a list of breakout schemes. One man promised he'd return after his release and use wire cutters to get to the jail wall where he'd then use a blow torch to cut open a metal window. He said he gave the man a cheque for $10,000 but nothing came of the plan. "I wrote him a letter and I asked him if he could give me the $10,000 back. He wrote me a letter back and told me he had spent the money."

Another plan involved an assault on a police paddy wagon used to transport prisoners to court. He said that a cheque for $5,000 had been sent to the mastermind of this plot. And again, nothing happened, he said.

Another variation saw an inmate's relative steal a bulldozer and smash through the jail wall. Buxbaum would clamber through the debris, then race to a waiting motorcycle. The $8,500 cheque endorsed to another inmate's girlfriend and the $5,000 he gave to son Phillip were to be used for that getaway, he said. Yet another scheme had him transferred to a psychiatric hospital from which he felt he might be able to escape without the aid of blow torches and bulldozers.

In all, he said he spent about $24,000 to be part of escape plots before deciding they were "rather silly approaches to scam me for money by other inmates." In the jury's absence, he told of one particularly spectacular plan in which a helicopter would drop into the jail yard and whisk him away.

Greenspan concluded his questioning ten minutes before the usual 1 p.m. lunch break on Tuesday, January 21. Buxbaum had been on the stand for nearly four days.

Ordinarily, court would recess for its lunch hour at about that time and Mr. Justice O'Driscoll asked prosecutor Martin if that was his preference.

But Martin was eager. He insisted on starting right away. He'd been waiting many months to tackle the millionaire.

He started by asking for more details on Buxbaum's plans once he escaped and got the witness to admit he had about $280,000 in several Swiss bank accounts.

Martin kept Buxbaum on the stand for two days, pointing

out the contradictions and admitted lies in his statements to the police whom Buxbaum had professed he'd tried to assist.

He got Buxbaum to reveal it was his view that the judge at his bail hearing, (Mr. Justice A.W. Maloney) had been "drinking...I thought he was slightly inebriated." Buxbaum claimed that that was yet another reason he felt he wouldn't get a fair trial.

"I knew what I had done," Buxbaum said. "I knew my womanizing was not right, that that was wrong. I knew that to take cocaine was very wrong."

He said he would have pleaded guilty to both adultery and cocaine use, "but charging me with murder of my wife, no, I can't plead guilty to that because I didn't do it, I had no part in it."

Martin then quizzed Buxbaum on the plan to get to a psychiatric hospital. Greenspan objected when the prosecutor asked Buxbaum what he had "done" to himself to draw the attention of the authorities and receive psychiatric assessment. (Martin was curtailed before the jury got to hear about the paper clips.)

The prosecutor was determined to reveal the sort of man Buxbaum was. Buxbaum admitted that his illegitimate child was the product of a back-seat liaison at a drive-in theatre with a 17-year-old kitchen helper at the Komoka nursing home. Martin had Buxbaum remind the jury that, at the time, he was a 30-year-old man with three children at home.

The defence's final witness then said that Corinne Willoughby was also seventeen when he first paid her for sex.

The prosecutor, continually sipping on a glass of water to punctuate his rapid-fire questions, had some concerns about Susan Ambrose.

Martin expressed amazement that Buxbaum hadn't called police when Ambrose allegedly suggested she poison Hanna and admitted she'd killed before.

"I don't know why I didn't. I should have, I guess," agreed the millionaire with the "flattened" emotional responses.

Pressed about how he overcame his shock at the proposal and still had sexual intercourse with Ambrose moments later, he replied: "That was the purpose of going to the motel room."

"I see," Martin continued, jotting something in his notes. "And further to that, you were going to employ her, at least you gave her an application for employment?"

Buxbaum explained that staff hiring was left to his administrators. He had no role in it.

"Well," Martin said, "the administrator of the nursing home could have hired this woman, then? You didn't have anything to do with it. She could have filled out the application, sent it in, and been hired?"

"I sort of doubted myself that she would have been hired," came the answer.

"Well, she *could* have been, for all you knew, because you didn't have anything to do with it?"

"Well," Buxbaum countered, growing uneasy, "she didn't have any medical qualifications. She didn't have any nursing-home experience."

"She could have been a maid in the kitchen, a dishwasher?" Martin asked, baiting his trap.

"Yes. I don't know."

"And she could have poisoned somebody's food while she was in the kitchen, couldn't she?" The self-made man was in a fix.

"That thought never crossed my mind," he offered.

Martin slowly turned him to the subject of divorce. The wary witness admitted that his wife had mentioned it once "very briefly" during a car trip in 1982 or 1983.

"'We can't go on with this lifestyle we're living,'" Hanna had said. "I knew what she meant and I agreed with her. I said you're not talking of divorce, and she said, no."

Then Hanna said that she was fully aware of his extra-marital activities, he said.

Martin expressed amazement that in his July 23 statement to

Detective-Inspector Ron Piers, Buxbaum had identified Barrett as "Bartlett."

"You knew your friend Barrett and what his proper name is?" Martin challenged.

"Yes. I had trouble spelling his last name."

"Well you didn't have any trouble pronouncing it, did you?"

"When?" Buxbaum asked evasively.

"You don't have any trouble pronouncing it now, you didn't have any trouble pronouncing it then, did you?," Martin asked, displaying some exasperation.

"No."

"But you called him Bartlett. Why did you call him Bartlett?"

"I think that was a mistake on my part."

"You made a mistake about the name of your good friend did you? Is that what you did? Is that what you're telling us, that you're trying to help these officers who were trying to find the murderer of your wife?" Martin's hands went to his hips.

"Yes. Yes, I did tell them that it was Barrett. First I thought it was Bartlett but it wasn't the right name. It was Barrett."

"And this is your good friend who you had known, like, for six months? That's right?"

"That's right."

Buxbaum went on to insist that the only reason he didn't tell Piers why Barrett was in Florida was because he was afraid of being charged with some conspiracy relating to cocaine.

The jury would have to assess how realistic this was from a man about to be charged in a murder. If he would lie to protect himself from a cocaine charge, what would he do facing a murder charge?

Martin directed Buxbaum's mind to the evening he stopped behind the blue Nova and Hanna's reaction when he suggested that the car was the Richardson's.

"Hanna agreed with me that we should stop," Buxbaum said.

Then Martin reminded him that he had told Piers that Hanna had said no such thing.

"How can you say your wife agreed to this stopping?" Martin asked, his arms outstretched toward the witness.

"Well, she did. That's why I say it."

"Well, why did you tell the inspector that your wife said: '...she didn't want me to, she said no, no, don't, don't stop.' Why did you say that to the inspector?"

"Because that day, on the 23rd when I went in, I was quite heavily drugged. (At this point he mentions three prescription headache pills and tranquilizers he'd taken that day.)

"Well, those pills don't stop you from telling the truth?"

"No, but they make you dizzy." The courtroom erupted in laughter at that response. "I told him the truth from what I remembered."

Martin then reminded Buxbaum that he had driven a blue rental car to the interview at the London OPP detachment.

"And you drove it, your drove there?" Martin asked, planting another land mine.

"I drove it, yes."

"And the pills you had taken didn't prevent you from driving a car, did they?," the wily prosecutor pressed, his hands returned to his hips.

"No, I shouldn't have driven, but I did drive."

Martin then wanted to know why Buxbaum hadn't told Piers about the pills and asked not to answer the questions.

"I told him. He knew I was drugged when I went for the interview and you can clearly hear it on the tape, you can hear the slurry speaking. I don't have slurry speech like that."

In a few moments, the prosecutor was expressing his puzzlement at why Buxbaum shut off the engine of his station wagon when he pulled up behind the Rent-a-Wreck Nova in the evening.

"Well, it would take a few minutes to check things out," Buxbaum offered. "Even if I come to an intersection and the light turns green I shut off my engine."

While spectators chewed that one over he said that he was in the habit of stopping for cars along the road and regularly, perhaps twice a week, stopped for hitch-hikers between London and Komoka.

Then Martin pointed out further inconsistencies in Buxbaum's statements: Buxbaum had told Piers that when he saw the man waving at the Nova: "(I) thought it would take the minute, and maybe he needed a lift to go for gas, er, I, I, normally don't do that."

To this, Buxbaum would only reply "I don't know why I told him that."

Then the proscecutor asked Buxbaum why he waited for two days after the killing before telling police about stopping for the blue car in the morning and yet had already suggested as a suspect a man who had broken into his home nearly two years before.

Martin suggested it would have been helpful to police to mention the name of Susan Ambrose, who — according to Buxbaum — had proposed poisoning Hanna just a few months before.

"There was no woman on the scene," Buxbaum countered, his voice starting to betray a hint of annoyance. "There was no woman in the morning. I never thought Susan Ambrose had any connection to it."

Following a brief argument in the absence of the jury about statements Buxbaum had made in jail, Martin abruptly concluded his questioning. A brief smile flickered on Buxbaum's face. This hadn't been so bad, after all. For his part, Martin had been low-key but persistent. The sometimes-abrasive prosecutor had deliberately stayed away from frontal assaults, preferring instead to relentlessly bring to light aspects of the millionaire's often contradictory story. Let the jury decide this case on the facts. He wasn't about to victimize a man who had a habit of being a victim anyway and who claimed Barrett had taken advantage of him. Martin didn't want the jury to develop any sympathy for Buxbaum. It would distract them from considering much more important things.

Greenspan was brief in re-examination. He wanted to undo some of the damage inflicted by the prosecutor. The lawyer wanted Buxbaum to talk about his truthfulness with Inspector Piers.

"I know that I never lied to Mr. Piers," Buxbaum responded. "I always tried to help the police whenever I could, as much as I could...I don't lie."

Late on January 23rd when O'Driscoll dismissed the jury until the following week for submissions by the defence and crown, he noted that the jurors were "probably happy to hear and interested to learn that that is all the evidence you'll hear."

The ten men and two women sitting in judgment of Helmuth Buxbaum had heard an earful about the millionaire in the previous fifty-nine days from sixty prosecution and twenty-nine defence witnesses. The trial had been a sensational one, and had also become one of the longest murder trials in Ontario history. The end was in sight.

It was time for the final submissions, and the defence had to go first because it called evidence.

Eddie Greenspan was ready. With his wife Susie, and teenaged daughter Juliana looking on, the Toronto lawyer laid out the facts in the case and methodically tried to show the jury that Buxbaum had nothing to do with the killing.

As a preamble, Greenspan warned the jury to disregard anything the presiding judge might say about the case. He noted that there are some places where judges are not permitted to comment on evidence because it is felt that the practice usurps the job of the jury.

As Mr. Justice O'Driscoll continued jotting down those remarks, Greenspan said that lawyers and judges have no particular insight that helps them to determine the facts in a case.

"You should disregard any comments made or his opinions about the facts," Greenspan warned the jury. Clearly the defence lawyer was concerned that the judge's remarks might not be flattering to his client.

Earlier, when he'd closed his case, Greenspan had argued unsuccessfully that O'Driscoll should make no comment on the facts he'd heard because it would restrict Buxbaum's right to a fair trial before the jury. Greenspan admitted that he had no law to cite in his bid to convince O'Driscoll. And, predictably, O'Driscoll was unimpressed, saying he would resign the day he could no longer share his views with the jury.

In his summation, Greenspan also took early aim at the prosecution, which he claimed had purposely tried to "blacken" Buxbaum's reputation by dwelling on the evidence of his extramarital escapades and cocaine use. "He does not seek through this trial to justify those unjustifiable actions," the lawyer said. Yet prosecutor Martin, he charged, had attempted to get the jury to "despise" Buxbaum.

Greenspan complained that the press had sensationalized the trial and was "not always scrupulously accurate."

In the next several days the lawyer pointed to what he called a "tissue of lies" created by prosecution witnesses Susan Ambrose, Rob Barrett, Terry Armes and Patrick Allen.

He dismissed Ambrose as "cunning and spiteful, a woman of outrageous theatrics, a woman who tells you by her demeanor she is lying."

The three men, he said, agreed to finger Buxbaum as the man behind the killing in exchange for deals that would get them out of possible convictions for first-degree murder which permit no parole eligibility for twenty-five years.

"People who would lie and cheat at the drop of a hat wouldn't likely have any trouble lying in a courtroom."

Greenspan's script was lengthy and detailed. Reading rapid-fire from a thick black binder in which he had inserted hundreds of tightly typed pages, Greenspan attempted to review every morsel of evidence in the case and show how Buxbaum was not involved, instead, how he was victimized by the street-smart Barrett and his friends.

Piling fact upon fact, punctuating his delivery with "there is more" and "that isn't all," he was working hard to show that all the evidence pointed toward acquittal.

He reminded the jury that the Helmuth Buxbaum they'd seen as a witness revealed the sort of man Buxbaum was. He was "an elemental person. What you see is what he is . . . what you saw is a weak person. He is not prone to displaying emotion. He is not the diabolical genius. He is, to put it crudely, a wimp."

There it was, *that word*, wimp. It described an image Buxbaum had struggled for years to shed. Here it was now being used to describe him in court. By his own lawyer. The press ate it up.

Greenspan went on to say that Buxbaum simply had no motive for murder. Hanna had forgiven him for his drug use and the prostitutes.

It was Barrett, he argued, the "small-time hustler with grand ambitions" who had reason to kill Hanna. The wife of this "millionaire-mark" had threatened to report Barrett to police. She was dangerous to Barrett.

"Someone stood . . . between him and all his dreams. It was Hanna Buxbaum.

"The bottom line is Hanna Buxbaum did not interfere with her husband's pursuit of women and cocaine . . . it was Barrett she tried to stop . . . it was Barrett and only Barrett who had reason to kill Hanna Buxbaum."

Greenspan highlighted the evidence that he felt showed his theory to be correct. Barrett went to Florida, "the drug capital of North America" to get cocaine, not a killer. And he was still in that state trying to get Paul Ringuette to kill Hanna in mid-June. The lawyer said that Barrett couldn't have known about the Buxbaums' upcoming June 19 departure for Europe, because he never told Ringuette about the need to hurry. Barrett was obviously working alone — without Helmuth, Greenspan said.

"How can you be morally certain about anything else in his

evidence?'' Greenspan asked the jury, surveying faces for a sign of support, or an appreciative nod.

Buxbaum's belief in hard money theories and his damaged brain were responsible for his actions at the banks immediately before and after the killing, he said.

And it wasn't likely that a man involved in the killing would be so helpful with police, providing several statements late into the same night despite his tiredness from two sleepless nights.

Greenspan rolled on. He said that Buxbaum was in no rush to get onto Highway 402 the morning of the killing. ''On the prosecution's theory, he is late for the murder he arranged... how likely is that?'' He added that if Buxbaum had truly been involved that morning there would have been no need to make the Nova appear disabled. He would have stopped anyway. Having the car jacked up only made a getaway more difficult.

In the evening, Helmuth and Hanna had agreed to stop for the Nova because they thought it was the Richardson's car, he said, pointing to the evidence of independent witness Roy Buxbaum, an ''accurate reporter.''

Greenspan also said that if Hanna had really screamed, ''No, honey, please, not this way,'' Roy would have heard it, but he hadn't.

Greenspan said that Armes' memory had gradually improved as he gave several statements to police following his arrest, until he came up with the ''honey'' quote. Once he remembered it, the lawyer charged, Armes got ''a honey of a deal.''

''No question that is a devastating remark if what Armes says is true. (But) Hanna would not possibly have reason to suspect anything involving her husband.

''Not even Hanna Buxbaum would put up with that and still call him Honey.''

Meanwhile, he continued, Barrett couldn't have received $5,000 from Buxbaum the day before the killing because he had no money left when the killers came visiting him at his Westbury Hotel room.

As Greenspan continued into his third day, the jurors were growing restless. Several had abandoned their notebooks while others merely doodled. Several times as Greenspan continued, Buxbaum closed his eyes and seemed to nod off. Spectator interest declined as revealed by empty seats in the courtroom. Greenspan tried a few small jokes but the jury sat stone-faced. They didn't want to be read by the hard-working defence counsel.

Greenspan was making good points but they were spaced far apart in his lengthy submission. His approach in dealing with all minutiae was beginning to take its toll.

The tedium was broken briefly during Greenspan's fourth day as a strong earth tremor shook the fourth-floor courtroom for about five or six seconds. Greenspan, in full flight, didn't notice the tremor at first and was stopped by O'Driscoll who called an abrupt recess. Twenty minutes later, court resumed and Greenspan broke up the jury and the court when he announced: "For my next trick, I am going to part the waters of Lake Ontario."

The wittiest line, however, was delivered by a spectator as he awaited resumption of court. Boris Petrovici, an elderly character who had become one of the dozens of Buxbaum-watchers addicted to the proceedings, took a reporter aside to share his somewhat cynical view.

"I thought when the building was shaking," he confided, in thick Yugoslav accent, "that Mr. Buxbaum's bulldozer had come for him."

But laughs were few as the defence wound up its case. At one point, Greenspan was arguing passionately about the "deals" received by Barrett, Allen and Armes, saying they were the result of the prosecution's zeal to nail Helmuth.

During the next recess, Buxbaum's sons, Paul, Mark and Phillip had sharp words for the prosecution. This was the first time they'd heard Greenspan's allegations about the deals, because earlier in the trial they'd been excluded from the courtroom because they were witnesses.

Led by Paul, the Buxbaum sons confronted Constable Mel Getty in the corridor outside court.

"You'll do anything to win, won't you?" Paul shouted at

Getty. "Anything to win, anything for your unethical deals."

Getty shrugged off the angry words. He knew that Paul and the others would naturally dislike the men who were trying to convict their father. Nothing he could say would change their opinion.

Greenspan's submission continued for five days. It was by far the longest the lawyer had delivered in his career. During the last day, with the end in site, he was able to moderate his rapid delivery, to insert pauses for effect.

He dismissed the evidence of Dawn Watson that Buxbaum had spoken to her of drowning, poisoning and kidnapping Hanna. Greenspan said that both she and Buxbaum were heavily stoned on drugs at the time and that he doubted the conversation had taken place.

Likewise, he attacked the evidence of Susan Ambrose, whom he described as "a very strange woman." She had delivered her evidence in a manner worthy of an Academy Award for best actress, he said.

"Three times with a prostitute and he's talking about getting his wife killed...a prostitute he doesn't know...does that make sense?"

Greenspan said that Ambrose was a woman with "grand dreams, grand illusions" and that she had tried to insert herself into Buxbaum's future by offering to dispose of his wife.

He stressed that Buxbaum had no possible motive to murder Hanna. Buxbaum was extremely wealthy and didn't need the proceeds from the insurance policy, he pointed out.

Buxbaum couldn't have killed Hanna for want of sex. He was getting plenty of that. And he wouldn't have killed his wife merely because she was overweight.

"If being overweight is a reason to be killed, a lot of us are in serious trouble and should start dieting immediately...this is a silly motive." The pudgy counsel drew a good laugh with this remark.

He then tackled the crown's contention that Buxbaum was afraid to divorce his wife for fear he would lose the "regard" of his children. Greenspan noted that Buxbaum had already lost the regard of his family because its members were fully aware of his use of cocaine and prostitutes.

The lawyer urged the jury to remember clearly the evidence of prison inmate Daniel Borland. Borland had "demolished" the evidence of Rob Barrett, he said. Greenspan said that Barrett had demonstrated shock at being exposed by Borland and had demanded to know where his former friend had gotten the information about the case.

"If Barrett didn't tell Borland, where in the world did Borland get all that information from?" the lawyer asked. "Daniel Borland knows because Barrett told him."

If the jurors chose to believe Borland they couldn't believe Barrett, he said. "Barrett is lying and Helmuth Buxbaum is innocent."

Greenspan said that even though they had already been sentenced, the confessed conspirators in the case had every reason to lie.

The hardworking lawyer was coming to his conclusion. His pace slowed further and he looked into the eyes of every juror.

"You're not here to try Helmuth Buxbaum for his morality or lack of morality," he reminded his audience of twelve.

"His conduct is strange at times," Greenspan conceded. "As a result of his stroke he is a strange man at times...but he is not a killer."

The lawyer said he expected prosecutor Martin to talk about the dead woman as one who was "virtuous and faithful."

"There was a lot of sex, drugs, the death of a virtuous woman. There is nothing to connect them."

He said that Buxbaum was frank with his friends and family doctor, sometimes too frank.

"Whatever else he is, he is not cunning, devious. He is without guile."

"He lost an awful lot on her death. His wife, a mother, his partner in business, his best friend."

"I can suggest you can fairly say that Helmuth Buxbaum has established his innocence."

Then Greenspan had a reminder for the jury about the fate

of the street-wise men who arranged the killing. He said that both Barrett and Pat Allen would be eligible for day parole by late in the year. He asked the jurors to think about looking Barrett and Allen in the eye on the street and say that they were morally certain these men had told the truth.

Greenspan was near the end of his marathon address. The jury sensed it and they obliged by paying closer attention to their note-taking. In the prisoner's box, Helmuth Buxbaum avoided the eyes of the jury.

The lawyer said that the prosecution would attempt to paint Buxbaum as a "cold-hearted killer or demented."

But he said that the millionaire was "a different man, yes. A weak man, certainly. But not a killer."

Greenspan said he'd worked hard to debunk the crown case and reminded the jurors that an acquittal would not be an endorsement of Buxbaum's lifestyle.

"He admitted conduct that is publicly humiliating. He has much to be ashamed of. His private life has been ruined."

Greenspan's voice grew soft as he described Buxbaum as "a pathetic man."

"He has seen his most intimate secrets disclosed not just to the public but to his children as well. Perhaps he deserves that, perhaps more. But he does not deserve to be convicted of murder."

When Greenspan completed his summation February 3rd, he'd covered nearly every morsel of evidence delivered up by the prosecution. He'd left little untouched.

It would be just a few days now until the jury would determine if the doubts the lawyer had sown were reasonable enough to warrant an acquittal.

But first, prosecutor Martin would have a few words to say.

It was now the sixty-fifth day of the trial and everyone was tired. The laughter that for so long had leaked into the courtroom from a happy jury room had ceased.

Martin was brief and his manner relaxed. He parked his lectern directly in front of the jury, unlike Greenspan who had chosen an oblique angle.

Immediately in front of Martin was the police model of the shooting scene on Highway 402 crossed by both the railway overpass and the County Road 14 interchange.

The white-haired prosecutor had one binder of typed notes from which he would frequently stray to embellish a point. He would pause for effect, using broad gestures to underline his remarks. Always his tone was measured, almost grandfatherly as he appealed to the common sense of the jury. He took four hours to make his points.

At the outset, Martin started by asking six questions arising from the evidence he wanted the jury to consider: How did the gunmen in the morning of July 5 know that Buxbaum would stop?; Why weren't those same gunmen disguised?; How did the evening gunmen know that Hanna would be delivered to them?; Why was Buxbaum permitted to move around freely during the shooting?; Why was Buxbaum initially reluctant to decide that the morning blue car and the evening blue car were the same vehicle?; How did Buxbaum know that his wife had been shot in the head (as he told the first trucker on the scene) if he'd never run to her side to see the bullet entry wound above her hairline?

"The case in which we have been engaged these past four months has given all of us a view of life and death which we would rather not have seen," Martin said.

"This view we have had is of the life of a decent and virtuous wife and mother who endured her marriage to an adulterous husband, and who, with the patience of a saint and martyr, tried to bring him back to a decent life and who — for her pains — met a tragic death in a roadside ditch. We have seen the life of a faithless husband who squandered the faith and affection of his truly good wife."

He noted that some of the crown case was based on evidence from drug pushers, thieves, prostitutes and murderers, but he reminded the jury that "if you were to go forth to hire a killer you would not go to the good citizens social club."

His hands moved from his hips to his chest where he clasped them across his chest.

Martin said he felt that he'd proved beyond reasonable doubt that Buxbaum had arranged Hanna's killing and drove her to the place of her death.

The prosecutor then spoke of the prostitutes, rejecting Greenspan's criticism that Martin had sought to blacken Buxbaum's reputation. Only four prostitutes were called as witnesses in an attempt to reveal the state of the Buxbaum marriage, he said.

"The state of his marriage was simply deplorable and he wanted to get out of it," Martin concluded. "She (Hanna) was virtuous and he was promiscuous."

Martin said that Rob Barrett hadn't "harpooned" Buxbaum on cocaine. Evidence was that Buxbaum was already injecting cocaine in front of Corrine Willoughby before the millionaire met Barrett. And after meeting Barrett, Buxbaum had repeatedly gone back to Kelly's for more women and more cocaine.

The prosecutor said that Buxbaum appeared to truly value and enjoy the company of the large number of prostitutes with whom he associated and at the same time "played the role of faithful hardworking Christian husband and father."

"His life then, was one of hypocrisy that continues into this courtroom."

Warming to his task, Martin then moved on to the evidence of Susan Ambrose and the two shocked motel maids who overheard the conversation about poisoning. He reminded the jury that one maid had said " 'I just know he was interested in what she was saying' " and the other that " 'they were trying to murder somebody.' "

He said it was incredible if Buxbaum were truly upset that he'd still have sex with Ambrose and later give her an application for employment at the Komoka nursing home.

Then Martin discussed Buxbaum's use of drugs. By early 1984, he said, "it was clear Hanna was trying to get him away from drugs" and the family had tried to interest him in Pine Rest hospital in Michigan.

"Everyone was begging Helmuth Buxbaum to go, but Helmuth was reluctant to do so...Poor Hanna died with Helmuth's application for Pine Rest still in her purse."

Martin paused for effect, holding aloft the plastic-wrapped application form police took from Hanna's purse that had been retrieved from the Thames River. The purse and its contents were exhibits in the trial.

The prosecutor went on to dismiss the defence contention that Rob Barrett was angry at losing the landscaping job at Buxbaum's nursing home (and therefore had his own motive for murder). Martin noted that Barrett was merely "down in the dumps" according to his brother, and had only worked two or three days a week while he had the job. "How could he be enraged at losing something he valued so little?"

Clearly, Barrett's trip to Florida was to find killers, he said, since the $3,500 he took with him at first was obviously "peanuts" for any big-time drug dealing.

His voice rising at times, falling at others, Martin said that it was fear of Buxbaum's money — not of Buxbaum himself — that finally prompted Barrett to seriously seek a killer. "If it could buy a killer for his wife, it could buy a killer for Rob Barrett if he crossed him. That's what Rob Barrett was afraid of."

Martin then directed the jury to what he called a subtle but significant error Buxbaum had made on the witness stand.

Buxbaum, he said, had been asked about leaving Barrett on the afternoon before the killing when Barrett was insistent that Buxbaum stay with him. " 'He wanted me to follow him out to the 402...he wanted to meet me the next day.' " Buxbaum had testified. That, Martin said, confirmed that Buxbaum was virtually making an appointment for the killing and then helped his companions to select the murder site.

"Buxbaum made his fatal slip in his attempt to recite his pat story to you," he told the jury.

Greenspan obviously didn't agree. He glowered at the back of the prosecutor's head and mumbled something to his assistant, Chris Buhr.

Martin then began suggesting answers to some of his opening questions. He said that the gunmen weren't masked in the morning because Buxbaum was the only witness expected to survive. And he wasn't about to identify the men he'd hired. There was, therefore, no reason to quickly flee from their accomplice.

Buxbaum had stopped in the first place, without being waved down, he said, "so the killers could do their murderous work."

In the evening, he said, the licence plate had to be covered and the hit-man disguised because, this time round, another witness was to survive — the nephew, Roy Buxbaum.

Likewise, he continued, with Roy ordered to keep his head down during the shooting, Helmuth Buxbaum was permitted an unmolested view of the execution, because he wasn't going to interfere. That's also how he knew his wife was shot in the head. He had witnessed it, as Armes had pointed out, on tip toes, Martin said.

Martin reminded the jury of Hanna's "particularly damning statement": " 'No, honey, please, not this way.' "

"In the face of all this, Buxbaum didn't even blink an eye. He just stood there and watched." Martin paused, again clasping his hands across his chest.

Then, changing gears, he said that the $13,000 Barrett gave to Buxbaum the day after the killing *had* to be for the murder.

It simply didn't make sense for Barrett to demand $20,000 from Buxbaum, settle for $13,000, return to face the men he feared, and also pick up cocaine at London airport if he were working on a huge cocaine deal in Toronto.

He then attacked the credibility of Daniel Borland, the convict who was so helpful to Greenspan and the defence.

Borland, he said, couldn't have learned the information about the crime from Barrett. The inmate was simply another criminal who "just joined the company of convicts...who were just scamming to make money off of Mr. Buxbaum."

"Mr. Borland, he's the actor...he does a pretty good job of trying to fool you when he's in the witness box."

The prosecutor then addressed the question of motive in the murder. Martin said that he wasn't relying on any particular motive to show why Buxbaum arranged to have Hanna killed. "Most crimes are senseless," he reminded the jury.

The $1 million life insurance policy may have been a factor in Buxbaum's thinking, but it didn't provide motive.

"If the wind is blowing and the river is rising you will make sure the premium on your house insurance been paid," Martin said, drawing a common-sense analogy.

Regardless, he said, by early 1984 when the insurance policy was purchased with Helmuth Buxbaum as beneficiary, "Helmuth Buxbaum enjoyed a lifestyle that was incompatible with marriage."

Hanna had tried to change her husband, who only "play acted" that he wanted to change, Martin said.

"Hanna stood in his way. Hanna had to be removed. (She was) an obstacle in his path to cocaine and to his women ...Hanna's death was the solution.

"We may never be able to unravel the twisted thoughts of Helmuth Buxbaum, but it is not necessary to do so."

As Martin moved toward his conclusion he came back to the events along Highway 402. He reminded the jury of the troubling fact that Buxbaum had pulled up behind the same blue car twice in one day. It was "an unbelievable coincidence," the prosecutor said.

The crown attorney slowed his pace even more as he conducted his own survey of juror faces. They seemed to be following him closely.

"When you ultimately retire to consider your verdict, I submit that you will be required to consider the evidence of the various witnesses who have been called to testify, including the evidence of Helmuth Buxbaum himself. You will have to sift the evidence and ultimately resolve the many conflicts which exist between Buxbaum's evidence and that of many of the witnesses called by the crown. Mr. Greenspan suggests to you that those conflicts can be resolved simply by choosing to believe that all of the other witnesses are lying wherever and whenever their evidence conflicts with that of Buxbaum. In other words, Susan Ambrose is lying; Dawn Watson is lying; Corrine Willoughby is lying; Robert Barrett is lying; Patrick Allen is lying; Terry Armes is lying; Anita Pitcher is lying;

Debbie Barber is lying; Kelly Barrett is lying; even Heinz Wagner is lying. It is interesting to note that some of Helmuth Buxbaum's evidence actually coincides with the evidence of some of these witnesses.''

Martin then took aim at the accused man who had averted his eyes from the jury for most of the prosecutor's address.

''You may recall that Helmuth Buxbaum was the last witness to testify at this trial — he heard the evidence of all of the witnesses called not only at this trial but also at the preliminary hearing. Of course, as an accused person, he has every right to be present throughout his preliminary hearing and trial, and to hear the evidence called both for and against him. I would not deny him that right. But the fact remains, that Helmuth Buxbaum has heard all of the evidence — some of it twice — before he took the stand. That gave him the best chance in the world of altering his evidence to suit the facts that have gone before. And he has the greatest reason of all to lie — to avoid conviction on this charge.''

The seasoned lawyer then took another common-sense tack. And a closing shot at his adversary, Greenspan.

''There is an old magician's trick in which, while the theatre audience watches, the magician makes an elephant disappear upon a stage. The essence of that trick — and it is a trick — is to distract all of the audience's attention while the elephant is simply led off the stage.

''Well, in this case the elephant is the guilt of Buxbaum as shown by the unanswered questions I have given you. The distraction is presented by Mr. Greenspan when he condemns Barrett, Allen, Armes, Mrs. Ambrose, Dawn Watson, the crown, the police. In effect, Buxbaum — who admits he lies — says ''do not believe them for they are liars'' and then goes on to say ''believe me because I never lie'' and that statement is a lie.

''Therefore, do not lose sight of the elephant, look upon the conduct of Helmuth Buxbaum for what it is, the conduct of a guilty man.''

Martin closed his binder, asking the jury for a conviction.

Mr. Justice O'Driscoll excused the jury for a week, saying that he needed time to digest his 2,800 pages of handwritten notes before delivering his own closing address.

On the weekend, Paul, Mark and Phillip Buxbaum conducted an invitation-only, mini-press conference for three female reporters they viewed as sympathetic to the family. The Buxbaum sons complained about the deals made by prosecutors and Paul complained that Barrett and Allen would soon be back on the street, showing "you can get away with murder." The remarks were reported after the trial ended.

On February 11, the sixty-sixth day of the trial, O'Driscoll began his six-hour charge to the jury. Buxbaum watched the bespectacled judge as O'Driscoll read from his carefully prepared notes. In a front row seat sat three of the Buxbaum children, Paul, Mark and Phillip. They were joined by sixteen-year-old Esther and the children's guardian, Reverend Douglas Dakin, who had moved into the Buxbaum house.

O'Driscoll asked the jury to consider the central question in the case: had the Crown proved beyond a reasonable doubt that Buxbaum had arranged the killing of Hanna. The judge dismissed evidence of Buxbaum's drug use and adultery, his hard-money economic theories and evidence from his accountant as "background music" in the case.

"Keep your sights trained on the issue," he admonished jurors, "don't run down blind alleys. You're not here to pass judgement on anyone's morals or lack of morals or their sexual proclivities."

The killing itself had been "vicious, brutal and cold-blooded," he said.

He then took a swipe at Greenspan's warnings to the jury that they should disregard O'Driscoll's opinions on the evidence. "The trial judge is not to be reduced to a large piece of blotting paper who is reduced to the role of timekeeper for the recesses." O'Driscoll said he agreed with the defence lawyer that the only important opinion of the evidence is that held by the jury, not himself or Greenspan. He said that the jury should therefore be able to dismiss Greenspan's opinions about who was lying in the case.

O'Driscoll noted there had never been any suggestion that Buxbaum was insane at the time of the killing, therefore he could be found either guilty or not guilty and no finding on any reduced charge would be possible. "There is no half-way house, or quarter-way house," he said.

The judge then retraced the evidence of possible motives, saying that most crimes are committed for some reason. He reminded the jury that Susan Ambrose, Dawn Watson and Rob Barrett had all testified that Buxbaum was tired of his wife and complained that he couldn't divorce her.

He reviewed Barrett's evidence about Buxbaum's giving him money for the killing and for photographs. The jury would have to decide if those events actually transpired, he said.

The defence, he said, had admitted that Buxbaum "had unfortunate appetites that led him to the bar stool at Kelly's" where he met Barrett, a man who viewed him as "the most unbelievable mark of all time."

He reminded the jury that Buxbaum had testified it was Barrett who first introduced him to the cocaine needle and got him hooked.

Thumbing through his notes and occasionally reading large sections of trial transcript, O'Driscoll reminded the jury that the defence, through psychiatrist Malcolm, contended that Buxbaum became "hypersexual" after his stroke.

And the defence, he said, contended that Hanna had tried to pry her husband away from the clutches of Barrett.

O'Driscoll turned his attention briefly to Patrick Allen, the man Buxbaum testifed he was unsure whether he'd met before the morning confrontation along Highway 402. The judge reminded the jury that Allen said he'd seen Buxbaum at a party one time at the Park Lane Hotel. He said that the jury would have to decide whom they believed about that.

"If the evidence convinces you the accused knew the man on the morning of July 5 ... what does that do to the credibility of Helmuth Buxbaum? If he recognized Allen why didn't he tell the police?"

Greenspan's constant doodling was beginning to be punctuated by bursts of frantic scribbling. The last statement had gotten his attention. The next few moments produced even more scribbling.

O'Driscoll asked the jury if they believed that the morning stop was pure coincidence and if Buxbaum really hadn't recognized Allen.

"How is it that two out of three of the same creeps just happened to be on the side of 402 Highway some ten hours later when Helmuth Buxbaum is returning home ... is there more than one answer to that question?"

The jury could hear Greenspan's pen scratching at his paper and could see his deeply furrowed brow as he recorded these remarks.

There was more. "If you accept the crown's allegation and you conclude beyond a reasonable doubt that Helmuth Buxbaum, the accused man, bankrolled the murder of his wife from away back, then something else emerges from that, namely that he delivered her up not only once but twice on the same day to her executioners."

More scribbling.

O'Driscoll continued to paw through a mountain of red-bound transcripts from the trial as he reviewed other evidence and cautioned the jury about how it should weigh the evidence of jail inmates.

He noted that Barrett, Allen and Armes, a cocaine addict, a speed freak, and an alcoholic, all had lengthy records. But all three, he said, had pleaded guilty to their role in the killing and were serving their sentences. O'Driscoll reminded the jury that it was Armes who had testified that Hanna had pleaded with her husband "No, honey, please, not this way," a damning phrase that Armes said he'd never forget. The defence had claimed, O'Driscoll said, that the words were invented to get Armes a deal with prosecutors.

He also warned about Daniel Borland, the convict so helpful to the defence.

"Each and every one of these four witnesses...is from, and has an unsavory background," he said. The first three, he agreed, may have "springboarded" to deals with the prosecution. But those three were now serving sentences and — unlike Borland — they had actually been involved in the killing.

He asked jurors if they believed that Borland had come forward with his story out of a sense of justice. "I suppose that suggestion would be hard to swallow after you have seen him and heard him," O'Driscoll said, answering the question himself.

Doodling had long since been abandoned at the defence table.

"Crown counsel does not have the luxury of calling sanitized witnesses," the judge continued, indicating clearly whom he believed.

He then turned his attention to Helmuth Buxbaum and advised the jury that if they felt that the accused man had told significant lies, either to police or in his trial evidence, they could infer a consciousness of guilt on his part. Buxbaum could have been lying immediately following the killing "to throw the police on a false scent," he suggested.

The judge was nearing the end of his charge. He said he hoped that the jury would be able to reach their required unanimous verdict without becoming a "hung jury."

"I sincerely hope that such will not happen in this case," he said. He pointed to the fifty-five days of actual evidence, six days of defence and crown submissions and his own charge. "No other jury would be in a better position to reach a verdict than you are now," he said.

O'Driscoll dismissed Greenspan's warning to jurors that they must be able to look Barrett and Allen squarely in the eyes and say they were morally certain that the two crown witnesses had told the truth. ''That is not the test,'' O'Driscoll continued. The test to be applied was whether the prosecution had proved beyond a reasonable doubt that Helmuth Buxbaum had arranged the killing of Hanna. ''I wouldn't worry about looking Barrett or Allen in the eye,'' he said, adding that it was more important that each juror be able to look himself in the eye and say that he had been true to his oath to try the case fairly on the evidence.

At 1:13 p.m. on February 12, the jury was sent out to begin deliberations. When court recessed briefly, Greenspan stormed out, lit a Belmont Mild and groused: ''It was the worst charge I've heard in my life. Is that any way to end seventy days?''

Court resumed and Greenspan complained bitterly to O'Driscoll about the charge. He started by asking the judge to halt deliberations before they started because he had ''many, many submissions to make.'' Greenspan didn't want the jury to return with a verdict while he was making his pitch for an entirely new charge. O'Driscoll declined, saying that he had no intention to interfere with the jury. But Greenspan could make his submissions.

For the next two hours, Greenspan reviewed his complaints, arguing that O'Driscoll's charge unfairly overlooked the defence evidence and theories.

The judge, he said, had made it clear to the jury ''that you felt Mr. Buxbaum was guilty and should be convicted.''

He was particularly upset at the quote about Buxbaum's stopping for the ''creeps'' for the second time in ten hours and thereby delivering Hanna into the hands of her executioners.

''The jury may be over-awed by that quote,'' Greenspan said, adding it amounted to ''a complete rejection by your lordship of the defence theory.''

''The conclusion your lordship has arrived at is clearly that he is guilty...the charge is irretrievably lost.''

O'Driscoll heard out the lawyer and turned to the prosecution for its views. Assistant prosecutor Brendan Evans said that the crown had no objection to the charge and reminded O'Driscoll that the jury had been warned by the judge to disregard any opinions from the bench if they chose.

At 5:45 p.m., the judge recalled the jury and cleared up a minor point in his charge concerning the defence's position that Buxbaum believed the July 6 payout of $13,000 at London airport to be for drugs, not murder. The jury was sent back to its work.

Shortly before 10 p.m. the jury was sequestered for the night at a city hotel and resumed its deliberations twelve hours later.

About forty reporters, photographers and cameramen were on hand for the conclusion to the case that had by now attracted nationwide attention. They were beginning to get bored. Some played cards, others listened to Greenspan's continuing complaints about O'Driscoll's charge. Others began interviewing each other about their coverage of the case. The tedium was relieved briefly with word that Esther Buxbaum had been seen entering the building and was visiting her father in the basement cell area. She was captured on film while leaving the building shortly after noon. The pretty, shy teenager was rejoining her brothers at a hotel to await the verdict, safe from the prying eyes of the press.

During the noon recess, the jury announced that it had a verdict and jurors began shredding their notes.

At 1:53 p.m., February 13, the jury was led back into court to announce the fate of Helmuth Buxbaum. Despite short notice, an instant crowd packed the courtroom. An expectant hush fell over those assembled.

Buxbaum had moved a few feet closer to the jury in his prisoner's box so that he could carefully inspect the faces of the ten men and two women as they took their seats and attendance was taken. The tired-looking jurors did not return his inspection.

When jury foreman Keith Hancock stood to announce his verdict, it was as though, for just a moment, time stood still. The quality control inspector at a local General Motors plant was asked if the jury had found the accused man, Helmuth Buxbaum, guilty or not guilty.

"Guilty," he replied.

A murmur rippled across the courtroom and all eyes turned to Buxbaum. The millionaire, suddenly branded a murderer, cocked his head to the side and looked at Greenspan. The lawyer, ashen-faced, tapped on his table with a pen and then asked that the jury be polled to ensure that each juror agreed with the verdict. Buxbaum betrayed no emotion, just as on the night Hanna died.

The jurors agreed with the verdict, then Buxbaum studied O'Driscoll.

The judge asked him if he had anything to say before sentence was passed.

Buxbaum stood stiffly, gripping the front of his box.

"Your lordship, I am not guilty of the charge," he said, softly.

O'Driscoll paused for a moment, as if to say something, shuffled his papers instead and imposed the mandatory life sentence with no eligibility for parole for twenty-five years. He also added the automatic lifetime ban on owning firearms and explosives that accompanies first-degree murder sentences.

"Remove the prisoner, please," the judge told court officers. Buxbaum was led out, head slightly bowed, his usual quick gait slowed somewhat. He was crushed. His faith in the system, in his million-dollar lawyer, had failed him. But, as usual, he wouldn't — and couldn't — show it.

By 2:05 p.m. it was all over. Reporters beat it out before the spectators to file their news bulletins.

Later, at a hastily convened news conference, prosecutor Martin expressed satisfaction that the hard work of police and crown lawyers had paid off with a conviction. Asked about the cost of the prosecution, which unofficially had been pegged at nearly $1 million, Martin said that it was "impossible to figure out," but the expensive case was "part of the price the taxpayers pay for the administration of justice."

Reverend Dakin went before the cameras and microphones to say that he felt a "sort of numbness" and to say that he was commenting on behalf of the children. Paul, Mark, Phillip and Esther had stayed away from court, he explained, because they didn't know how they could cope with the verdict. Danny, fourteen, and Ruthie, seventeen, were in school, he added.

Helmuth, Dakin said, "has been a public disgrace to his family. He wanted to apologize, and has, to them."

The children weren't prepared for a guilty verdict, he said, although some of them might have thought about it in "the back of their minds."

Dakin was asked if *he* felt that Helmuth was guilty. "I don't know," he said, adding that he had yet to talk to his long-time friend about the verdict.

Next to the microphones was a perturbed-looking Greenspan, clutching a legal document listing what he said were forty-seven errors made by O'Driscoll. Buxbaum had just signed it and Greenspan said that he was immediately appealing the case.

"Round one, and only round one, is over. Round two begins," he said, in carefully measured tones.

The appeal would proceed "forthwith," he said. Many of the forty-seven points dealt with O'Driscoll's charge to the jury and his rulings about the admissibility of evidence in the case. The judge also erred by not warning the jury to ignore press coverage of the case, he said.

Greenspan conceded that his team had been compiling its list of complaints throughout the trial. The still-determined lawyer said he expected it to be "many months" before the appeal would be heard. Eddie Greenspan, the man with the well-deserved reputation for hard work, wasn't going to give up without further fight.

Buxbaum's legal battles were clearly not yet over. His family got another jolt several hours later when they learned that Helmuth's older brother, Isbrandt, had plans for his own legal action.

A few hours after the verdict, Isbrandt announced to a

reporter that he was planning to sue Helmuth for the mental anguish caused to his son, Roy, the backseat passenger during the shooting.

Isbrandt noted that Roy, now sixteen, had been terrified when the barrel of a gun was thrust into his face and that the boy had been put through the trauma of hearing his favorite aunt plead with her executioner, imploring him to spare her life, before she was finally slain.

"He was using my son," Isbrandt complained of his brother's murder scheme. "Roy still has nightmares," he said.

He added that he thought it clear that Helmuth was guilty: "He was seeding it and now he is harvesting." He said that he had been awaiting a verdict before launching his action.

The following day, February 14, 1986, Spider, the accused hit-man, appeared in a London courtroom. There he was granted a change of venue for his first-degree murder trial. It would be held in Toronto.

With an appeal still to be heard, a possible civil suit waiting in the wings and a related trial not yet held, it was evident that it would be some time before the last would be heard of Helmuth Buxbaum.

One thing, however, was clear by Valentine's Day, 1986 as Buxbaum started a sentence that, if upheld, would keep him behind bars until he is seventy. Twelve men and women had spoken. And they'd decided, beyond a reasonable doubt, that Helmuth had arranged the killing of Hanna, his long-time sweetheart.

EPILOGUE

The Tragedy

Helmuth Buxbaum proved himself to be a naive, much-flawed man rather than truly evil or diabolical.

He could, of course, be cynical and manipulative in his dealings with his church, in business and with family. But he could also be overly trusting with near-total strangers. He was vulnerable once outside his element; his work and his religion.

With his complex personality, he felt he could run and hide from responsibilities when they became too much to bear. He found escape in the bars of London, the women and the cocaine.

When he felt guilty about his indulgent lifestyle, he would compensate with acts of generosity through his church. He wore his religion like a shield and tried to project an image of loving husband and father.

Helmuth Buxbaum struggled for recognition, to overcome the difficult life situation into which he was born. He had broken out of the shadow of his brothers and sisters and established himself as the pre-eminent Buxbaum. The little kid who had been determined to show he wasn't a wimp had gone far beyond that. He was a success, the talk of the family. And he had a big, fine-looking family of his own.

Feelings of insignificance had been replaced by feelings of omnipotence. Money made the difference. It was important to him: it was a benchmark of success and an effective tool.

He worked hard for it and used it as a club to get his way. He observed how others would do almost anything for his money. If he wanted things he would judiciously give or withhold money to ensure his will prevailed.

Money bought him respect in the community, political influence, a prominent role in his church, a comfortable lifestyle. It also brought him escape on the backstreets of London which were filled with hookers and cocaine dealers.

He lived in two entirely different worlds, with a life that was carefully compartmentalized. He could just as comfortably sit amid his friends on a pew at West Park Baptist Church as on a bar stool among an entirely different crowd at Kelly's Hotel. Those worlds collided when his wife became concerned about the cost of his habits. When that happened, it was perhaps only natural Helmuth Buxbaum would think that money could buy him a solution: the death of his wife.

Aside from insecurity, his other fatal flaw was an insatiable appetite for attractive young members of the opposite sex, fantasy and real. From his first extra-marital escapade in 1967 to the bizarre sexual excesses of 1984, Buxbaum's libido was the common thread linking nearly all his activities.

The sex led to cocaine, which in turn increased his desire for sex. His stroke in 1982 merely enhanced his appetite and his restraint was gone. He was trapped in a vicious circle, fed in his appetites by loose women and Rob Barrett. As the speed of that circle increased, it was almost pre-determined that only something dramatic would happen to pry the weak-willed man away.

Helmuth Buxbaum wanted to be held accountable to no man. With his ingrained religion, he felt accountable only to God. And with his knowledge of the Bible, he could find passages to convince himself he was right.

He chafed at the controls placed on him by his family in the months following his stroke. When called to account by his minister, Paul Fawcett, he would fire back some justification culled from the pages of the Bible, criticize his minister and then ignore him. In the end, he didn't want to be accountable to his wife, who for years had permitted him a long leash. He couldn't stand her meddling in his affairs, complaining about his drug use, invading his shower looking for needle marks, cutting off his contact with Barrett and others. He was still determined to show he wasn't a wimp. The sign of the wimp, he felt was to let others control one's life.

Yet to operate in the nether world of drugs and hookers, he clearly allowed himself to be manipulated. He knew that Barrett was short-changing him on drugs. He knew that some of the drug crowd considered him an oddball and had taken advantage of him. But he wanted to be accepted in their easygoing lifestyle, a world in which responsibility was only a seldom-used word.

The effect of cocaine on Buxbaum was similar to its control on others who abuse the drug. But Buxbaum could afford so much more and its effects were dramatic. Injected cocaine, unlike cocaine that is snorted, can increase the sexual appetitite. It kicked Buxbaum's already considerable drive into overdrive. He enjoyed the drug's other very pleasant effects, including a sense of well-being, self-confidence, a feeling of strength and exhilaration. The sense of omnipotence that money provided him in his straight life, he found in cocaine with the London crowd.

A stable personality would not need such escape. But Buxbaum craved escape.

Friends felt that the stroke altered Buxbaum's personality. In fact, it merely revealed aspects of his character that previously had been kept well-hidden. The apparent remarkable physical recovery masked some subtle mental changes, which even he didn't understand.

The psychological aspects of the stroke in a man so relatively young at the peak of his successes, were perhaps more understandable. Buxbaum was determined to enjoy the time that was left to him. He realized the preciousness of each day and he wanted to eliminate his feelings of emptiness, unhappiness and insignificance. He made a conscious effort to maximize his pleasure. It was just a couple of months after he was back on his feet that he signed on with the Taurus Escort Service to dramatically increase his supply of women.

A few friends, staff, fellow Baptists and other members of his family had known he wasn't the upright citizen he claimed to be. In fact, when word of the Highway 402 shooting first spread, many of them instinctively assumed it was Helmuth who had been shot because he was the Buxbaum with enemies.

After his arrest, his associates began falling away. He was stripped of church membership, his staff openly rejoiced, watching his trial in evident glee, and even some of his family members expressed their certainty there would be a guilty verdict. Buxbaum had been a hypocrite, a manipulator, a religious zealot with these people and this was their chance to sit back and enjoy the discomfort of the self-made man.

Comparisons were made with the Christine Demeter murder case, but in some ways the life and trial of Peter Demeter paled in comparison with that of Helmuth Buxbaum. Buxbaum was, of course, far richer, and had publicly played the role of model citizen, benefactor, family man, pillar of church and community. Demeter had been a busy contractor who lived an exotic lifestyle. Buxbaum was a study in contrasts. Both men were hardworking immigrants from war-torn Europe who had found considerable success in a new land but had chosen to throw that success away because of bad relationships with their wives.

Buxbaum's victim was a good, religious, simple woman, a stark contrast to Demeter's; the gorgeous, leggy, jet-set model, Christine.

Hanna Buxbaum spoke little of the troubles she'd faced in her life. She turned inward, telling few others about her wandering husband. She also prayed that God would bring him back from his indulgences. Just as faith in the Bible and her Mennonite convictions had helped Hanna and her family to cope with the cruelties of Russian refugee camps, she looked to the word of God to help her through a strained marriage. She wouldn't believe the worst until the very end, when she uttered the unforgettable "No, honey, please, not this way." The pain she must have felt in her heart in that terrible instant had to surpass that caused by any bullet.

With her death, she left $3,000 to each of her nieces and nephews and $200,000 to a variety of religious, charitable and missionary groups. Her family solicited contributions in her memory to Mennonite relief work, so that her charity could continue past her death.

The woman who had suffered so much in silence during her life died a very public and cruel death. Thousands upon thousands of total strangers would learn intimate details of her relationship with Helmuth and marvel at her Christian compassion for the man who would take her life.

Her headstone inscription is prophetic and it will be for her husband. Their works *do* follow them.

With twenty-five years until parole, Helmuth Buxbaum has surely lost what could have been his golden years, a time to sit back and enjoy his comfortable life. Instead, he will be behind bars, a seeming eternity before him to reflect on the things that might have been. In the end, his money, the one sure commodity that had bailed him out of trouble, was unable to buy him the votes of ten men and two women in a St. Catharines courthouse. He had to have been shocked with the grim reality that the system of justice, the great leveller, has no respect for wealth or religious affiliation no matter how loudly demonstrated.

The tragic irony in the case of Helmuth Buxbaum is that he wanted his wife dead because he feared he would lose the children to her through divorce. No divorce proceeding, no matter how bitterly contested, could have matched the notoriety of his arrest and trial. He has lost contact with the children for whom he professed so much love. And he lost his wife, a good woman and fine mother whom the children loved. His time with Hanna's children will be limited to their prison visits. The shame the children feel is a heavy burden. Some of them have considered changing their surnames.

Helmuth Buxbaum may not live to complete his sentence. He will be eligible for parole in the year 2009. By then, his children will have children of their own.

Paul, Mark, Phillip, Esther, Danny and Ruthie . . . the living losers in Helmuth Buxbaum's murderous affair.